# Voices from the Zulu War

# Voices from the Zulu War

## Campaigning Through the Eyes
of the British Soldier, 1879

## Ian Knight

FRONTLINE BOOKS

A Greenhill Book

*Voices from the Zulu War: Campaigning Through the Eyes of the British Soldier, 1879*

**A Greenhill Book**

This edition published in 2011 by
Frontline Books, an imprint of Pen & Sword Books Limited,
47 Church Street, Barnsley, S. Yorkshire, S70 2AS
www.frontline-books.com, email info@frontline-books.com

Copyright © Ian Knight, 1992

ISBN: 978-1-84832-590-6

PUBLISHING HISTORY
This book was first published by Greenhill Books in hardback in 1992
under the title *"Under the Orders of the Great White Queen"*.

A CIP data record for this title is available from the British Library.

For more information on our books, please visit www.frontline-books.com,
email info@frontline-books.com or write to us at the above address.

Printed in Great Britain by CPI Mackays, Chatham ME5 8TD

# Contents

# LIST OF ILLUSTRATIONS

# ACKNOWLEDGEMENTS

THIS volume would not have been possible without the help of a number of Zulu War enthusiasts, who made their own painstakingly-compiled libraries available to be plundered by me: my thanks especially to Keith Reeves and Ian Castle for their advice and encouragement, to Rai England, for access to his incomparable collection of contemporary newspaper engravings, and to Cliff Meek, for help in tracking down Lord Grenfell's account. Colonel Ian Bennett kindly read the manuscript and made several useful suggestions, whilst in South Africa, 'SB' Bourquin once again allowed me full access to his invaluable collection. Chard's letter to Queen Victoria is reproduced by kind permission of Her Majesty the Queen. Claire Colbert's help with the photographic copying was much appreciated, as ever. Finally, no list of acknowledgements would be complete without mention of Dave and Nicky Rattray of Fugitives' Drift Lodge, without whom my own travels in Zululand would have been far more trouble and much less fun!

# INTRODUCTION

O N 11th January 1879, the British forces under the command of Lieutenant-General Lord Chelmsford, crossed the border from the British colony of Natal into the independent African kingdom of Zululand, and embarked upon one of the most famous campaigns in British Colonial history. When troops from the Centre Column advanced to their first engagement, an attack on the homestead of the border chieftain Sihayo kaXongo, a Zulu called out a challenge, asking them by whose orders they had come. According to George Hamilton-Browne, commandant of the 1st Battalion, 3rd Regiment of the Natal Native Contingent, one of his staff replied: 'By the orders of the Great White Queen'.

This response seems particularly appropriate as a title for a book of eye-witness accounts, drawn mainly from the reminiscences of British officers who fought in the war. Today, more than a century later, it's difficult not to see the Anglo-Zulu War as a particularly cynical piece of Imperial expansionism. Certainly, it was a very brutal and destructive war: it cost the lives of 76 British officers and over 1,000 NCOs and men killed in action, and a further 17 officers and 330 men who succumbed to disease. Of the black Africans from colonial Natal who joined them as auxiliaries, the official toll was given as 600 dead, but it was probably considerably higher. One can only estimate the Zulu losses: 7,000 killed in action would be a conservative estimate. In addition, their king was deposed, their government overturned, and their homes and crops laid waste.

Yet few of the men whose stories are told in this book questioned the morality of British policy. They were by no means brutal or insensitive men – they were drawn from the best educated and most cultured strata of Victorian society, after all – but they were very much part of the establishment, and the officer class was essentially conservative in outlook. They may have found in their enemies many of the virtues which they themselves championed – courage, discipline, patriotism and honesty – yet for most of them the British Empire was an article of faith. They believed implicitly in its moral superiority, in its right to rule those which it considered lesser breeds, and that by expanding its boundaries they were spreading the just cause of Christian enlightenment. Like professional soldiers the world over, they went where they were sent, and did the job expected of them; for them, it was indeed enough that they had come 'by the orders of the Great White Queen'.

With one or two exceptions, the accounts in this book are taken from memoirs written at the end of long and successful careers. For most of the British participants, the Zulu War was merely one chapter in their adventurous lives: they fought it, and moved on to police other hot-spots around the Empire. Some of their reminiscences, like those of Sir Evelyn Wood, who commanded a column throughout the war, or Horace Smith-Dorrien, who, as a young lieutenant, was one of only a handful of regular officers to survive the massacre at Isandlwana, are of the greatest historical importance, and have been well-thumbed by historians over the years. Others, like Major Harcourt Bengough's account of life with the Natal Native Contingent, are less well-known, but equally significant. Almost all of them were published about the turn of the century, and most have been virtually unobtainable since. The current and seemingly unabating interest in the Zulu War, I believe, justifies taking them off the shelf, blowing away the dust, and collecting together the relevant passages into one volume.

Although the present work tells the whole story of the Zulu War through British eyes, it cannot be an exhaustive compilation. It is a collection of accounts that seemed particularly important or entertaining to the editor; it is obviously not possible to include every memoir from every officer. Nor, indeed, did every officer write his memoirs, even though it was clearly fashionable to do so; many a promising career was cut short by battle or disease in later campaigns, whilst other important players in the Zulu drama simply remained reticent. Of the senior commanders, neither Chelmsford, Buller nor Pearson left autobiographies, and of the officers who defended Rorke's Drift – whose fame must have assured them a place in the literary market – only one, Colonel (then Assistant Commissary) W. A. Dunne, wrote down his story at any length; this appeared in an obscure edition of the *Army Service Corps Journal*, and, more recently, formed the basis of Colonel Ian Bennett's *Eyewitness In Zululand*. Lieutenant Chard left only his official report and a longer letter written at Queen Victoria's request, which is included here. Lieutenant Bromhead apparently left no account at all.

There are, of course, limitations to approaching a subject as complex as the Zulu War in this way. Like most eye-witness accounts, they present a very narrow perspective of events. Apart from 'Harry O'Clery of the Buffs' and Archibald Forbes, the war correspondent, all of these accounts are from British officers: although literacy was rising amongst the lower ranks, the fashion for autobiography was obviously more appropriate to the upper classes. Not that the Other Ranks didn't provide some extraordinarily vivid accounts of the Zulu War, mostly in letters written to their families at home, and often subsequently published in the British press: Frank Emery's *The Red Soldier* (1977) includes an excellent selection of these. It makes interesting reading to compare the preoccupations and attitudes of the ordinary soldier with those of his leaders. Nor, of course, is there any Zulu viewpoint in the current selection: Zulu was not a written language in the nineteenth century, and, although many Zulu accounts were recorded and translated by interested whites in the years after the war, it's really only in the last twenty years that writers and historians have accorded them their proper importance in the literature of the war. John Laband has collected and edited some in *Fight Us In the Open* (1985), and the serious student is recommended to the four thick volumes of Zulu testimony, covering a wide range of historical and cultural topics, currently published by the University of Natal in the *James Stuart Archive*. For a general history of the war, which I hope presents a balanced picture, the reader is recommended to Ian Knight's *Brave Men's Blood* (1990).

Although the passages here have obviously been selected for inclusion, it has been decided to let them speak for themselves, and not to introduce copious footnotes. Those footnotes which do appear are from the original texts. No other editing has taken place beyond the removal of some terms, in common use at the time, referring to other races; racial attitudes were very different in the 1870s, and terms which would be considered offensive today were not necessarily believed to be so then. Nevertheless, in fairness both to the contemporary writers and to modern sensitivities, appropriate terms have been substituted here in square brackets.

It should also be said that in 1879 there was no standard spelling of Zulu names, and writers simply recorded them phonetically, each as the word sounded to him. Cetshwayo, with its click sound represented by the letter 'c', and the frictive sound in the middle, must have seemed virtually unpronounceable to most British tongues, and was often simplified as 'Cetewayo', 'Cetywayo' or 'Ketchwayo'. Isandlwana was often written Isandhlwana, Isandwhlana or Isandula, and Eshowe, which also has a slight frictive sound at the beginning, was rendered Etshowi, Eschowe, or even Ekowe; the latter originated in the reports of the Scandinavian missionaries who first established a post on the site, and who represented a guttural 'ch' sound with a 'k'. In the modern text, the currently accepted spellings have been used, whilst in the old spellings are retained in the contemporary accounts. Not only does this give a flavour of the period, it also gives a good idea of the problems that plague historians on the question of orthography! It's interesting to note that even some of the European names are mis-spelt, even by colleagues who knew those concerned well. The question of rank perhaps requires some clarification, too. Many officers held Brevet ranks which were different from their regimental ranks: a Brevet was an immediate advance in

14

rank and Army seniority, given as a reward for gallantry or other outstanding service. A recipient was known by this rank, and took precedent over his contemporaries for further promotion, but received no extra pay. Throughout this book all ranks are listed as appropriate to their Zulu War service.

Finally, it must be noted that many of the accounts published here were written by old men, looking back on their adventures of twenty or even thirty years before. In some cases, time has blunted their memory, and they have had ample opportunity to reflect on their experiences, to re-arrange their impressions over the years, and to make a sense of them that they didn't necessarily have in the white-hot chaos of battle. Evelyn Wood's account of Khambula, for example, has a classic error in that it precisely transposes the dispositions of the Zulu regiments: those who fought in the left horn being placed on the right, and vice versa; one can only follow John Laband's supposition that such an error arose when Wood perhaps confused references to the Zulu right and left with his own right and left when questioning prisoners. Nevertheless, whatever their faults, these accounts present a very vivid picture of the war in the field, filtered through the personalities and writing styles of some of its participants. Hamilton-Browne tells his grim story of Isandlwana with all the verve of a novelist, whilst the anecdotes of Bindon Blood are full of jaunty humour. Wood's account of Hlobane and Khambula, and Molyneux's description of Gingindlovu, are classic battle narratives, with a sharp eye for detail. Sir Richard Harrison's reminiscences echo both the sad responsibilities of command and the unglamorous drudgery of keeping a fighting army supplied in the field. Together they are a hugely important contribution to our knowledge of the war and the men who made it.

For more than a century, historians have sifted and analysed the evidence in an attempt to piece together the truth about the events of the Anglo-Zulu War. Perhaps it's an impossible task; the focus of understanding is constantly shifting, throwing some aspects into the shadows and highlighting others, whilst the unrelenting silence of many a key participant leaves yawning gaps in our knowledge which are unlikely, now, ever to be filled. Hopefully, however, the present collection will enable the reader to peel back at least a corner of the curtain of time, and understand just a little of how the war seemed, and sounded, and felt, to a handful of those 'red soldiers' who marched through the blue-remembered hills of old Zululand in 1879.

The illustrations have been chosen from contemporary newspaper and magazine engravings, not only for their dramatic and informative content, but to suggest something of the way the Zulu War was presented to the British public back home, excepting those from Hamilton-Browne's *A Lost Legionary In South Africa*.

Such newspaper and magazine illustrations were worked up by a team of skilled engravers in the UK, using sketches made on the spot, either by participants, or by trained 'special artists' such as Melton Prior and Charles Fripp. Although such a process obviously allowed for considerable room for error, most of the finished products were surprisingly accurate. Nevertheless, the images clearly followed certain conventions in their depiction of conflict, and these are more apparent in the down-market papers, such as the *Penny Illustrated*, rather than the more famous and restrained *Illustrated London News* and *Graphic*. Most of those reproduced here are from the *Penny Illustrated*, which have the added bonus of being 'fresh' images; few have been reproduced since their original publication. They are all from the collection of Rai England, apart from Nos. 1. 2. 3, and 4 (which are taken from Hamilton-Browne's *A Lost Legionary In South Africa*) and No. 6, which is in the editor's collection.

Ian Knight, 1992

CHAPTER ONE

# THE ZULU WAR

THE Anglo-Zulu War was the direct result of a forward policy adopted by Britain in the 1870s in an attempt to rationalise her southern African entanglements. Britain had been at the Cape since 1806, displacing the Dutch, who had arrived a century and a half before, as the resident colonial power. The Cape had little to interest rival European empires per se, but it was an important staging post on the long haul round Africa to India and the East.

Like the Dutch before them, the British were reluctant to embark on expensive imperial adventures, and tried to seal off their possessions from the limitless and largely unexplored tracts of black Africa that lay beyond. They were no more successful at this than the Dutch: the Boers, the descendants of the original Dutch settlers, were a hardy and independent breed, who flouted colonial strictures and wandered restlessly beyond the frontier in search of new grazing lands for their cattle. This brought them into conflict with the black groups of the interior and the eastern coastal strip, who were already in possession of those lands.

To complicate matters, the Boers soon conceived a hearty dislike for their new political overlords, and in the 1830s a large section of the Boer community at the Cape simply packed its possessions into its ox-wagons, and crossed out of the colony, in search of pastures new. Their passage was marked by a series of bitter conflicts with inland African groups, which dragged British authority marching reluctantly in their wake.

By the time the dust had settled in the 1860s, the British found themselves in possession of the Cape, and stretches of the well-watered eastern coastal strip, extending as far as a territory known as Natal, whose northern boundary was the Thukela river. Inland, the Boers held two republics, the Orange Free State and the Transvaal, and scattered in between were a variety of African states and kingdoms, which increasingly felt the pinch as white settlement encroached more and more on their lands. The largest and most powerful of these kingdoms was that of the amaZulu, which lay north of the Thukela.

In the 1820s, at about the time that the juggernaut of white expansion was building up steam in the south, the black groups lying between the Drakensberg mountains and the sea had been torn by a series of violent upheavals. Quite what caused them is still a matter of debate: perhaps they were unsettled by Portuguese slave-trading further north in Mozambique; perhaps these pastoral societies had simply outstripped the capacity of their environment to support them. Organised into clans – each clan tracing a theoretical descent to a common ancestor – the clans began to band together for support, and to attack their enemies. Under Shaka kaSenzangakhona, an inspired general and a ruthless political survivor, the Zulus emerged as the dominant power, incorporating most of the clans between the Thukela and Phongolo rivers, and driving out many of their rivals. The shock waves from the period of Zulu expansionism reverberated as far south as the borders of the Cape Colony.

Under Shaka, the Zulu kingdom had a highly centralised state apparatus which overlay the clan structure of which it was composed. At the heart of this system was the army, which provided the basis of monarchical power; young men from across the nation, regardless of clan origins, were recruited at regular intervals to form amabutho, age-grade regiments. These were effectively the state labour force, and the warriors were required to spend a period of national service quartered at barracks (amakhanda, known to the British as 'military kraals') before the king gave them permission to marry and establish their own homes. Shaka kept his army mobilised for much of his reign, but in subsequent years the warriors spent most of their time living with their families, and only mustered

18

at the barracks when the king called up a particular regiment. Thus the Zulu army was an armed citizenry rather than a standing army in the European professional sense; nevertheless, by the 1870s, Britain chose to make much of its potential threat.

In fact, Zulu relations with the British colony of Natal had generally been good. The first British adventurers had made their way to Shaka's court in 1824, and Shaka had granted them the land around Port Natal (now Durban), the only viable harbour on the coast. On this slender basis all subsequent British claims to the area rested, and in 1842 Britain formally annexed Natal, largely to prevent the Boers from getting it. Over the subsequent decades it filled up with a scattering of white settlers, and a large black population, many of whom were historically antagonistic towards the Zulu kingdom across the river. For the most part, however, the Home Government continued to regard South Africa as a drain upon both the Treasury and the War Department.

In 1867, however, diamonds were discovered north of the Cape, and at last South Africa offered the prospect of some return on Britain's years of investment. In order to exploit the economic potential, it would be necessary to build a new infrastructure, which was clearly impossible when the area consisted of so many independent and mutually antagonistic groups. The solution adopted by the Colonial Office in London was Confederation, a bringing together of these groups under one authority: British. This was easier said than done, since the Africans had little enough cause to give up their autonomy to any whites, whilst the Boer Republics had been born of a desire precisely to escape British authority – and even the most self-sufficient British possession, the Cape, saw few reasons why it should support the burden of its more backward colleagues.

Nevertheless, Britain went ahead with the scheme. In 1877, the alleged bankruptcy and inefficiency of the Transvaal Republic was used to justify British annexation. At the same time, a new High Commissioner, Sir Henry Bartle Frere, was sent to South Africa with instructions to implement Confederation. Frere had not long been in Africa when he decided that the quickest way to do so was by breaking the power of the

Zulus. There was a certain logic to his argument. He maintained that the Zulus were the strongest of the independent black groups in South Africa, and that their existence inevitably encouraged black resistance elsewhere. The Zulu army, in his view, was so large that it was clearly a threat to its neighbours, a point that was no longer just hypothetical, since, with the annexation of the Transvaal, Britain had inherited a source of potential conflict with Zululand. The Transvaal and Zulu kingdom were locked in dispute over a festering border wrangle which dated back to the 1840s. Prior to annexation, when scheming against the Transvaal, Britain had supported the Zulu claim, but since the slice of territory in question was now arguably British, the Imperial position underwent a dramatic volte face. If the Zulu threat could be removed, Frere reasoned, the Transvaal Boers, hitherto less than enthusiastic about the advantages of British rule, could surely be made to change their minds? Under such circumstances, it would be difficult for reluctant republics and colonies alike to oppose the Confederation scheme.

North of the Thukela, at his principal homestead of Ulundi, in the heart of Zululand, King Cetshwayo kaMpande watched the changing mood amongst his neighbours with unease. Cetshwayo had come to the throne in 1873, and since then had instituted a number of reforms designed to strengthen the state apparatus. He was aware that some of these reforms caused concern beyond his borders, but he had always tried to stay on good terms with the British. He was adamant, however, that the disputed territory in the north-west belonged to the Zulus, and had attempted to reinforce his claim by building small royal homesteads in the area. He failed to grasp that such actions were inevitably bringing him into confrontation with his former allies.

In 1878, a Border Commission was established to look into the dispute. Frere was determined to use its findings to provoke a war against the Zulus. The Home Government was ambivalent about any such war: it recognised that it was probably an inevitable result of the Confederation policy, but it wanted to postpone it as long as possible. Frere, on the other hand, anticipated a quick and successful strike which would

20

be over before far-away London could object. To his dismay, however, the Border Commission found largely in favour of the Zulus, and Frere had to hunt around for an alternative casus belli. He seized upon a series of border incidents which took place in late 1878, and when the Zulu representatives were summoned to hear the result of the commission's findings in December 1878, they found themselves presented with a British ultimatum. King Cetshwayo was required to surrender a number of individuals for trial for violating Natal territory, and to disband his army within thirty days. Since the army was the prop which held the Zulu kingdom together, this was clearly an impossible demand. No answer was given to the British ultimatum, and on 11th January 1879 British forces began to invade Zululand.

In his book *A Sketch of the Kafir and Zulu Wars*, published in 1880, Captain Henry Hallam Parr devoted a chapter to justifying British policy towards the Zulus. There is little talk of confederation, and a good deal on the supposedly threatening attitude of King Cetshwayo. 'Why', wondered Parr, 'should a petty barbarian monarch be allowed to embarrass the British Empire at such a time?' Yet Parr had been Frere's military secretary, and clearly felt the need to defend his superior against an increasingly hostile public perception of the war at home. Hallam Parr is unusual in considering British policies at such length. Bindon Blood, who, as a major in the Royal Engineers, was sent out with the reinforcements after the Isandlwana debacle, provided an interesting summary of the war in his lively autobiography *Four Score Years And Ten* (1933). Like most soldiers, he did not give much space to politics, and saw Zulu history in terms of a series of atrocities which inevitably brought them into conflict with the Crown. Yet Blood's account of the war itself can serve as a concise and perceptive introduction, and he casts a professional's eye over the relative merits of the opposing armies:

*

The Amazulu – the 'Celestials' – commonly called the Zulus, were an unimportant tribe until the early years of the nineteenth century. At that time they inhabited the pleasant and fertile country in the north-east of what is now Zululand, about the Black and White Umvolosi Rivers, and seem to have been chiefly known as producers and peddlers of tobacco. About AD 1800 they were ruled by a chief who had a nephew named Utshaka – 'Daybreak' – commonly called Chaka; and this nephew having managed to collect a following, killed his uncle the chief, took his place, and organised the fighting men of the tribe in a few years into the most formidable native army in South Africa.

With his army, before 1830, Chaka occupied the whole of what is now Zululand, and also took possession of the territory that is now Natal, exterminating or driving out the previous inhabitants of both areas as he proceeded. In Natal he first came in contact with white men, 'Boers' from the Cape Colony, which we had taken from the Dutch, and from which there was an extensive migration of Boers to the interior, commencing about 1825, and followed by the formation of the states which are now included in the Union of South Africa.

But Chaka saw little of this, as his oppressive rule had aroused discontent, so that his younger brother Dingaan – the 'Poor Creature' – murdered him about 1830 and took his place. Dingaan attacked the Natal colonists at once, destroyed Durban, and was also guilty of more than one treacherous massacre. But he was defeated ultimately in 1840 by a rising of Zulus under his younger brother Panda, assisted by 400 mounted Boers; and thereupon he took refuge with a small tribe near Delagoa Bay, who promptly murdered him to curry favour with his pursuers.

After this, on the 14th February 1840, the Natal Boers proclaimed Panda King of the Zulus, and also declared their own sovereignty over Natal. Then, after some fighting, the British Government occupied Natal in 1842, and the colony settled down under the consequent reign of law and order.

Panda reigned over the Zulus until his death in 1872, when he was succeeded by his son Ketchwayo. Ketchwayo added to the efficiency of the Zulu army in various ways, but specially by acquiring for it a large proportion of rifles, which he was foolishly permitted to do; and before long it became evident that he had made up his mind to try conclusions with the white men, and that his army and most of his subjects were at one with him about this.

Accordingly our relations with Ketchwayo soon became strained. Many unpleasant occurrences took place and insolent replies were received to reasonable and just requests on several occasions up to 1878, when the climax was reached. In July of that year a body of armed Zulus entered Natal territory, took two refugee Zulu women out of the huts of British subjects, and killed them when they had conveyed them into Zulu territory which was near. When remonstrances and demands were sent to the Zulu King, insolent replies were returned; and when a final message was sent to Ketchwayo, demanding, *inter alia*, the surrender of the men who had violated British territory, no satisfactory reply was received; and so, on the 4th January 1879, Her Majesty's High Commissioner, Sir Bartle Frere, placed the enforcement of all demands in the hands of Lt-General Lord Chelmsford, who commanded the troops in South Africa. Lord Chelmsford was originally a Guardsman, and in the days of the 'extra rank', when captains in the Guards ranked as lieutenant-colonels and lieutenants as captains, he exchanged while comparatively a young man to command a line battalion. He was adjutant-general in India when I first met him, being universally liked and respected, and considered one of the best adjutant-generals there had ever been.

The forces at Lord Chelmsford's disposal at the front were as under, the numbers given being close approximations, namely:

| | |
|---|---:|
| British Infantry, with 200 Naval Brigade (2 gatlings) | 5,800 |
| White mounted troops | 750 |
| RE one company | 120 |
| Natives on foot | 9,000 |
| " " mounted | 250 |
| Guns 7-pdr on wheels | 8 |
| Rocket tubes | 2 |

This force was divided into four 'columns', three of them being of about 2,000 white men each, and the fourth of about 3,500 natives; the 1st column, under Colonel Pearson of the Buffs, at the mouth of the Tugela; the 4th under Colonel Evelyn Wood, VC, in front of Utrecht; the 3rd under Colonel Glyn about Helpmakaar and Rorke's Drift; and the 2nd under Colonel Durnford to the south of the 3rd, on the strong position called Kranz Kop.

Ketchwayo's army was said to amount to some 40,000 efficient men, all foot-soldiers trained to fight at close quarters with the stabbing assegai and ox-hide shield. They had been lately equipped with a considerably proportion of rifles, including many breech-loaders of different patterns, but fortunately for us had no idea of the tactical methods and arrangements required to make long-range fire-arms useful. It was generally believed that some 20,000 of Ketchwayo's army watched Lord Chelmsford's 3rd column, that the large part of the rest lay towards the mouth of the Tugela about Etshowe, and that some 5,000 or 6,000 watched Colonel Evelyn Wood's command – the 4th British column.

Now perhaps it will be interesting if we devote a page or two to considering the composition and capabilities of these two forces.

The Zulu army as I have stated was a body of infantry trained to fight hand to hand with the stabbing assegai and ox-hide shield. The men were little encumbered by clothing or equipment, and were very active and capable of rapid movement. Also they were kept in good condition, and were excellent marchers and hill climbers, and they were full of courage and enthusiasm.

Of late years considerable numbers of rifles of various descriptions had been acquired and issued to the Zulu army, but it had not taken to them, and very few of the men could shoot at all well, while the leaders had no idea of the tactics which have to be adopted with fire-arms, in order to develop their powers fully. Thus the Zulus' idea of a normal attack was to advance in masses in crescent formation, to get close to the enemy, and then to charge home, enveloping him as far as possible. In cases where there was cover close up to a negligent enemy, and other special circumstances favoured the Zulus, these tactics succeeded. But it was very different when the force attacked was properly composed and handled, so as to give effect to the power of destroying mass formations which is possessed by modern rifles in the hands of well trained men, and to the capabilities of artillery and cavalry. And similarly it was repeatedly proved that Zulu forces were helpless against fortified positions, even when they were fortified in the most elementary manner.

I always understood that the Zulus managed with a minimum of transport, and that what they had was arranged on the 'coolie' system, men being utilised for it who had not come up to the physical standards of their regiments, and also women to some extent.

Turning to the British army, we find that the six battalions in it of British infantry were an excellent lot of men. They had all been some time in South Africa and so had not been affected, like our newly mobilised troops, by the short-service-and-reserve system lately introduced in England. Their officers were of the well known sort, who could be depended upon to lead their men anywhere. Under an absurdly mistaken idea that the South African country was too difficult for field artillery, Lord Chelmsford had only 7-pdr mountain guns on light carriages, and very few of them – only eight in all – for a force liable to be attacked at any time by concentrations of 20,000 foot-soldiers, working in mass formations and full of courage and enthusiasm. This of course was due to remarkable ignorance in high places of the powers and capabilities of artillery.

Again in Lord Chelmsford's army there was equal neglect of cavalry. Lord Chelmsford had, it is true, seven or eight hundred mounted men, all gallant volunteers in small bodies fit for anything that small bodies could do, but useless for such an enterprise as, say, the destruction of a Zulu mass by the operation of all the arms of the service in due combination, on any sort of suitable ground. In such a case what could the Zulus have done, practically having no firearms, absolutely no artillery, no cavalry, nothing but trumpery assegais four feet long or so, with leather shields that would only have been in their way?

Of course Lord Chelmsford's mounted men might easily have been made into six or seven squadrons of splendid cavalry, if he had had cavalry officers fit to teach and handle them. But nothing of the sort was ever thought of.

The British force was organised in columns, the normal brigades and divisions having been entirely given up. To my mind this was a great mistake, as a complete change of organis- ation on starting on active service cannot be sound. Ever since I have been in the British service it has been the regular practice to organise armies anew in brigades and divisions, etc., when they are mobilised, and to furnish them with staffs newly put together for the occasion. I have always regarded this practice as one of the chief causes of the many 'regrettable occurrences' that have taken place in our campaigns.

There is no doubt that the art of field fortification might have been utilised in Natal and Zululand with much advantage, both for the defence of the Natal border, and on the lines of communication at such positions as Rorke's Drift and Isandhlwana; and consequently it was strange that there was only one weak company of engineers with Lord Chelmsford's force, and that it was not with the column designated for the main advance. It is conceivable that if it had been with that column, the placing of the positions of Isandhlwana and Rorke's Drift in a state of defence might have been thought of, and the history of South Africa in 1879 might then have been quite different from what it was.

But the greatest defect in the composition of Lord Chelms- ford's army was the utter unsuitability of its transport. This consisted practically altogether of ox-wagons, which were very cleverly constructed four-wheel vehicles, each drawn by six or eight pairs of fine oxen and requiring the services of two men. These vehicles and their draught arrangements had been evolved to meet the requirements of colonial life in South Africa, and were admirably well adapted thereto. Those re- quirements never made it necessary, as field service require- ments do, for *great masses of transport to move and camp together*, and so to make the feeding of the consequent enor- mous number of bullocks an actual impossibility; as the only possible mode of feeding them was to graze them for five or six hours of daylight each day on suitable grass. Our officers did their best to get over this difficulty, but it will easily be understood that their efforts were vain, owing to the great numbers of animals involved, and that the long delays and some of the other regrettable occurrences of the Zulu War were the inevitable result.[1]

Lord Chelmsford advanced into Zululand with the 3rd Column on the 11th January 1879, and soon realised that it was impossible for him with his transport and supply arrangements as they were, to make a rapid march at that season into the middle of the Zulu country. He therefore decided to move all his columns a short distance forward only, and apparently, then to await events. Accordingly, on the 20th January the 3rd Column was encamped at Isandhlwana, and next day a force of native police and mounted volunteers was sent some fourteen miles out to feel for the enemy, and reported the presence of Zulus in considerable strength. At daylight on the 22nd a battalion of British infantry, the Mounted Infantry and four guns started to re-inforce the troops reconnoitring, the Commander-in-Chief accompanying them; whilst Colonel Durnford, with the 2nd Column, having been ordered out to Isandhlwana, was on the way. Meanwhile, in the night of the 21st/22nd, 20,000 Zulus moved undiscovered to within about one and a half miles of Isandhlwana Camp, which had not been put in a state of defence. In the course of the morning the Zulus attacked the camp and captured it with ease in an hour, killing about 800 white officers and men and great numbers of natives, soldiers and others; and capturing the guns, rocket-tubes, stores of ammunition, etc., together with the transport cattle, wagons and everything else.

A large number of the Zulus pursued the fugitives for a long distance, and a considerable detachment went to attack Rorke's Drift, which had not been made into a defensible post, but was strengthened by means of biscuit boxes, mealie bags and so forth, as soon as fugitives brought news of the disaster at Isandhlwana. The defenders were 139 of all ranks in number, of whom 33 were patients in hospital, and their losses were

[1] After Isandhlwana, great efforts were made to bring mules to Zululand from various parts of the world, and they were very useful in the final advance on Ulundi.

25 killed and wounded in the defence, which was completely successful, although in the course of the night some buildings were evacuated and burnt which had been held at first. The officer in command was Lieutenant Chard, RE, and he was ably assisted by Lieutenant Bromhead of the 24th Regiment and the Rev Mr Smith, one of the military chaplains who happened to be at the post.

The defence of Rorke's Drift post was, of course, a most remarkable exemplification of the helplessness of the Zulu army against the most trumpery fortification, owing to their deficiency of fire-arms big and little, and this though it was composed of some of the finest fighting men to be found anywhere!

While the events described above were in progress, part of No. 1 Column comprising about 1,200 British troops under Colonel Pearson of the Buffs, having crossed the Tugela by the lower drift near the sea, proceeded on the 18th January towards Etshowe about 30 miles distant. Their progress was slow, owing to transport difficulties, and on the 22nd January, the day of Isandhlwana, they were attacked on the line of march, near the Inyezane River, by about 5,000 Zulus who had been lying in wait for them. After an action lasting one and a half hours, in which all arms were brought into play by the British commander, the Zulus were defeated and put to flight, and the British column marched on to its biovouac, about three miles from the field of battle. The British loss was 10 killed and 16 wounded, while over 300 Zulus were slain. The Zulus made considerable use of fire-arms in this action, but ineffectually of course owing to want of training.

The day after the action the column reached and occupied the position at Etshowe, with the intention of making it a base for the further advance on Ulundi, but on the 29th news arrived of the disaster at Isandhlwana. Thereupon Colonel Pearson decided to hold on to Etshowe with about 1,300 white and 60 native fighting men, and to send all the mounted men and spare natives back to the Tugela. By the 10th February the fort was completed on a sound scheme, in a most creditable manner, by the company of engineers in the garrison, ably assisted by the other soldiers and sailors, all under the orders of that brave and able commander, Colonel Pearson of the 'Old Buffs'. No attack was ever made on the fort, although it was watched by large numbers of Zulus, until it was finally relieved on the 3rd April, after the garrison had been nearly six weeks on reduced rations, and after additional troops had arrived from England. The successful action of Ginginhlovo was fought by the relieving force, nearly 6,000 strong, against an army of Zulus said to have been 20,000 strong, which attacked the British entrenched camp early in the morning of the 3rd April, but was beaten off easily, with heavy loss, by rifle and artillery fire. On this occasion also the Zulus fired off many cartridges with trifling effect, while they suffered severely from the British fire, 773 of their dead bodies being found within 1,000 yards of the entrenched camp. One battalion of the reinforcements just landed, consisting largely of raw recruits, formed part of this relieving force, which had as artillery two 9-pdr guns, four 24-pdr rocket-tubes and two gatlings, one in each of the two divisions into which it was formed.

It will be remembered that Colonel Durnford was killed and his (2nd) Column of natives was destroyed with the 3rd Column at Isandhlwana. Colonel Evelyn Wood's 4th Column was not attacked at the same time as the columns at Isandhlwana and Inyezane, and operated afterwards in defence of Utrecht and the Transvaal. Colonel Wood established himself in an entrenched camp at Kambula Hill, and after meeting with a rather severe reverse on the 27th March, owing to a surprise due to bad outpost work, in a cattle raid at a place called Hlobane Mountain, he was heavily attacked at Kambula Hill on the 29th by a force said to be 20,000 strong, which was eventually repulsed and driven off with severe loss. The British loss on these two occasions together was about 200, of whom about 150 were killed.

The shocking disaster at Isandhlwana naturally caused some panic in Natal and the Transvaal; but the Zulus did not follow up their victory, and nothing occurred beyond minor raids and convoy attacks until the events at Hlobane Mountain, Kambula and Ginginhlovo at the end of March and beginning of April 1879, which are described in the last chapter.

By the end of April, the reinforcements which had been sent from Home on the arrival of the news of Isandhlwana, had gone to the front, and Lord Chelmsford found himself in command of a force of over 22,500 of all arms, which he organised into two divisions and a Flying Column, the 1st Division, about 9,200 strong, under Major-General H. H. Crealock, having its headquarters at the mouth of the Tugela; the 2nd, about 10,200 strong, under Major-General Newdigate at Doornberg on the Buffalo River; and the Flying Column, about 3,100 strong, under Brigadier-General Evelyn Wood, at a new camp near the Sand Spruit, one of the sources of the white Umvolosi. After this there was little progress made until the last days of June. On the 1st July the 2nd Division and Flying Column had arrived within 10 miles of Ketchwayo's Kraal at Ulundi, when some futile negotiations took place and an armistice was arranged till the 3rd July. On that day after the armistice had expired, there was a reconnaissance by a considerable body of mounted troops, which nearly fell into an ambuscade and had to make a helter-skelter return to camp. Next day, on the 4th of July, the British army, just over 4,000 strong, with 12 guns and 1,000 natives, moved out in hollow square formation and were attacked by the Zulu army, said to be 20,000 strong. The Zulus advanced to within 70 yards of the British square, which must have shot badly, and then gave way to the fire that was poured into them. The 17th Lancers and Irregular Horse then attacked and pursued for some distance until the enemy were dispersed or had found shelter. The Zulu casualties were estimated to be about 1,000 in killed alone. The British casualties were 12 killed and 70 wounded.

When the pursuit was over the mounted troops were sent to destroy the Ulundi kraals, which they burnt, and, later in the day, the British army returned to camp without making any attempt or arrangement to follow up their victory, or to capture the king. Stranger still, they commenced at once a retrograde march on Natal, Lord Chelmsford resigning his command and proceeding with a large staff direct to Pietermaritzburg. Thus was the bubble of the Zulu military power burst! The Zulus made no visible attempt at a rally, although, thanks to Lord Chelmsford's arrangements, or rather to his neglect of obviously advisable precautions, there was nothing to prevent such an attempt.

It will be remembered that the ridiculously named Flying Column on which the energy and activity of Evelyn Wood were wasted, acted with the 2nd Division in the advance of Ulundi and in the final action there.

## CHAPTER TWO

# ISANDLWANA AND RORKE'S DRIFT

T HERE were a number of good strategic reasons why Chelms-ford had decided to invade Zululand with more than one column. True, he risked diluting his greatest asset, his fire-power, and maintaining several independent columns in the field would prove a logistical nightmare, but Chelmsford had been deeply concerned about the almost complete absence of defensive arrangements in Natal, and was worried that unless he could tie down the Zulus over a wide area, a lightly-encumbered impi might slip past him and wreak havoc in the colony.

In any case, neither Chelmsford nor many of his officers believed that the Zulus were really capable of pressing home a sustained attack across the sort of open country which characterised much of Zululand. Chelmsford had arrived in South Africa in early 1878, and had supervised the final stages of the Ninth Cape Frontier War, where large bodies of Xhosa warriors had shown themselves distinctly reluctant to stand and fight. The prevailing military opinion was that the Zulus would have to be driven into a corner and made to fight: and three powerful columns, converging on Ulundi, obviously had a greater chance than one of achieving that.

When Chelmsford decided to join the Centre Column (No. 3), he effectively displaced the nominal commander, Colonel Glyn of the 24th, and confirmed the general feeling that this column would be in the forefront of the advance, and bear the brunt of the fighting. The backbone of the column was the two battalions of the 24th (2nd Warwickshire) Regiment. It was unusual for two battalions of the same regiment to be serving together (in theory one battalion was supposed to

1. In one of the illustrations to *A Lost Legionary in South Africa*, Hamilton-Browne has shown himself in typically heroic mode, at the forefront of the attack on Sihayo's homestead.

2. At dawn on the 23rd January, Hamilton-Browne salutes the body of Col. Pulleine on the field of Isandlwana.

3. *Left* 'Collecting Information For The O.C.': Hamilton-Browne riding down a Zulu scout in pursuit of intelligence. For the first few weeks after Isandlwana, stray Zulus could expect an unsympathetic reception at the hands of the remainder of the Centre Column – and Hamilton-Browne was less sympathetic than most.

4. *Right* 'The Crime Of The Naturalist': one of the illustrations in Hamilton-Browne's book, depicting Lt. Harford's dastardly deed with the gin bottle!

5. The claustrophobic fight for the hospital at Rorke's Drift, an incident which caught the imagination of the Victorian public, and became one of the legendary feats of arms of the era. In this version of the scene, a sick patient is helped to safety in the nick of time, even as a wounded Zulu clutches at his blanket.

6. In the cold light of dawn, the defenders of Rorke's Drift eagerly await the arrival of the remainder of Lord Chelmsford's column.

7. *Left* How the *Penny Illustrated* saw Midshipman Coker, of H.M.S. *Active*, directing the Gatling gun at the battle of Nyezane on January 22nd. The scene is broadly accurate, but Coker was eighteen at the time of the battle – not quite the jaunty youth depicted here. Coker was one of those who succumbed to disease during the siege of Eshowe.

8. *Right* An alarm at Eshowe; members of the Naval Brigade rush to man the ramparts. Although alarms were common, the Zulus in fact made no attack on the defences.

9. *Left* The *Penny Illustrated* depicts an incident in the siege of Eshowe described by Shervington; Zulus set off a booby-trapped 'torpedo' left by Engineer work-parties. It's unlikely that the Zulus would have worn the ceremonial finery depicted here, but this engraving has nonetheless depicted Zulu costume with surprising accuracy.

10. *Right* Saving the day; a heroic image of Sergeant Anthony Booth, 80th Regiment, who rallied the survivors of the disastrous action at Ntombe Drift in March 1879. In fact Booth's men were not so well prepared – with full accoutrements! – as this sketch suggests, though the background details capture something of the chaotic nature of the fighting.

11. A surprisingly accurate rendition of the death of Captain Campbell, Wood's Staff Officer, at the battle of Hlobane: Lieutenant Lysons and Private Fowler are poised to drive off his assailants, an act which won them both

the VC. Although the Zulus are wearing too much regalia – a common fault in many newspaper illustrations at the time – the overall scene is well conveyed.

12. Major Hackett is carried, severely wounded, back from the sortie which saved the day at Khambula. Although clearly based on a description of the incident, the officers' uniforms have been decidedly romanticised in this engraving.

13. Trooper Grandier's heroic escape from his captors; a nice rendition of the scene, which nonetheless probably never happened!

14. Field punishment inflicted with the Cat; flogging was no longer permitted in the British Army during peacetime, but was allowed on active service.

Both black and white soldiers were flogged during the Zulu War, as Bindon Blood's account confirms.

15. Captain Cecil D'Arcy won the VC for heroism during Buller's skirmish at Ulundi on the 3rd July. During the retreat, Lance-Corporal Raubenheim of the Frontier Light Horse fell from his horse, and D'Arcy turned back to rescue him, though the Zulus were pursuing close behind. Raubenheim had been badly stunned, and, although D'Arcy managed to haul him onto his own horse once, the animal threw both of them off, and D'Arcy couldn't lift him a second time. D'Arcy managed to escape, but Raubenheim was killed. This sketch gives a surprisingly accurate impression of the scene – although it is unlikely that Raubenheim would have been wearing a sword.

16. Lord William Beresford rescues Sergeant Fitzmaurice during Buller's skirmish on July 3rd. Such heroic deeds were exactly what the British public expected of their heroes, and provided the special artists and correspondents with Chelmsford's column with plenty of dramatic copy.

17. Gatling guns in action at Ulundi. The Gatling proved unreliable but effective; it was prone to jamming, but when it worked it cut a swath through the Zulu ranks, as Grenfell described.

remain on garrison duty in the UK whilst the other served overseas) but the 1/24th had arrived in South Africa in 1876, and played a prominent part in the suppression of the Xhosa uprising, whilst the 2/24th had arrived just in time to take part in the mopping up operations at the end of the campaign. Both battalions were therefore used to fighting in South African conditions, and the 1st Battalion, in particular, had earned a reputation as seasoned veterans who could be relied upon to rise to any task. To support the infantry, the column included a battery of six 7-pdr guns of N Battery, 5th Brigade, Royal Artillery, a number of small mounted units from the Natal Volunteer Corps, and both battalions of the 3rd Regiment, Natal Native Contingent. The NNC were recruited from Natal's black population who were often very willing to fight against the Zulus, but since the colonial authorities were nervous of arming and training them properly, and many of their officers held them in contempt, their fighting potential was largely wasted.

Nonetheless, the column was undeniably strong, and this was apparent even to King Cetshwayo. He had been stunned by the British ultimatum, which had been clearly designed to make compliance impossible and to give him no room for manoeuvre. At first he prevaricated, but when it became apparent that British troops were about to cross into his territory, he called up his warriors. After consulting the ibandla, his council of powerful men representing the various groups within the kingdom, the king resolved to wage an essentially defensive war. He would strike at the British so long as they were in Zululand, but, in keeping with the Zulu view that they were the innocent victims of foreign aggression, and in the hope of winning political advantages in any future negotiations, he would not allow his warriors to cross into Natal. When news of the skirmish at Sihayo's homestead on 12th January reached Ulundi, it confirmed the king's suspicion that the Centre Column was the strongest and most dangerous of the enemy incursions, and Cetshwayo disposed his troops accordingly. Those warriors who lived in the northern and coastal reaches were ordered to concentrate near their homes and harass the British flanking columns, whilst the main strike

49

force, consisting of some 20,000 warriors of the youngest amabutho, was sent against Chelmsford.

These events are best told by Commandant George Hamilton-Browne, who lived through them. Hamilton-Browne was an Irish adventurer who had seen a good deal of active service against the Maoris in the New Zealand Wars (where he had the nickname 'Maori Browne'), and he held a command with a tough irregular unit, Pulleine's Rangers, in the closing stages of the war on the Eastern Cape. In the Zulu War he commanded the 1/3rd NNC. His reminiscences, *A Lost Legionary in South Africa*, published about 1912, suggest he was a both garrulous and scurrilous storyteller, a courageous and reliable soldier by his own account at least, and a man of strong prejudices, which he frequently voiced. He was quite capable of brutalising both his own men and the enemy. His story takes us from the column's advance into Zululand on the morning of 11th January (he says the 10th – presumably a memory slip), to the terrible aftermath of Isandlwana just eleven days later. Were his doubts about the choice of camp a case of being wise after the event? Perhaps. But his story is chilling none the less:

*

Before daylight on the morning of the 10th January 1879, the headquarter column of the Zululand Field Force began to cross the Buffalo River at Rourke's Drift and enter Zululand.

I had a few days before been appointed Commandant of the 1st Battalion of the 3rd Regiment of the Natal Native Contingent, composed of ten companies. Each company consisted of three white officers, six white non-commissioned officers and one hundred or more Natal natives. The exact number of natives I never knew but I had about twelve hundred of them in all.

The officers were chiefly a smart lot of young colonials, most of whom spoke Zulu, all of them good shots and fine horsemen.

The non-coms were a motley crowd, a few of them old soldiers and ex-clerks, the majority of them runaway sailors, ex-navvies, and East London boatmen. They were an awful tough crowd, but they looked a hard-fighting lot and though their language was strong, and they were evidently very rough, they looked also very ready, and I afterwards found that most of them did not belie their looks. The greater number of both officers and non-coms had served through the Gaika and Galeka wars of 1877 and 1878, and many of them had been under me before.

The column was commanded by General Lord Chelmsford and was composed of both battalions of the 24th Regiment, one battery of Royal Artillery, two companies of Mounted Infantry, the Natal Mounted Police, the Natal Carbineers, and the 3rd Regiment of Natal Native Contingent, of which Commandant Lonsdale was commandant-in-chief, I commanding the 1st and Commandant Cooper the 2nd Battalion. Of course we had doctors, ambulances, commissariat officers and the usual miles of wagons, without which no column can march in Africa.

The morning was very cold, the dense morning fog, for which Zululand is famous, hung close to the ground, and although it was midsummer the cold bit, causing us to shiver in our thin khaki clothing, whilst the naked natives turned blue, their teeth chattering like stone-breakers at work.

There were four crossing-places to the river, a very rapid one and on that day in flood.

Two of these were fairly practicable drifts (fords), and two ponts that had been put together by the Royal Engineer officer and some of my non-coms. These drifts were above and below the ponts and my orders were that I was to cross at the lower drift, line the ridge on the other side and hold it while the 24th, the guns and the wagons were got across by the ponts.

The Mounted Infantry were to cross after my men and the mounted volunteers were to cross after Commandant Cooper at the upper drift.

Well before daylight in the bitter fog, we came down to the drift. The river was full, rapid and very cold and looked far from tempting. However orders must be obeyed so we hardened our hearts and dashed at it, the natives all locking arms and rushing in en masse. My horse was nearly carried off his feet but having been used to crossing bad rivers in New Zealand, I kept him up and over we got. I do not know how many of my natives were lost. I had never received a long roll of them when I took over the command, and but few returns were ever sent in.

A most dashing act was done at the drift by Captain Hayes who was in command of my rear company.

One of the Mounted Infantry, a poor horseman, lost control of his horse, and horse and man were swept down the river. Captain Hayes who had crossed, dashed in and saved both. This was done under the eye of the General who mentioned it in dispatches, and who rode that night to my camp to thank Captain Hayes personally.

Now we were in Zululand, cold, wet through and shivering with our tempers short and crisp. The Colonial can grumble just as well as an old Tommy, and he has, as a rule, more command of language. However it did not take me long to get my men into line, and we pushed on, up the rise, and took possession of the top of the ridge, which we lined.

Just then the sun came up and away went the fog. For the first hour or so we enjoyed it. But when our clothes were dry we began to get dry ourselves and I may say we dried very quickly and soon began to scorch.

There was no shade and as the sun increased in heat, there we lay on that bare ridge and roasted all that live-long day. Certainly we had plenty of water nearly as warm as ourselves, but that scorching sun would have been less intolerable had we been on the move.

There was no enemy in sight, nothing to do, conversation died away, it was too hot to sleep, even the East London boatmen could not curse, and the only thing I could do was to stick four assagais into the ground, rest a shield on them, lie with my head in the shade of the latter and think of iced drinks.

How we white men longed for the enemy or anything to break this monotony, but no enemy came. Although Serhio (one of Cetewayo's principal *indunas* (chiefs) and one of the chief causes of the war) had his kraal only a few miles off, he refused to call on us for afternoon tea, but we called on him for early coffee next morning.

However the longest day must have an ending and at dark the pickets were posted, and we were ordered down to the camp that had been pitched in a long line on the Zulu bank of the river.

Now I do not want to rake up old stories or say anything unkind about men, most of whom are dead. But in the book of Standing Orders, issued to all commandants, the first order was that no camp should be pitched without being laagered. Yet here was a camp, stretching away in a long line, without any attempt at a laager or any other defence.

After a feed of bully beef and biscuit washed down by a pannikin of muddy coffee, the first food that day, I had just finished my pipe and was rolling myself up in my blankets when the orderly officer arrived with the order that I was to parade eight companies of my men before daylight and join the party that was to attack Serhio's kraal next morning.

It seemed I had hardly been to sleep, when the faithful Quin roused me up with a pannikin of coffee and it was a case of turn out and get my men together. We had some trouble in turning out the natives but it was done at last and we marched off, being ordered to take post in rear of the mounted advance guard, the sun rising as we crossed the ridge and advanced on the precipitous Krantz where Serhio had his stronghold.

As we got nearer we could hear the lowing of cattle, the sound coming from a deep cleft running into the precipice. Just then the screen of mounted men moved away to the right and left and I received orders to advance to the front.

It may be as well here to say something about the arming of my motley gang. My officers and non-coms were each armed with MH rifles and each carried seventy rounds of ammunition. Fifty more MH rifles were distributed amongst the natives, but as they were quite ignorant of the use of rifles, and the MH is not a rifle to be played with by a duffer, we were ourselves in far greater danger of our own men than the enemy were. Fifty more old muzzle-loading rifles were provided but I did not fear these so much, as the natives usually forgot to tear off the end of the paper cartridge or placed it in ball part first, so that the rifle refused to go off. We certainly had no time to instruct them in musketry but as only five rounds, per man, was issued, I trusted, with luck, to get through the job without being shot by my own [men].

The rest of the force had shields, assagais and knobkerries and I made up my mind that the closer the action was the safer it would be for me. I therefore determined to charge the first moment I could. But alas! I did not know then, in what an awful funk the Natal [African] was of the real fighting Zulu.

Anyhow the mounted men cleared my front and I pressed on, passing Lord Chelmsford and his staff who up to that time had accompanied the advance guard. The General returned my salute and calling me over to him said, 'Commandant Browne, those Krantzes are full of cattle; go down and take them but on no account are you to fire before you are fired at.' He also said, 'I shall hold you responsible that no women or children are killed.'

He then wished me luck in the most kind and courteous manner – a manner that endeared him to all of us. No general that I ever served under in South Africa, was so respected and liked as he was, and certainly, no Colonial officer ever said a word against him or blamed him for the awful disaster that came later on.

Well I got my men into line and advanced to the first fight in Zululand. Previous to moving off I repeated the General's orders to my captains, at the same time telling them to impress on their men that any man who hurt a woman or a child would be shot at once. I then gave the order to advance, and we moved on to the Krantz in what might be called a line, but a very crooked one, as a South African native cannot walk in a line, draw a line, or form a line, and if placed in a line will soon mob himself into a ring.

The Krantz was a precipitous mountain about 500 feet high, and where the enemy and the cattle were located was in a deep cleft running in V shape, the foot of the hill being covered with boulders and bushes.

My men advanced leaping and jumping, singing war-songs, sharpening their assagais, and looking so bloodthirsty that I feared they would kill every woman and child we came across. But as we drew nearer the scene of action their zeal for fighting – like Bob Acre's courage – oozed out of them. Their war-songs dwindled away and they seemed indisposed to come on. In fact some of them suddenly remembering they had important business to transact towards the rear had to be encouraged with the butt of the rifle or the ready boot of my non-coms. As the native must be led, myself and all the officers were in front. This being the case, and we being far more in funk of our playful savages armed with MH rifles than of the enemy, I gave orders that there was to be no firing but that we must trust to the steel.

As we neared the place I observed I could send a party to the right and left of the V-shaped entrance. I therefore detached the two flank companies, and when they had moved off to their assigned places I again advanced.

A voice hailed us asking by whose orders we came. My interpreter and right-hand man (Captain R. Duncombe) answered 'by the orders of the Great White Queen' and the enemy, or those of them who had exposed themselves, at once ran back to cover. I again ordered the advance; a few shots were fired at us, and I immediately gave the word to charge and led it, followed splendidly by No. 8 Company, commanded by Captains R. Duncombe and O. Murray. A ragged volley was fired at us by the enemy, but we charged on through it and up the rising ground to the mouth of the V which we found to be full of boulders. I had gained the mouth when I looked back. Ye gods of war, what a sight for a commandant! No. 8 Company, led by two of the best Colonial officers I have ever met, were on my heels, but the rest! I saw their backs in a mad stampede while among them raged their furious officers and non-coms.

Above the rifle shots rang out their wild imprecations while with butt, fist and boot they tried to instil courage into that awful mob of cowardly [men].

Now I must say a word about No. 8 Company. Among my 1200 men I had 300 real Zulus. They were the remains of a young Zulu regiment that had been destroyed by Cetewayo's orders the year before. He had ordered a fight to take place, with sticks, between them and his own royal regiment. The youngsters had beaten their seniors, and this so enraged the king that he turned Serhio's regiment, armed with shields and assagais, on to them who had decimated them. This was not cricket, as the boys had only their sticks; however some of them had escaped to Natal with Esikota, the king's youngest brother, and these 300 men were quite game to return and play another match, backed up by white men, with their destroyers. Their contempt for the Natal [African] was unbounded, and they were splendid fighting men. They formed three of my companies, Nos. 8, 9 and 10. No. 9 was in camp. No. 8 was with me and No. 10 was one of the companies I had sent to work round the enemy's flank.

I left off, as our charge swept into the mouth of the V. Here the Zulus, who had up to this time been firing at us from under cover, met and for a time we had a sweet hand-to-hand fight. Shield clashed against shield, assagai met assagai and the hissing word 'Guzzie', as the stab went home, was answered by the grunt or yell of the wounded man. I had my hands full and had to use freely both sword and revolver. The enemy fought splendidly but my men would not be denied. Had not Serhio been the *induna* (chief) of the Impie who had killed their brothers, and would they not have their revenge?

My white officers and non-coms also fought like fiends and we drove them back over the rocks and round the rocks until at last they took refuge in rear of the cattle jammed into the narrow end of the V. These had to be driven out before we could get to them again and it was done; also a lot of women and children were brought out. Thank the Lord none of them hurt, and they with the cattle were removed to the open. We now found that the enemy had retreated by a narrow path to the top of a cliff about 60 feet high and had blocked the path by rolling big boulders into it.

They opened fire on us, which although hot was very badly directed and my officers and non-coms returned it with interest.

Just then Lieutenant Harford of the 99th Regiment, who was acting as SO to Commandant Lonsdale, came up to me. He was a charming companion, one of the very best, but he was a crazy bug and beetle hunter, and would run about on the hottest day with a landing-net to catch butterflies and other insects. He moreover collected and treasured snakes, scorpions and loathsome beasts of all sorts. He had never been under fire before and had on two or three occasions talked to me about a man's feelings while undergoing his baptism of fire, and had expressed hopes he would be cool and good while undergoing his. Well we were in rather a hot corner and he was standing to my right rear when I heard an exclamation, and turning round saw him lying on the ground having dropped his sword and revolver. 'Good God, Harford,' I said, 'you are hit!' 'No, sir,' he replied, 'not hit but I have caught such a beauty.' And there the lunatic, in his first action, and under a heavy fire, his qualms of nervousness all forgotten, had captured some infernal microbe or other, and was blowing its wings out, as unconscious of the bullets striking the rocks all round him as if he had been in his garden at home. He was just expatiating on his victory and reeling off Latin names – they might have been Hebrew for all I knew or cared – when I stopped him, and told him to get as quick as he could to the right flanking company and hurry them up. He looked at me with sorrow, put his prize into a tin box and was off like a shot.

All this time my bold runaways had been absent, but now they returned in this manner.

There was in the second 24th a major (Wilson Black by name), and Commandant Lonsdale having been knocked over by sunstroke during the previous day, Major Black had been placed, for the time being, in full command of the 3rd NNC.

He was a Highlander, brave as his own sword, tender-hearted as a woman, hospitable as a Maori, but with a temper well, may I say it, just a little peppery. He had served through the Crimea and Mutiny with, I think, the Black Watch, and I had only met him the night before.

Up to this time he had been with the 2nd Battalion of the 3rd, but when he saw the undignified retreat of the greater part of my men, he drew his sword, and quickly bringing forward a strong party of the 24th, with fixed bayonets, he rode right at them. They were now between the devil and the deep sea. They were already catching toko badly from their own white officers and non-coms, and as if that was not enough here comes a man on horseback followed by a lot of those red soldiers, who with flashing steel, were rushing right at them. It was too much. They had to turn back and with their officers trying to get them into some sort of shape they were driven at the point of the bayonet back to me. When they arrived Black burst through them and joined me. At once they halted. Forward they would not come, back they could not go, for there was that awful line of the red soldiers with fixed bayonets, and among them raged their own white men. So they did just what I expected they would do; every man of them who had a gun let it off, quite regardless as to the direction of the business end pointed, and they fired away as fast as they could load.

In vain their officers ordered them to cease fire, in vain their non-coms kicked and cuffed them; fire they would and fire they did so long as they had a cartridge left.

Well that was a very sultry spot indeed for the time being but there is an end to most things in this world and, thank the Lord, their fire-play soon ended.

Some of them rammed their cartridges down bullet first so they became harmless as their rifles refused to go off, and as it does not take a raw savage long to let off five rounds of MH ammunition when he aims at nothing the firing died away and we were again able to pay attention to the Zulus. We also counted our dead and wounded and I found that my beauties had bagged thirty-two of themselves, but I could well spare them.

I do not believe that the enemy were responsible for a single one, their fire having been kept down by my officers who perforated every head that was raised to fire at us, so the firing ceased. Yet we were at the base of a 60-foot perpendicular cliff and could not get at them and I saw at once that we must wait for the flanking companies to work round. They were having a hard job getting at the spot on account of the roughness of the ground but there was nothing else to do.

Major Black thought otherwise. How he expected to scale the cliff I know not, but he got to the foot of it and shouted for rifles to come on. He was standing with his back turned to the rock and was waving his sword when the Zulus hearing him rolled over some stones; one struck the gallant major on the – well, not on the head – and he fell on his knees and poured out a volume of Gaelic that filled my non-coms with delight.

It might have been prayers he was letting go, but the volubility and unctuousness forbid that idea, and they all thought, though they could not understand one word of his orison, that he was using very bad language indeed and all the more they admired him.

A few minutes before Colonel Glyn and Major Cleary had come up and were standing by me. We were unable to restrain our laughter and burst into a roar as Black limped up to us cursing, in good Anglo-Saxon, the Zulus for wounding a gentleman in a place he could not show to anyone but the doctor.

However he was not much hurt and soon recovering his temper joined in the laugh.

The flanking companies had by this time worked round and Lieutenant Harford who had joined one of them shouted to the Zulus that if they surrendered they would not be killed.

This they did, and the fighting, as far as I was concerned, was over for that day.

The mounted men who had gone to the top of the hill had a sharp skirmish with a large party of the enemy, these being joined by the Zulus who had escaped from me. But they were easily routed, the troopers pursuing some distance and killing a good few.

Leaving one company behind me to collect our own wounded, I joined the main command with the rest of my men and we returned to camp for the night. Serhio had been well punished, his big kraal had been burned, two of his sons were among the dead, some of his daughters among the prisoners, and his pet herd of cattle had been captured.

If you wish to know the cause of the war I must refer you to Blue Books for the information. It was no business of mine and my opinion was not asked on the question.

Next day (the 12th) we rested in camp, and my natives asked for an ox, to medicine themselves with. This I gave them hoping the ceremony might instil some courage into them, as they swore it would, but I had no idea of the diabolical cruelty they were going to practise on the poor beast or I would have seen them in Hades first. Anyway, something must have gone wrong with the performance as their courage did not increase but rather diminished. However I will not touch on the subject of [African] witchcraft, but pass on.

During the day the General visited my camp and kindly thanked me for the work of the day before. He also requested me to present to him Captains Duncombe and Murray.

The same evening I received orders to strike camp, and at daylight to move out to the scene of the late fight, and camp there with the object of making a road over a swamp, so as to allow the heavy wagons to advance.

We moved out and camped, but when it came to road-making trouble began.

The Colonial officers turned sulky. They had come out to fight not to make roads. None of the natives had ever used pick or spade before, and it took me all my time to get them turned to. Certainly it is not a pleasant job to make roads in Zululand during the summer-time, the sun hot, flies bad, and men sulky. The Colonial officers were not at their best, and men who would willingly stand up to their middles all day long in the drift of a river plugging oxen over, grumbled and swore. It required no small amount of tact to get them started, but when they saw me off shirt and turn to, they could not hang back and once started we soon made things hum and the road grew apace.

In this manner things went on till the 19th of January. On that morning I was visited by the General and his staff. He informed me that news had been received that the Zulu army was to leave Ulundi that morning to attack us, and ordered, in case he was attacked, I was to move down and attack the right flank of the enemy. I suggested that as I lay in their road, they would eat me up long before they reached him. He thought not, but I requested the chief of the staff to allow me to take my men off work and laager my camp.

This he refused, but as soon as the staff left I altered the position of my wagons, told off my white men to their respective posts and made what preparations I could in case of a fight. I took no precautions, for my natives, with the exception of the Zulu companies, as I knew that the Natal [men] would bolt at the first onset.

That afternoon I received a note from Captain Duncombe who was in command of the picket on the top of the hill, informing me that there was a large number of cattle in the valleys on his right, and requesting me to come up at once. This I did, taking with me two companies of my Zulus, the other one being on picket with him. On joining him on the top of the pass we moved carefully to the edge of some very rough ground consisting of deep valleys, and on looking into these we saw a large number of cattle herded by a few unarmed Zulus, who called to us to come down, as they wished to surrender themselves and the cattle. This was a temptation, a very nice bait indeed, but I saw through it. I had matriculated an ambush work in New Zealand, had had more than my share of it and with all my faults I have never been deemed a greedy or covetous man, so directed Captain Duncombe to shout to them ordering them to come up and surrender on the top, but this they refused to do. Captain Duncombe then at my request called Umvubie, the head fighting *induna* (chief) of my Zulus and asked him what he thought of it. He at once replied, 'That is a trap, those bushes are full of Zulus. If we descend they will kill every one of us, but we shall have a good fight first. I and my brothers are ready to descend with the chief.'

Now this was startling. I had no doubt that what Umvubie stated was true, and if so a large body of the enemy – how large I knew not – must be on the General's right flank.

I immediately sent off a runner to the HQ camp, with a note to that effect, and, as it was approaching sunset, retired to my camp, leaving Captain Duncombe with a few good men (well hidden) to keep watch for any moves they (the Zulus) might carry on.

The Zulus, seeing I had retired, came out of their ambush, some 1,500 strong, and started towards a large military kraal which we knew to be several miles down the river. I partook of early coffee at that kraal later on.

Seeing they left the cattle behind, Duncombe and his men,

61

as soon as they lost sight of the enemy, descended into the valley, captured some 150 head of them and brought them into my camp.

On reaching my camp I found Major Black had arrived, bringing with him two companies of the second 24th. I reported to him what I had seen and Captain Duncombe coming in shortly afterwards, Major Black at once sent a report into the HQ camp.

The night passed quietly, but my natives were very restless and evidently in a great funk.

Next morning Captain Hallam Parr, one of the staff, came out with orders to Major Black and myself that we were to get ready to march as the whole column was to move forward, so we struck camp and packed wagons. On the General reaching us, he questioned myself and Duncombe as to what we had seen and we reported fully. This interview being over, I was ordered by the CSO to move my men on and clear the road, a rough wagon track over the pass, of any boulders and stones that might be lying on it and was to be supported by a party of the second 24th, under Lieutenant Pope.

Away we went and after a few miles came to a queer-shaped mountain that looked like a sphinx lying down, by the same token I have never seen the beast depicted standing up, anyhow the road ran between this mountain and a kopje when we at once came out on a big plain.

I had just reached here when Major Cleary rode up, who directed me to move to my left so as to be ready to encamp, he riding with me, and pointing out the ground on which my camp was to be pitched, which would be on the extreme left of the line.

The column came up, and the camp was arranged in the same form as it had been on the bank of the river, only it was much more extended. As soon as the tents were pitched, and we had had some food, I was joined by Commandant Lonsdale, who had that day come out of hospital. I was talking to some of my best officers when he joined us and his first words to me were, 'My God, Maori, what do you think of this camp?' I replied, 'Some one is mad.' The Colonial officers were loud and long in complaint, and Duncombe said, 'Do the staff think we are going to meet an army of school-girls? Why in the name of all that is holy do we not laager?'

In the evening I strolled over to the 24th lines to have a chat with the officers, all of whom I knew well. Whilst there, I had a yarn with Colonel Glyn who was acting as brigadier-general, and would have had command of the column had not the General and staff decided to join us at the last moment. He was a very old friend of my family's and had served as a lieutenant under my father. He did not seem to be in good spirits, but said nothing about the camp and on my remarking it looked very pretty though rather extended, he looked hard at me, shook his head and said 'Very'.

That night Lonsdale came to my tent and told me that myself and Cooper were each to parade eight companies before daylight, and to clear the rough broken valleys to our right front. He would take command, and that Major Dartnell, with the Natal Mounted Police and volunteers were to act in concert with us, keeping on the high ground. I inquired if any orders had been given to laager the camp. He answered 'No', adding language not very complimentary to certain members of the staff, which I fully endorsed.

Before daylight we moved out of camp, and while doing so I saw and spoke to Lieutenant-Colonel Pulleine of the first 24th. We were old friends, and he chaffed me, saying, 'A lot of you [black] leaders will be knocked over to-day.' I answered, 'If that is so, when I return to camp I shall not find one of you alive.' We laughed and parted. Which prophecy was to come right you shall hear.

At the head of my men I crossed a donga to join up with Lonsdale who was with the 2nd battalion, and on doing so he instructed me to make a detour of a hill and descend into some valleys, he working round the other side in such a manner so as to catch anything or any one who might be between us.

The movement was carried out and we captured some hundreds of head of cattle, though all the kraals we passed contained only old men, women, girls and children.

To a girl, I returned some goats which one of my men had taken from her and, through Duncombe, questioned her as to the movements of all the men. She replied, 'That they had been ordered to join the king's big army.' We again asked 'where that was'. She pointed with her chin over to the NE, at the same time saying, 'They would attack us in two days' time.' This bore out the opinion I had formed, after hearing the news on the 19th that the army had left Ulundi.

In our next drive I captured two young men and questioned them. They had no goats to be given back to them, but there are more ways than one of extracting information.

They were led apart and well questioned. War is war and you can't play at savage war with kid gloves on. The information amounted to this. They had both left the big army and had come over to see their mother. We inquired, 'Where is the big army?' They pointed in the same direction as the girl had done. 'When was the attack to take place?' They did not know, but the moon would be right in two days' time.

This information tallied with the girl's and Lonsdale, Cooper and myself discussed it.

The day wore on. The valleys became as hot as furnaces. We captured more cattle. So towards evening we left the low country after the most trying day and made for the high land.

On reaching it, I at once suggested we should return to the camp and inform the General of what we had learned. This was decided on and as we were then seven miles from camp Captain O. Murray was immediately dispatched, with two companies, to drive the captured cattle there. The remainder of us rested; as the white non-coms, most of whom were on foot, were very tired after their rough day's work in the stony, rugged valleys.

Poor Murray! I never saw him again. He was one of the very best stamp of Colonials, brave, loyal and true, always ready for hard work, a splendid shot and horseman. I know before he went down in the awful hell of the 22nd that he did his duty to the last, and that very many of the enemy fell to his rifle.

Evening was drawing on. We had fallen in and were preparing to return to camp when two mounted men rode up, informing us that Major Dartnell had sent them to find us, and ask us to come and support him as he had 300 Zulus in front of him, the ground in rear of the enemy being so rough, he was unable to use his horses to advantage.

I requested Lonsdale not to think of doing such a thing, pointing out at the same time that we had no food or reserve ammunition, also that we were seven miles from camp, our white men worn out and that it would be night before we could reach Dartnell, who was over three miles from us and at least that distance further away from camp than we were.

Again was not this party of Zulus the advance guard of the big army? a trap to catch us or a small party of men on their way to join the big army who would clear out directly they saw Dartnell reinforced.

Duncombe who was asked to give an opinion fully agreed with me, but Lonsdale, who had not got over his sunstroke, was simply spoiling for a fight, so orders were given for us to advance, and away we went.

I regret to say that as we moved off four of my officers left me without leave and returned to camp. Their punishment came quickly, they were all killed next day.

Well on we went till we came to an open valley and saw the mounted men drawn up at one end of it, while at the other end were from 200 to 300 Zulus with very rough ground just in their rear and at this moment the sun set.

I again pointed out to Lonsdale the folly of our joining the mounted men. If it was a trap and we descended, our men, or rather our white men who had been on foot all day were too much exhausted to put up a good fight.

If it was not a trap, the enemy would never stand and allow about 1,400 more men to join the mounted forces but would fall back into the rough ground where it would be impossible to follow them in the dark.

However Lonsdale decided to descend, so down we went. As we advanced, the Zulus drew off into the rough ground and the night fell. There is no twilight in Zululand.

Here we were at least eleven miles from camp, no food, no spare ammunition, well knowing that a huge army of Zulus must be in our close vicinity. Well I was not in command, but I begged Lonsdale even at that hour to return to camp. I said, 'We know the camp is going to be attacked, every cock fights best in his own yard. When the General hears our news he will order the camp to be laagered and we can put up a fight there against the whole Zulu nation, whilst out here we shall be stamped flat in a minute.' But no, Lonsdale would not grasp the situation, and decided to stay where we were with the intention of going for those few Zulus in the morning.

Major Dartnell concurred with him. They decided to form two squares, our men in one, Dartnell's in another, and we were to bivouac there for the night.

My Colonial officers were furious. Colonial officers are given to speaking their minds. Even Captain Duncombe came to me and asked me if everyone had gone mad. 'What in God's name are we to do here?'

The squares were formed. We had in our square about 1,400 natives armed as I have before mentioned, with their complement of white officers and non-coms, but few of the officers had brought their rifles, and very many cartridges had been lost while scrambling over the rocks and rough ground during the day. I of course disarmed the natives, who had MH rifles, and gave them to the officers but the ammunition was very short.

The natives were made to sit down in a square, two deep, the white men being inside. Ye Gods of war! as if Natal [Africans] in a formation two deep would stand for a moment against a rush of Zulus. Sick with disgust, as soon as the square was formed, I lay down and, strange to say, fell asleep. I had loosened my revolver belt for a minute, meaning to buckle it again, but went to sleep without having done so. I do not know how long I slept when I felt myself rushed over and trampled on. I tried to get to my feet, but was knocked down again. I then tried to find my revolver, but was unable to do so. I never let go of my horse's bridle which I was holding in my hand, and at last staggered to my feet.

The square was broken, natives rushing all ways mixed up with plunging horses, while the night was horrible with yells, shouts and imprecations. 'My God,' I thought, 'why am I not assagaied?' as half-mad natives rushed by me jostling me with their shields. In a flash I saw it was a false alarm. To wrench a knobkerry out of a native's hand, and to lay about me, was the work of a moment. My white men fought their way to my shout and backing me up splendidly we soon quelled the uproar and thrashed the cowards back to their places.

To pick up my revolver and buckle the belt did not take long, and then it was time to inquire the cause of the row. It seems that one of the natives had gone to sleep and had dropped his shield and assagais, and this was enough to frighten the bold Natal blacks into a stampede.

Yet with *these cowards* I was expected to stop a rush of the finest fighting savages in the world!

As soon as I met Lonsdale I again urged him to return to camp even at this hour, and perhaps he might have done so, when Major Dartnell came over to us and informed us that he had sent an orderly back to camp to request the General to reinforce us. This would be worse and worse, with a force of men barely strong enough to meet 30,000 to 40,000 Zulus, even when in laager. It certainly was not the game to break up that force into two parts at a distance of quite eleven miles and just before a big fight was expected to take place.

Again I sat down, sick to the very heart, but of course I could say no more. Lonsdale was my chief, and it was my duty to loyally back him up and obey his orders.

About an hour afterwards, one of the horses shook himself, and immediately the cowardly hounds of Natal [Africans] again stampeded, but we were ready for them this time, and thrashed them back to their places. I then informed them that the next man who moved would be at once shot and that the two Zulu companies should charge and kill off the company to which the delinquent belonged. This threat put the fear of the Lord into them, and for the rest of the night they sat tight.

The weary night dragged on, no chance of sleep, no chance of rest, as we had to watch our wretched [men], and I was very pleased to see the east lighten and grow pale.

Just after daybreak, to my unbounded surprise, the General, staff, four guns, the Mounted Infantry and I think six companies of the second 24th reached us.

Colonel Glyn rode over to me and drawing me aside said,

'In God's name, Maori, what are you doing here?' I answered him with a question, 'In God's name, sir, what are you doing here?'

He shook his head and replied, 'I am not in command.' And fine old soldier as he was, I could see he was much disturbed.

As we were speaking, I received orders to get my men into line and advance into the rough ground, into which the enemy had retreated the night before. We were now going further away from the camp; but orders must be obeyed, so getting my crowd under way, we advanced.

After moving forwards about two miles I found a party of the enemy in caves and behind a good cover of rocks and stunted bush. They appeared to be well supplied with firearms, and opened out on us, making fairly good practice.

I was just going to try to kick a charge out of my beauties, when a mounted orderly rode up with orders for me, which were that I was at once to report myself with my battalion to the General, and that he was to guide me to the place where the General was waiting for me.

Getting my men together and advising Lonsdale of my orders, I requested him to take over my skirmish, and on his relieving me with the 2nd battalion I moved down a valley and found the General and staff quietly at breakfast.

Never shall I forget the sight of that peaceful picnic. Here were the staff quietly breakfasting and the whole command scattered over the country! Over there the guns unlimbered, over the hills parties of Mounted Infantry and volunteers looting the scattered kraals for grain for their horses, a company of the 24th one place, and another far away, and yet I knew that an army of from 30,000 to 40,000 of the bravest and most mobile savages in the world were within striking distance of us, and that our camp was some thirteen miles away; left with but few horsemen and only two guns to defend, and it a long straggling camp, hampered with all the wagons and impedimenta of the column.

As soon as I halted my men, the General rose and kindly greeting me asked me if I had had any breakfast. I replied, 'No, nor had any of my men had any.' I might have added, 'and no dinner or supper the night before.' Of course he understood, that as commandant, I could not eat in presence of my fasting men.

I said, 'Are you aware, sir, I was engaged when I received your order?' He said 'No,' and turning to the CSO said, 'Crealock, Browne tells me he was engaged when he received the order to come here.' Colonel Crealock came to me and said, 'Commandant Browne, I want you to return at once to camp and assist Colonel Pulleine *to strike camp and come on here.*' I nearly fell off my horse. Could these men know of the close proximity of the enemy? Were we all mad or what? However I was only a poor devil of a Colonial commandant and as a simple irregular not supposed to criticise full-blown staff officers, so I saluted and said, 'If I come across the enemy?' 'Oh,' said he, 'just brush them aside and go on,' and with this he went on with his breakfast.

So I kept on down that valley which presently opened out into a big plain, and on the far side of it, about thirteen miles off, was a queer-shaped mountain, the ground gently rising to the base of it. With my glasses I could discern a long white line which I knew to be tents. The name of that mountain was Isandlwana and the time was then 9 a.m. on the 22nd January 1879.

We marched very slowly on, the day was intensely hot, and my white non-coms who were on foot very fagged. They had had a very hard day the day before. They had had no sleep and no food, and somehow over the whole command there seemed to hover a black cloud.

However push on was the word, and at 10 o'clock myself and Adjutant-Lieutenant Campbell, who were riding some distance in front, flushed two Zulus. They bolted and we rode them down. Campbell shot his one, but I captured mine and on Duncombe coming up we questioned him.

He was only a boy and was frightened out of his life so that when asked where he came from, he pointed to the line of hills on the left flank of the camp saying 'he had come from the King's big army.' 'What are you doing here?' we asked, to which he replied 'that he and his mate had been sent by their *induna* to see if any white men were among the hills' we had just left, 'but as they were sitting resting under the shade of a rock they did not hear the white men and were caught.' 'What was the size of the army?' He answered, 'There were twelve full regiments' (about 30,000 or perhaps 36,000 men).

Now here was the fat in the fire with a vengeance.

The big Zulu army within four miles of the left flank of the camp, Colonel Pulleine without mounted men, or only a few, only two guns, not more than 900 white men in all, the camp not laagered and the General away on a wild-goose chase, at least thirteen miles from him.

I was unaware, at the time, that Colonel Durnford, RE, had, that morning, reached Isandlwana; he had some hundreds of natives and a rocket battery with him.

I at once wrote a note to the following effect:

10 a.m. – I have just captured a Zulu scout who informs me the Zulu army is behind the range of hills on the left flank of the camp. Will push on as fast as possible. The ground here is good for the rapid advance of mounted men and guns.

This note I sent by a well-mounted officer with orders he was to ride as fast as possible.

The next thing was to try and advance as fast as I could. I rode forward and used my glasses, but everything so far was peaceful.

Just then I met two boys loaded with food. They had been sent out to me by the kind fore-thought of Lieutenant Beuie of my battalion.

They also brought me a note from a great chum of mine, Lieutenant Anstey, first 24th, who told me he and Lieutenant Dailey had gone to my tent the night before, and as they had found a good dinner spoiling, they had eaten it, but sent in return a couple of bottles of whisky. I was never fated to see any of these kind-hearted men again but it is the fortune of war. Well these loads were indeed a godsend, and I divided the food and drink among my non-coms who were on foot and it just bucked them up and gave them heart to further exertions. I would not have minded having some myself, but I was mounted, and they were on foot, so after a ten minutes' halt I again gave the word to move on.

At about 11 o'clock I was on ahead and looking through my glasses when I saw a puff of smoke rise from the hills on the left of the camp. It was followed by another. They seemed to come from a huge black shadow that lay on the hills. Presently another puff and in a moment I knew they were bursting shells. Not a cloud was in the sky, and I knew that the black shadow resting on the hills must be the Zulu army moving down to attack the camp.

At once I dispatched the second message:

11 a.m. – The Zulu army is attacking the left of the camp. The guns were opened on them. The ground here still suitable for guns and mounted men. Will push on so as to act as support to them.

This I dispatched by a mounted officer, and at the same time my first messenger returned. He informed me he had delivered my note to a SO who had read it, and told him to rejoin me, and that I was to push on to camp.

But now my brave barbarians, with their wonderful eyesight, had seen the dreaded foe, and they refused to march. They could not run away as the Zulus were between them and safety, but it took all the muscular persuasion of my officers and the dauntless blackguardism of my non-coms to kick a crawl out of them.

Umvubie of No. 8 Company helped me at this juncture to solve the problem. He said he and his men would march in rear and kill everyone who lagged behind, so at last I got a crawl out of them. I rode on and used my glasses.

I could now see the troops lying down and firing volleys, while the guns kept up a steady fire. The Zulus did not seem able to advance. They were getting it hot, and as there was no cover they must have suffered very heavy losses, as they shortly afterwards fell back. The guns and troops also ceased firing. At about midday I was looking back anxiously to see if the mounted men and guns were coming up, when I heard the guns in camp reopen again; and riding forward, we were then about four miles from the camp. I saw a cloud of Zulus thrown out from their left and form the left horn of their army. These men swept round and attacked the front of the camp, and I saw the two right companies of the 24th and one gun thrown back to resist them. There was also plenty of independent firing going on within the camp, as if all the wagon men, servants, and in fact everyone who could use a rifle was firing away to save his life.

I at once sent another messenger with the following note:

The camp is being attacked on the left and in front, and as yet is holding its own. Ground still good for the rapid advance of guns and horses. Am moving forward as fast as I can.

My second messenger joined me shortly after this and told me he had delivered my note to a staff officer and had received orders for me to push on to camp.

At 1 o'clock the camp was still holding its own and the Zulus were certainly checked. The guns were firing case and I could see the dense mass of natives writhe, sway and shrink back from the steady volleys of the gallant old 24th.

I had given orders to my men to deflect to their left so as to try to get into the right of the camp, and the officers and non-coms were forcing the brutes on, when about half-past one I happened to glance to the right of the camp. Good God! what a sight it was. By the road that runs between the hill and the kopje, came a huge mob of maddened cattle, followed by a dense swarm of Zulus. These poured into the undefended right and rear of the camp, and at the same time the left horn of the enemy and the chest of the army rushed in. Nothing could stand against this combined attack. All formation was broken in a minute, and the camp became a seething pandemonium of men and cattle struggling in dense clouds of dust and smoke.

The defenders fought desperately and I could see through the mist the flash of bayonet and spear together with the tossing heads and horns of the infuriated cattle, while above the bellowing of the latter and the sharp crack of the rifles could be heard the exulting yells of the savages and the cheers of our men gradually dying away. Of course I saw in a moment everything was lost and at once galloped back to my men.

There was no time to write, but I said to Captain Develin, a fine horseman and a finer fellow, 'Ride as hard as you can, and tell every officer you meet, "For God's sake come back, the camp is surrounded and must be taken."'

Then getting my officers together, I said to them, 'Our only chance is to retreat slowly,' and ordered them to form their companies into rings, after the Zulu fashion, and retire, dismounting themselves and hiding all the white men among the natives. This we did, and although there were large parties of the enemy close to us, they took no notice of us, and we gradually retired out of their vicinity. When we had got to a place, about five miles from the camp, where I thought my white men and Zulus could put up a bit of a fight in case we were attacked, I halted and determined to await the course of events. During the retreat I had often looked back and seen that the fighting was over in the camp, but that one company, in company square, was retreating slowly up the hill surrounded by a dense swarm of Zulus. This was Captain Younghusband's company. They kept the enemy off as long as their ammunition lasted, then used the bayonet until at last overcome by numbers they fell in a heap like the brave old British Tommy should.

Well here we were. The white men worn out and hungry, but most of them determined and I had the satisfaction to read on the grim, dirty faces of my roughs, that no matter what they had been in the past, they meant to stick to their work, do their duty like men and if necessary die game.

Curses not loud but very deep, went up for a time, and one or two of Lord Chelmsford's staff must have felt their ears tingle.

We sat and lay where we were. There was nowhere to go, nothing to be done, we had no food, and very little ammunition, but we had some water and tepid and muddy as it was it was thankfully used as there was no shade and the sun shone like a ball of fire. As soon as I had made what few arrangements I could I told the men to get some rest, as I was convinced that later on, we should be called upon to retake the camp, as through that camp was the only possible retreat for the General's party and ourselves.

After a time Captain Develin rode up to me. 'Well,' said I,

'who did you see?' 'I first saw Major Black with the second 24th and repeated your message – he at once turned back. Then I saw Colonel Harness with the guns – he at once turned back. Then I saw the mounted men, and they turned back.' 'Well,' said I, 'where are they?' 'Why, sir,' he replied, 'as we were marching back we met the staff and the troops were ordered to go back again, so I came on alone.'

Why had this been done? Those who want to know had better get the book Miss Colenso wrote in defence of Colonel Durnford, and if they study the evidences recapitulated in that book, especially that of Captain Church, they may find out. I am only writing of what I actually saw myself, and have no wish to throw mud at anyone.

Some time later I saw the MI come out from the hills on to the open ground, form up and dismount. I at once sent an officer to their OC to tell him that if he would support me I would again advance. He acknowledged my message but sent no reply, and shortly afterwards he again mounted his men and returned to the hills.

The long afternoon passed slowly away, and towards evening I saw a small body of horsemen riding towards us. On using my glasses I discovered it was the General and his staff and I at once mounted and rode to meet him.

He looked very surprised when he saw me and said, 'What are you doing here, Commandant Browne? You ought to have been in camp hours ago.' I replied, 'The camp has been taken, sir.'

He flashed out at once, 'How date you tell me such a false-hood? Get your men into line at once and advance.' I did so and led my 700 miserables supported by the staff against the victorious Zulu army.

We moved on about two and a half miles until we had opened out a good view of the camp, when he called me to him and said, in a kindly manner, 'On your honour, Comman-dant Browne, is the camp taken?' I answered, 'The camp was taken at about 1.30 in the afternoon, and the Zulus are now burning some of the tents.'

He said, 'That may be the quartermaster's fatigue burning the debris of the camp.' I replied, 'QM's fatigue do not burn tents, sir,' and I offered him my glasses. He refused them, but said, 'Halt your men at once,' and leaving me, rode back to the staff and dispatched an officer to bring up the remainder of the column.

I had just halted my men and placed them in the best position I could, when to my utter astonishment I saw a man on foot leading a pony, coming from the direction of the camp, and recognised him as Commandant Lonsdale.

He came up to me and said, 'By Jove, Maori, this is fun; the camp is taken.' 'Don't see the humour,' I said, 'but go and tell the staff; they won't believe me.'

He had had the most wonderful escape. As I have said before he was still suffering from sunstroke and having somehow lost the battalion he was with, had ridden towards the camp. More than half stupefied by the great heat, he rode into it, and all at once awoke to the fact that the camp was full of Zulus, some of them wearing soldiers' tunics, and that the ground was littered with dead men. He then realised the situation at a glance and in less time than words can tell, he turned his pony's head and rode as hard as he could away. He was pursued, but the ground was good-going, and his pony 'Dot' a very smart one, so he got clear away and joined us.

Well, again a weary halt. As we lay we could see long lines of Zulus marching along the hills on our right flank. They had with them many of our wagons, most probably loaded with their wounded men, or plunder out of the camp.

At last just as night fell, we were joined by the remainder of the column that had been sent for and we were then formed into line of attack. The guns were in the centre, flanking them parties of the second 24th, my battalion in line on the left, Cooper's battalion in line on the right, and the mounted men in front and on the flanks.

The General spoke a few words to the men and then ready once more, away we went to recapture the camp, or as Umvubie would say, 'To die, but have a good fight first.'

The night, as we were nearing the camp, became very dark and I received orders that I was to retake the kopje at all costs being at the same time warned that if my men turned tail the party of the 24th (under Major Black) who supported me, were at once to fire a volley and charge. This was pleasant for me but of course I recognised the necessity.

The word was now given to move on. At the same time the guns opened fire so as to clear the ground in front of us of any large bodies of Zulus who might be there.

I dismounted and made for the kopje, dragging with me the principal Natal *induna*, whom I had clawed hold of by his head ring, swearing I would blow his brains out in case his men turned tail. He howled to them not to run away, but behind them came the 24th with fixed bayonets so that no matter what funk the natives were in, they had to come on.

It was as dark as pitch, and soon we were stumbling and falling over dead men (black and white), dead horses, cattle, ruined tents and all the debris of the fight. But up and up the kopje we had to go, for every now and then Black's voice would ring out, 'Steady the 24th – be ready to fire a volley and charge.' Up and up we went as the shells came screaming over our heads; the burning time-fuses in the dark looking like rockets. Every time one came over us my wretched natives would utter a howl and try to sit down, but bayonets in rear of them will make even a Natal [African] move on, and they had to come.

At last we arrived at the top, no living man was there and as the shells just passed over us I told my bugler to sound the 'cease fire'. He could not sound a note, so I shouted to Black that we were on the top and asked him to have the 'cease fire' sounded. This was done and up rushed the 24th, who, when they reached the top of the hill, broke out into cheer after cheer. My Zulus to keep them company rattled their shields and assagais, for had not we retaken the camp; or rather perhaps I ought to say, reoccupied it. Anyhow we were there.

*The disaster at Isandlwana was stunningly comprehensive. Accurate casualty figures are notoriously difficult to compile, but according to the official narrative, there had been 67 officers and 1,707 men in the camp at the start of the battle; 52 officers, 806 NCOs and Other Ranks were killed along with 471 black auxiliaries – though the latter figure is almost certainly an underestimate. Both Durnford and Pulleine were amongst the dead, and not one officer of the 24th who had been present in the camp survived.*

*Hamilton-Browne had seen something of the fighting from a distance, but what had it been like to be in the terrible midst of the blood-letting? One of only five regular officers who survived to tell the tale was Horace Smith-Dorrien, a young lieutenant in the 95th Regiment, who was attached to the column as transport officer. It was Smith-Dorrien's baptism of fire, and his story, published in* Memories of Forty-Eight Years' Service *(1925), is one of the classic accounts of the battle and its frightful aftermath. He began the fateful morning of the 22nd attending to his duties at Rorke's Drift, where a company of the 2/24th under Lieutenant (not Captain) Gonville Bromhead, had been left to guard a supply depot established at the old mission station:*

I had several arrangements to make for Transport at Rorke's Drift, amongst others the erection of a gallows for making riems. This gallows was some 15 feet high, and the process consisted of cutting hides of bullocks into strips about an inch wide, working in a circle; the strips then had the appearance of the peel of an apple all coiled up, and in order to be fashioned into straight straps had to be passed over the gallows and through a weighted wagon-wheel below. These strips were then worked over the gallows and through the wheel, stretched and rubbed with fat until the curves were lost, resulting in very long, soft strips of hide, which could eventually be cut into lengths for tying to the horns of oxen as head-ropes. It is interesting to relate that the first use I saw the gallows put to was for hanging Zulus who were supposed to have behaved treacherously the day after the Rorke's Drift fight.

After starting the gallows, I went up to see Captain 'Gonny' Bromhead,[1] in command of the company of the 24th, and I told him a big fight was expected, and that I wanted revolver ammunition. He gave me eleven rounds, and hearing heavy

---

[1] Captain Bromhead and Captain Chard, RE, were awarded VCs for their defence of Rorke's Drift.

guns over at Isandhlwana, I rode off and got into that camp about 8 a.m., just as Colonel Durnford's force arrived. Colonel Durnford was having a discussion with Lieutenant-Colonel Pulleine of the 24th, who had been left by Lord Chelmsford in command of the camp, Lord Chelmsford and all the troops, including the 2/24th, having gone out to attack the Zulus. Lieutenant-Colonel Pulleine's force consisted of six companies of the 1/24th, two guns under Brevet-Major Smith and Lieutenant Curling, and some native levies.

As far as I could make out, the gist of Colonels Durnford and Pulleine's discussion was that the former wished to go out and attack the Zulus, whilst the latter argued that his orders were to defend the camp, and that he could not allow his infantry to move out. Colonel Durnford and his rocket battery under Russell, RA, and his mounted Basutos under Cochrane (32nd), then rode off towards a small hill, apparently a spur of the main range, and 1½ miles from the camp (see A on sketch). Of the 24th, one company (Lieutenant Cavaye) was on picket out of sight of the camp and about a mile to the north on the main range. We could hear heavy firing in this direction even then (8 a.m.). This company was reinforced later by two more (Mostyn's and Dyson's), and the three fell back fighting about noon and covered the north side of the camp. The remaining three companies present (for two under Major Upcher, with Lieutenants Clements, Palmes, Heaton, and Lloyd, only reached Helpmakaar on the 22nd from the old colony) were extended round the camp in attack formation, covering especially the front and left front. Two battalions of native levies were also in this line, but they were not to be relied on and were feebly armed, only one man in ten being allowed a rifle, lest they should desert to the enemy. In consequence of the heavy firing to the north and the appearance of large numbers of Zulus on the main range of hills, and partly, I believe, to support Colonel Durnford's movement, the line was pushed out on a curve, but to no great distance from the tents. Farther than this it never went. Our two guns were at the same time pushed out into the firing-line to the north-east of the camp (see sketch).

At about 12 a.m. the Zulus, who had apparently fallen back

behind the hills, again showed in large numbers, coming down into the plain over the hills with great boldness, and our guns and rifles were pretty busy for some time, causing the Zulus again to fall back. It was difficult to see exactly what was going on, but firing was heavy. It was evident now that the Zulus were in great force, for they could be seen extending (i.e. throwing out their horns) away across the plain to the south-east, apparently working towards the right rear of the camp. As far as I can make out, Colonel Durnford with his force never actually left the plain, but was close under the foot of the small spur he originally went to seize.

Nothing of importance occurred, beyond the constant increase of the Zulus and the spreading out of their horns, until about 1 p.m., when they started their forward movement direct on the camp. Our troops were in the positions they had occupied hours before, our two guns busy throughout shelling the enemy.

Forty-five empty wagons stood in the camp with the oxen in. It was a convoy which I was to have taken to Rorke's Drift for supplies early in the morning, but which was stopped until the enemy should be driven off. These wagons might have at any time been formed into a laager, but no one appeared to appreciate the gravity of the situation, so much so that no steps were taken until too late to issue extra ammunition from the large reserves we had in camp.

I will return to the advancing Zulus' line at about 1 p.m. It was a marvellous sight, line upon line of men in slightly extended order, one behind the other, firing as they came along, for a few of them had firearms, bearing all before them. The rocket battery, apparently then only a mile to our front, was firing, and suddenly it ceased, and presently we saw the remnants of Durnford's force, mostly mounted Basutos, galloping back to the right of our position. What had actually happened I don't think we ever shall know accurately. The ground was intersected with 'dongas',[1] and in them Russell with his rocket battery was caught, and none escaped to tell

---

[1] A donga is a deep dry watercourse.

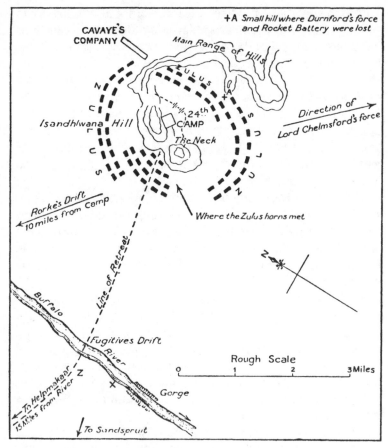

ISANDHLWANA, 22ND JANUARY, 1879.

the tale. I heard later[1] that Durnford, who was a gallant leader, actually reached the camp and fell there fighting.

And now the Zulu Army, having swept away Durnford's force, flushed with victory, moved steadily on to where the five companies of the 24th were lying down covering the camp. They were giving vent to no loud war-cries, but to a low musical murmuring noise, which gave the impression of a gigantic swarm of bees getting nearer and nearer. Here was a more serious matter for these brave warriors, for the regiment opposed to them were no boy recruits, but war-worn, matured men, mostly with beards, and fresh from a long campaign in the old colony where they had carried everything before them. Possessed of splendid discipline and sure of success, they lay on their position making every round tell, so much so that when the Zulu army was some 400 yards off, it wavered.

After the war the Zulus, who were delightfully naïve and truthful people, told us that the fire was too hot for them and they were on the verge of retreat, when suddenly the fire slackened and on they came again. The reader will ask why the fire slackened, and the answer is, alas! because, with thousands of rounds in the wagons 400 yards in rear, there was none in the firing line; all those had been used up.

I will mention a story which speaks for the coolness and discipline of the regiment. I, having no particular duty to perform in camp, when I saw the whole Zulu army advancing, had collected camp stragglers, such as artillerymen in charge of spare horses, officers' servants, sick, etc, and had taken them to the ammunition-boxes, where we broke them open as fast as we could, and kept sending out the packets to the firing-line. (In those days the boxes were screwed down and it was a very difficult job to get them open, and it was owing to this battle that the construction of the ammunition-boxes was changed.)

When I had been engaged at this for some time, and the 1/24th had fallen back to where we were, with the Zulus fol-

---

[1] Durnford's body was eventually found on the neck with many other heroes of this desperate fight; 130 dead of the 24th were counted there, and amongst them the only recognisable officers were Captain Wardell and Lieutenant Dyer.

lowing closely, Bloomfield, the quartermaster of the 2/24th, said to me in regard to the boxes I was then breaking open, 'For heaven's sake, don't take that, man, for it belongs to our battalion.' And I replied, 'Hang it all, you don't want a requisition now, do you?' It was about this time, too, that a Colonial named Du Bois, a wagon-conductor, said to me, 'The game is up. If I had a good horse I would ride straight for Maritzburg.' I never saw him again. I then saw Surgeon-Major Shepherd, busy in a depression, treating wounded. This was also the last time I saw him.

To return to the fight. Our right flank had become enveloped by the horn of the Zulus and the levies were flying before them. All the transport drivers, panic-stricken, were jostling each other with their teams and wagons, shouting and yelling at their cattle, and striving to get over the neck (see sketch) on to the Rorke's Drift road; and the red line of the 24th, having fixed bayonets, appeared to have but one idea, and that was to defeat the enemy. The Zulu charge came home, and, driven with their backs to the rock of Isandhlwana, and overpowered by about thirty to one, they sold their lives dearly. The best proof of this is the subsequent description of the Zulus themselves, who, so far from looking on it as a decisive victory, used to relate how their wagons were for days removing their dead, and how the country ran rivers of tears, almost every family bemoaning the loss of some near relative.

When this final charge took place, the transport which was in-spanned had mostly cleared the neck, and I jumped on my broken-kneed pony, which had had no rest for thirty hours, and followed it, to find on topping the neck a scene of confusion I shall never forget, for some 4,000 Zulus had come in behind and were busy with shield and assegai. Into this mass I rode, revolver in hand, right through the Zulus, but they completely ignored me. I heard afterwards that they had been told by their King Cetywayo that black coats were civilians and were not worth killing. I had a blue patrol jacket on, and it is noticeable that the only five officers who escaped – Essex, Cochrane, Gardner, Curling, and myself – had blue coats. The Zulus throughout my escape seemed to be set on killing natives who had sided with us, either as fighting levies or transport drivers.

After getting through the mass of Zulus busy slaying, I followed in the line of fugitives. The outer horns of the Zulu Army had been directed to meet at about a mile to the south-east of the camp, and they were still some distance apart when the retreat commenced. It was this gap which fixed the line of retreat.

I could see the Zulus running in to complete their circle from both flanks, and their leading men had already reached the line of retreat long before I had got there. When I reached the point I came on the two guns, which must have been sent out of camp before the Zulus charged home. They appeared to me to be upset in a donga and to be surrounded by Zulus.

Again I rode through unheeded, and shortly after was passed by Lieutenant Coghill (24th), wearing a blue patrol and cord breeches and riding a red roan horse. We had just exchanged remarks about the terrible disaster, and he passed on towards Fugitives' Drift. A little farther on I caught up Lieutenant Curling, RA, and spoke to him, pointing out to him that the Zulus were all round and urging him to push on, which he did. My own broken-kneed transport pony was done to a turn and incapable of rapid progress.

The ground was terribly bad going, all rocks and boulders, and it was about three or four miles from camp to Fugitives' Drift. When approaching this drift, and at least half a mile behind Coghill, Lieutenant Melvill (24th), in a red coat and with a cased Colour across the front of his saddle, passed me going to the drift. I reported afterwards that the Colour was broken; but as the pole was found eventually whole, I think the casing must have been half off and hanging down. It will thus be seen that Coghill (who was orderly officer to Colonel Glynn) and Melvill (who was adjutant) did not escape together with the Colour. How Coghill came to be in the camp I do not know, as Colonel Glynn, whose orderly officer he was, was out with Lord Chelmsford's column.

I then came to Fugitives' Drift, the descent to which was almost a precipice. I found there a man in a red coat badly assegaied in the arm, unable to move. He was, I believe, a mounted infantryman of the 24th, named Macdonald, but of his name I cannot be sure. I managed to make a tourniquet with a handkerchief to stop the bleeding, and got him half-way down, when a shout from behind said, 'Get on, man; the Zulus are on top of you.' I turned round and saw Major Smith, RA, who was commanding the section of guns, as white as a sheet and bleeding profusely; and in a second we were surrounded, and assegais accounted for poor Smith, my wounded MI friend, and my horse.

With the help of my revolver and a wild jump down the rocks, I found myself in the Buffalo River, which was in flood and eighty yards broad. I was carried away, but luckily got hold of the tail of a loose horse, which towed me across to the other bank, but I was too exhausted to stick to him. Up this bank were swarming friendly natives, but I only saw one European, a Colonial and Acting Commissariat Officer named Hamer, lying there unable to move. I managed to catch a loose horse, and put him on it, and he escaped. The Zulus were pouring in a very heavy fire from the opposite bank, and dropped several friendly natives as we climbed to the top.

No sooner had I achieved this than I saw that a lot of Zulus had crossed higher up and were running to cut me off. This drove me off to my left, but twenty of them still pursued for about three miles, and I managed to keep them off with my revolver.

I got into Helpmakaar at sundown, having done twenty miles on foot from the river, for I almost went to Sandspruit. At Helpmakaar I found Huntley of the 10th, who had been left there with a small garrison, and also Essex, Cochrane, Curling, and Gardner, from the field of Isandhlwana, all busy placing the post in a state of defence. We could see that night the watchfires of the Zulus some six miles off, and expected them to come on and attack, but we knew later they had turned off to attack Rorke's Drift.

I at once took command of one face of the laager, and shall never forget how pleased we weary watchers were when, shortly after midnight, Major Upcher's two companies of the 24th, with Heaton, Palmes, Clements, and Lloyd, came to reinforce. These two companies had started for Rorke's Drift that afternoon, but had been turned back to Helpmakaar by Major Spalding, a staff officer, as he said Rorke's Drift has been surrounded and captured, and that the two companies would share the same fate. Luckily, his information proved to be wrong.

*In the confusion, Smith-Dorrien did not see Melvill and Coghill's end, though it was to become one of the most famous incidents in the Zulu War. Coghill reached the river first, and spurred his horse into the torrent. He had just struggled out on the Natal bank, when he turned and saw Melvill, still holding the Colours, plunge in from the Zulu side. A bullet struck Melvill's horse and he was swept clear, fetching up against a large boulder which was just breaking the surface. An officer in the NNC named Higginson was swept by, and Melvill called out for him to help with the Colour. The current was too strong, however, and the heavy flag in its leather case was torn from Melvill's grasp and disappeared into the foam. Coghill saw Higginson and Melvill clinging to the rock midstream, and turned back to help them. A Zulu bullet struck his horse in the head and it collapsed under him, pitching him into the water, but Coghill struggled out to the rock, and together all three men swam across and clambered onto the Natal bank. Ahead of them a steep hill rose sharply out of the Mzinyathi valley, and as they stumbled up, Higginson left Melvill and Coghill to search for horses. He'd only been gone a few minutes when he heard a scuffle behind him, and Melvill and Coghill were caught and killed.*

*Was the ammunition supply to blame for the catastrophe, as Smith-Dorrien believed? His account was taken by a generation of historians to support the view that the 24th line collapsed because the men were starved of ammunition, which was stored in boxes secured by metal bands, and which could not be opened in a hurry. Certainly, runners had a long way to go from the supplies in camp to the line. Yet Smith-Dorrien's memory was at fault: boxes with a sliding easy-access panel in the lid, retained by just one screw, had been standard issue for many years before Isandlwana. Perhaps, over the years,*

*Smith-Dorrien had sought to make sense of his impressions of that dreadful day. He was much in demand as a public speaker in later life, and no doubt his audiences would have pressed him many times to provide an easy explanation for the disaster, and he found one, to his own satisfaction, in the memory of his exchange with Bloomfield. Probably, however, Bloomfield was simply showing a proper concern for the ammunition reserves of the 2nd Battalion, which had already been loaded for despatch to Chelmsford's men: it is significant that Smith-Dorrien's letters to his family, written in the immediate aftermath, make no mention of ammunition boxes. The real cause of the disaster lay elsewhere; the Zulus had simply outmanoeuvered Chelmsford, and caught the camp on the hop.*

*What of Chelmsford? We've already heard, from Hamilton-Browne, of how the news of the disaster reached him, and of the bleak march back to the devastated camp. Hallam Parr, Frere's apologist, who was present on Glyn's staff, takes up the story of the grim night spent amongst the dead on the battlefield, of the return to Rorke's Drift, and of the surprises that awaited them there:*

We were lying in a hollow square, the native battalions being posted on the kopjes on our right and left.

The men were wearied out, and it was a great relief for them to lie down and know that, as the Zulus never attacked until after midnight, they would probably get some rest before they had to cut their way to Rorke's Drift.

For it seemed to us, after hearing the accounts of the overwhelming force of the Zulu impi and its complete success, that the victorious Zulus were only waiting their usual time for attack (shortly before dawn) to endeavour to complete the destruction of No. 3 Column.

The night wore on. Some of the officers took snatches of sleep, some talked in low voices; the men lay tired out by their long day's marching, during which they must have covered over thirty-two or thirty-three miles.

The first part of the night was very black and dark, but about one a.m. the sky cleared and the stars shone out, and I received orders to serve out the rations of biscuit and tinned meat we luckily had with us.

It was disagreeable work moving about inside the square; in the dark it was difficult to walk without stumbling over the dead and the debris of all kinds with which the ground was strewn.

After the Regulars and Volunteers had drawn their rations, the officers and non-commissioned officers of the Natal Contingent came for theirs. One officer – I could not see his face and have no notion who he was – asked leave to draw for six or seven of his comrades, and as he had forgotten to bring a haversack, and could not carry six or seven rations of loose biscuit and tinned meat in his hands, I told him he had better hold out his hat for the biscuit. 'Sir,' said he stiffly, 'I must object to your suggestion. I should prefer to go without my rations than carry them in my hat.' As it then seemed highly probable that before long there would not be many of us with either a head to put a hat on or a mouth to put a biscuit into, and as there was not any time to waste, I sent him away to fetch some one else to draw rations; but felt grateful to him for infusing for the moment a slight tinge of humour into the proceedings, a quality which they certainly had lacked.

Just after rations had been issued – not very long before dawn, but while it was still quite dark – a yell was heard from below the kopje on our right, where was posted a battalion of the Native Contingent; then a rush of naked feet and the rattle of assegais and shields, and the clatter of accoutrements and rifles of the men in the ranks as they rose from the ground, and then a confused volley.

It seemed as if the attack we had been expecting had come at last. The men in square were quite steady – the 24th not firing a shot, but merely rising to the knee; the artillery standing to their horses. After a few anxious minutes it was found to be a false alarm, caused by the native battalion on the right running in upon the square, fancying the Zulus were advancing.

When the first streak of dawn gave enough light to enable the track to be seen, the column, or rather the remains of it, resumed its march. It was bitter leaving the bodies of our comrades still unburied, but the living had to be thought of first. Even if we had had ammunition and ration wagons with us, the fires we could see on the Natal side of the Buffalo showed plainly that the Zulus were in Natal, and we were bound to hurry back to assist in protecting the colony.

Dawn in South Africa breaks quickly, and before the rear-guard, with which my duties lay, left the ridge, there was light enough to show the state of the camp and what had been concealed by the darkness. It was a sight not easily forgotten.

During the first two hours of our march our path lay through broken and hilly ground, and we expected, before we reached the open country, that an attack would be made upon us. None, however, occurred, and we arrived at the other side of the little Bashee spruit, at which the men were glad to drink and refill their water-bottles.

Till then we had hardly time to realise what had happened; it had seemed so very unlikely that the Zulus would forgo the advantages offered by attacking a tired force bivouacking in an enclosed country, after they had been so completely victorious in their first onset, that we had been speculating on the future more than thinking on the past. But now, when we got into the open ground and found our way open to Rorke's Drift, we had time to think of those we had left behind on that fatal ridge, and a host of familiar faces rose to our recollection with a tightening of the heart as we rode along.

Soon we saw that the post at Rorke's Drift was on fire, and feared the worst, and made sure that at any rate the ponts had been wrecked.

We advanced on the river, and our scouts, to the surprise of all, reported the points standing. The cavalry crossed below them at the shallows, as it had done twelve days before, and the first files advanced up to where the mission station had stood, at the best gallop their weary and hungry horses could muster after having been under the saddle nearly thirty hours.

We expected to find a repetition on a smaller scale of Isandlwana camp, but as we came in sight of the commissariat stores, a cheer sounded from the top of a wall of mealie sacks, from a man on the look-out, and was taken up by the remainder of the little garrison, and to our delight we found that there was no more bad news to be expected, at any rate at present.

To relate what had occurred here we must retrace our steps.

About 2.30 that afternoon, when the sack of Isandlwana was complete, when the Zulu regiments who had been engaged were scattered all over the camp – some helping themselves to booty and ammunition; some stabbing each dead man, so that the corpse should not swell (the Zulu superstition is that if this is not done, as the body swells and corrupts, the right hand and arm of its slayer also swells and corrupts); some carrying away those wounded Zulus who could be moved, and shooting those who could not; some throwing their dead into holes, ravines, and dongas; about this time the Undi corps, the crack corps of the Zulu army (which, with the exception of the Nkobamakosi regiment, had been held in reserve), arrived, fresh and eager for fighting, near the camp.

Finding there was nothing for them to do here, and being ignorant that the whole of the column was not destroyed, this corps continued its march in the direction of the Buffalo. After crossing, the corps split up into regiments. The crack regiment, the Royal Tulwana, in whose ranks Cetywayo had fought in his younger days, and to which he still nominally belonged, advanced to attack Rorke's Drift, accompanied by portions of three other regiments, making up a force of between three and four thousand men. The other portions of the Undi corps dispersed in search of the plunder and cattle.

At Rorke's Drift there was stationed, to guard the ponts, stores, and hospital, the B Company of the second battalion 24th, under Lieutenant Bromhead. The ponts were in charge of Lieutenant Chard, RE.

News of the disaster at Isandlwana reached these officers about 3 p.m., and they began at once hurriedly strengthening the position which Bromhead had already begun to place in a state of defence.

A worse position could hardly be imagined. Two small thatched buildings, about thirty-nine yards apart, with thin walls, commanded by rising ground on the south and west, completely overlooked on the south by a high hill. On the north side an orchard and garden gave good cover to an enemy up to within a few yards of the houses.

The force which was about to defend this position against three or four thousand Zulus consisted of 104 officers and men, and 35 sick. Luckily the men were seasoned soldiers and were commanded by two capable and brave officers, who upheld indeed the prestige of the British subaltern.

*The subsequent events at Rorke's Drift were the stuff of Victorian military legend. Chard himself described the battle in a remarkably detailed and explicit letter which he wrote at Queen Victoria's request a year after the fight. He was sitting at his tent by the drift, having just finished lunch, when he noticed two horsemen approaching from the direction of the column:*

From their gesticulation and their shouts, when they were near enough to be heard, we saw that something was the matter, and on taking them over the river, one of them, Lieutenant Adendorff of Lonsdale's Regiment, Natal Native Contingent, asking if I was an officer, jumped off his horse, took me on one side, and told me that the camp was in the hands of the Zulus and the army destroyed; that scarcely a man had got away to tell the tale, and that probably Lord Chelmsford and the rest of the column had shared the same fate. His companion, a Carbineer, confirmed his story – he was naturally very excited and I am afraid I did not, at first, quite believe him, and intimated that he probably had not remained to see what *did* occur. I had the saddle put on my horse, and while I was talking to Lieutenant Adendorff, a messenger arrived from Lieutenant Bromhead, who was with his company at his little camp near the commissariat stores, to ask me to come up at once.

I gave the order to inspan the wagon and put all the stores, tents, etc., they could into it. I posted the sergeant and six men on the high ground over the pont, behind a natural wall of rocks, forming a strong position from which there was a good view over the river and ground in front, with orders to wait until I came or sent for them. The guard of natives had left some time before and had not been relieved. I galloped up at once to the commissariat stores and found that a pencil note had been sent from the 3rd Column by Captain Allan Gardner to state that the enemy were advancing in force against our post – Lieutenant Bromhead had, with the assistance of Mr Dalton, Dr Reynolds and the other officers present, commenced barricading and loopholing the store building and the missionary's house, which was used as a hospital, and connecting the defence of the two buildings by walls of mealie bags, and two wagons that were on the ground. The Native Contingent, under their officer, Captain Stephenson, were working hard at this with our own men, and the walls were rapidly progressing. A letter describing what had happened had been sent by Bromhead by two men of the Mounted Infantry, who had arrived fugitives from Isandhlwana, to the officer commanding at Helpmakaar. These two men crossed the river at Fugitives Drift, with some others, and as they have since reported to me, came to give notice of what had happened, to us at Rorke's Drift, of their own accord and without orders from anyone.

I held a consultation with Lieutenant Bromhead, and with Mr Dalton, whose energy, intelligence and gallantry were of the greatest service to us, and whom, as I said in my report at the time, and I am sure Bromhead would unite with me in saying again now, I cannot sufficiently thank for his services. I went round the position with them and then rode down to the ponts where I found everything ready for a start, ponts in midstream, hawsers and cables sunk, etc. It was at this time that the Pontman Daniells, and Sergeant Milne, 3rd Buffs, who had been employed for some time in getting the ponts in order, and working them under Lieutenant MacDowell, RE, (killed at Isandhlwana), offered to defend the ponts, moored in the middle of the river, from their decks with a few men. Sergeant Williams 24th and his little guard were quite ready to join them.

We arrived at the commissariat store about 3.30 p.m. Shortly afterwards an officer of Durnford's Horse reported his arrival from Isandhlwana, and I requested him to observe the movements, and check the advance, of the enemy as much as possible until forced to fall back. I saw each man at his post, and then the work went on again.

Several fugitives from the camp arrived, and tried to impress upon us the madness of an attempt to defend the place. Who they were I do not know, but it is scarcely necessary for me to say that there were no officers of HM Army among them. They stopped the work very much – it being impossible to prevent the men getting around them in little groups to hear their story. They proved the truth of their belief in what they said by leaving us to our fate, and in the state of mind they were in, I think our little garrison was as well without them. As far as I know, but one of the fugitives remained with us – Lieutenant Adendorff, whom I have before mentioned. He remained to assist in the defence, and from a loophole in the store building, flanking the wall and hospital, his rifle did good service.

There were several casks of rum in the store building, and I gave strict orders to Sergeant Windridge, 24th Regiment, who was in charge (acting as issuer of commissariat stores to the troops), that the spirit was not to be touched, the man posted nearest it was to be considered on guard over it, and after giving fair warning, was to shoot without altercation anyone who attempted to force his post, and Sergeant Windridge being there was to see this carried out. Sergeant Windridge showed great intelligence and energy in arranging the stores of the defence of the commissariat store, forming loopholes, etc.

The Reverend George Smith, vicar of Estcourt, Natal, and acting Army chaplain, went for a walk (before the news of the disaster reached us) to the top of the Oscarberg, the hill behind Rorke's Drift. Mr Witt, the missionary, went with him, or met him there. They went to see what could be seen in the direction of the Isandhlwana camp. He saw the force of the enemy which attacked us at Rorke's Drift, cross the river in three bodies – and after snuff-taking, and other ceremonies, advance in our direction. He had been watching them for a long time with interest, and thought they were our own Native Contingent. There were two mounted men leading them, and he did not realise that they were the enemy until they were near enough for him to see that these two men also had black

faces. He came running down the hill and was agreeably surprised to find that we were getting ready for the enemy. Mr
Witt, whose wife and family were in a lonely house not very
far off, rode off, taking with him a sick officer, who was very
ill in hospital and only just able to ride. Mr Smith, however,
although he might well have left, elected to remain with us,
and during the attack did good service in supplying the men
with ammunition.

About 4.20 p.m. the sound of firing was heard behind the
Oscarberg. The officer of Durnford's returned, reporting the
enemy close upon us, and that his men would not obey his
orders but were going off to Helpmakaar, and I saw them,
about 100 in number, going off in that direction. I have seen
these same men behave so well since that I have spoken with
several of their conduct – and they all said, as their excuse,
that Durnford was killed, and it was no use. About the same
time Captain Stephenson's detachment of Natal Native Contingent left us – probably most fortunately for us. I am sorry to
say that their officer, who had been doing good service in
getting his men to work, also deserted us. We seemed very
few, now all these people had gone, and I saw that our line of
defence was too extended, and at once commenced a
retrenchment of biscuit boxes, so as to get a place we could
fall back upon if we could not hold the whole.

Private Hitch, 24th, was on the top of the thatch roof of
the commissariat store keeping a look-out. He was severely
wounded early in the evening, but notwithstanding, with Corporal Allen, 24th, who was also wounded, continued to do
good service, and they both when incapacitated by their
wounds from using their rifles, still continued under fire serving their comrades with ammunition.

We had not completed a wall two boxes high when, about
4.30 p.m., Hitch cried out that the enemy was in sight, and he
saw them, apparently 500 or 600 in number, come around the
hill to our south (the Oscarberg) and advance at a run against
our south wall.

We opened fire on them, between five and six hundred
yards, at first a little wild, but only for a short time, a chief on
horseback was dropped by Private Dunbar, 24th. The men

were quite steady, and the Zulus began to fall very thick. However, it did not seem to stop them at all, although they took advantage of the cover and ran stooping with their faces near the ground. It seemed as if nothing would stop them, and they rushed on in spite of their heavy loss to within 50 yards of the wall, when they were taken in flank by the fire from the end wall of the store building, and met with such a heavy direct fire from the mealie wall, and the hospital at the same time, that they were checked as if by magic.

They occupied the cook-house ovens, banks and other cover, but the greater number, without stopping, moved to their left around the hospital, and made a rush at the end of the hospital, and at our north-west line of mealie bags. There was a short but desperate struggle during which Mr Dalton shot a Zulu who was in the act of assegaing a corporal of the Army Hospital Corps, the muzzle of whose rifle he had seized, and with Lieutenant Bromhead and many of the men behaved with great gallantry. The Zulus forced us back from that part of the wall immediately in front of the hospital, but after suffering very severely in the struggle were driven back into the bush around our position.

The main body of the enemy were close behind the first force which appeared, and had lined the ledge of rocks and caves in the Oscarberg overlooking us, and about three or four hundred yards to our south, from where they kept up a constant fire. Advancing somewhat more to their left than the first attack, they occupied the garden, hollow road, and bush in great force. The bush grew close to our wall and we had not had time to cut it down – the enemy were thus able to advance under cover close to our wall, and in this part soon held one side of the wall, while we held the other.

A series of desperate assaults were made, on the hospital, and extending from the hospital, as far as the bush reached; but each was most splendidly met and repulsed by our men, with the bayonet. Each time as the attack was repulsed by us, the Zulus close to us seemed to vanish in the bush, those some little distance off keeping up a fire all the time. Then, as if moved by a single impulse, they rose up in the bush as thick as possible, rushing madly up to the wall (some of them being already close to it), seizing, where they could, the muzzles of our men's rifles, or they bayonets, and attempting to use their assegais and to get over the wall. A rapid rattle of fire from our rifles, stabs with the bayonet, and in a few moments the Zulus were driven back, disappearing in the bush as before, and keeping up their fire. A brief interval, and the attack would be again made, and repulsed in the same manner. Over and over again this happened, our men behaving with the greatest coolness and gallantry.

It is impossible for one individual to see all, but I particularly myself noticed the behaviour of Colonel Sgt Bourne 24th, Private McMahon, AHC, Privates Roy, Deacon, Bush, Cole, Jenkins 24th, and many others.

Our fire at the time of these rushes of the Zulus was very rapid – Mr Dalton dropping a man each time he fired his rifle, while Bromhead and myself used our revolvers. The fire from the rocks and caves on the hill behind us was kept up all this time and took us completely in reverse, and although very badly directed, many shots came among us and caused us some loss – and at about 6.00 p.m. the enemy extending their attack further to their left, I feared seriously would get it over our wall behind the biscuit boxes. I ran back with two or three men to this part of the wall and was immediately joined by Bromhead with two or three more. The enemy stuck to this assault most tenaciously, and on their repulse, and retiring into the bush, I called all the men inside our retrenchment – and the enemy immediately occupied the wall we had abandoned and used it as a breastwork to fire over.

Mr Byrne, acting Commissariat Officer, and who had behaved with great coolness and gallantry, was killed instantaneously shortly before this by a bullet through the head, just after he had given a drink of water to a wounded man of the NNC.

All this time the enemy had been attempting to fire the hospital and had at length set fire to its roof and got in at the far end. I had tried to impress upon the men in the hospital the necessity for making a communication right through the building – unfortunately this was not done. Probably at the time the men could not see the necessity, and doubtless also there was no time to do it. Without in the least detracting from the gallant fellows who defended the hospital, and I hope I shall not be misunderstood in saying so, I have always regretted, as I did then, the absence of my four poor sappers, who had only left that morning for Isandhlwana and arrived there just to be killed.

The garrison of the hospital defended it with the greatest gallantry, room by room, bringing out all the sick that could be moved, and breaking through some of the partitions while the Zulus were in the building with them. Privates Williams, Hook, R. Jones and W. Jones being the last to leave and holding the doorway with the bayonet, their ammunition being expended. Private Williams's bayonet was wrenched off his rifle by a Zulu, but with the other men he still managed with the muzzle of his rifle to keep the enemy at bay. Surgeon Reynolds carried his arms full of ammunition to the hospital, a bullet striking his helmet as he did so. But we were too busily engaged outside to be able to do much, and with the hospital on fire, and no free communication, nothing could have saved it. Sergeant Maxfield 24th might have been saved, but he was delirious with fever, refused to move and resisted the attempts to move him. He was assegaied before our men's eyes.

Seeing the hospital burning, and the attempts of the enemy to fire the roof of the store (one man was shot, I believe by Lt Adendorff, who had a light almost touching the thatch), we converted two large heaps of mealie bags into a sort of redoubt which gave a second line of fire all around, in case the store building had to be abandoned, or the enemy broke through elsewhere. Assistant Commissary Dunne worked hard at this, and from his height, being a tall man, he was much exposed, in addition to the fact that the heaps were high above our walls, and that most of the Zulu bullets went high.

Trooper Hunter, Natal Mounted Police, escaping from the hospital, stood still for a moment, hesitating which way to go, dazed by the glare of the burning hospital, and the firing that was going on all around. He was assegaied before our eyes, the Zulu who killed him immediately afterwards falling. While firing from behind the biscuit boxes, Dalton, who had been using his rifle with deadly effect, and by his quickness and coolness had been the means of saving many men's lives, was shot through the body. I was standing near him at the time, and he handed me his rifle so coolly that I had no idea until afterwards of how severely he was wounded. He waited quite quietly for me to take the cartridges he had left out of his pockets. We put him inside our mealie sack redoubt, building it up around him. About this time I noticed Private Dunbar 24th make some splendid shooting, seven or eight Zulus falling on the ledge of rocks in the Oscarberg to as many consecutive shots by him. I saw Corporal Lyons hit by a bullet which lodged in his spine, and fall between an opening we had left in the wall of biscuit boxes. I thought he was killed, but looking up he said, 'Oh, Sir! you are not going to leave me here like a dog?' We pulled him in and laid him down behind the boxes where he was immediately looked to by Reynolds.

Corporal Scammle (Scammell) of the Natal Native Contingent, who was badly wounded through the shoulder, staggered out under fire again, from the store building where he had been put, and gave me all his cartridges, which in his wounded state he could not use. While I was intently watching to get a fair shot at a Zulu who appeared to be firing rather well, Private Jenkins 24th, saying 'Look out, Sir,' gave my head a duck down just as a bullet whizzed over it. He had noticed a Zulu who was quite near in another direction taking a deliberate aim at me. For all the man could have known, the shot might have been directed at himself. I mention these facts to show how well the men behaved and how loyally worked together.

Corporal Scheiss, Natal Native Contingent, who was a patient in the hospital with a wound in the foot, which caused him great pain, behaved with the greatest coolness and gallantry throughout the attack, and at this time creeping out a short distance along the wall we had abandoned, and slowly raising himself, to get a shot at some of the enemy who had been particularly annoying, his hat was blown off by a shot from a Zulu the other side of the wall. He immediately jumped up, bayonetted the Zulu and shot a second, and bayonetted a third who came to their assistance, and then returned to his place.

As darkness came on we were completely surrounded. The

Zulus wrecked the camp of the Company 24th and my wagon which had been left outside, in spite of the efforts of my batman, Driver Robson (the only man of the Royal Engineers with us), who had directed his particular attention to keeping the Zulus off this wagon in which were, as he described it, 'Our things'.

They also attacked the east end of our position, and after being several times repulsed, eventually got into the kraal, which was strongly built with high walls, and drove us to the middle, and then to the inner wall of the kraal – the enemy occupying the middle wall as we abandoned it. This wall was too high for them to use it effectively to fire over, and a Zulu no sooner showed his head over it than he was dropped, being so close that it was almost impossible to miss him. Shortly before this, some of the men said they saw the red-coats coming on the Helpmakaar road. The rumour passed quickly round – I could see nothing of the sort myself, but some men said they could. A cheer was raised, and the enemy seemed to pause, to know what it meant, but there was no answer to it, and darkness came. It is very strange that this report should have arisen amongst us, for the two companies 24th from Helpmakaar did come to the foot of the hill, but not, I believe, in sight of us. They marched back to Helpmakaar on the report of Rorke's Drift having fallen.

After the first onslaught, the most formidable of the enemy's attacks was just before we retired behind our line of biscuit boxes, and for a short time after it, when they had gained great confidence by their success on the hospital. Although they kept their positions behind the walls we had abandoned, and kept up a heavy fire from all sides until about 12 o'clock, they did not actually charge up in a body to get over our wall after about 9 or 10 o'clock. After this time it became very dark, although the hospital roof was still burning – it was impossible from below to see what was going on, and Bromhead and myself getting up on the mealy sack redoubt, kept an anxious watch on all sides.

The enemy were now in strong force all around us, and every now and then a confused shout of 'Usutu' from many voices seemed to show that they were going to attack from one side and immediately the same thing would happen on the other, leaving us in doubt as to where they meant to attack. About midnight or a little after the fire slackened and after that, although they kept us constantly on the alert, by feigning, as before, to come on at different points, the fire was of a desultory character. Our men were careful, and only fired when they could see a fair chance. The flame of the burning hospital was now getting low, and as pieces of the roof fell, or hitherto unburnt parts of the thatch ignited, the flames would blaze up illuminating our helmets and faces. A few shots from the Zulus, replied to by our men – again silence, broken only by the same thing repeatedly happening. This sort of thing went on until about 4 a.m. and we were anxiously waiting for daybreak and the renewal of the attack, which their comparative, and at length complete silence, led us to expect. But at daybreak the enemy were out of sight, over the hill to our south-west. One Zulu had remained in the kraal and fired a shot among us (without doing any damage) as we stood on the walls, and ran off in the direction of the river – although many shots were fired at him as he ran. I am glad to say the plucky fellow got off.

Taking care not to be surprised by any ruse of the enemy, we patrolled the ground around the place, collecting the arms, and ammunition, of the dead Zulus.

Some of the bullet wounds were very curious. One man's head was split open, exactly as if done with an axe. Another had been hit just between the eyes, the bullet carrying away the whole of the back of his head, leaving his face perfect, as though it were a mask, only disfigured by the small hole made by the bullet passing through. One of the wretches we found, one hand grasping a bench that had been dragged from the hospital, and sustained thus in the position we found him in, while in the other hand he still clutched the knife with which he had mutilated one of our poor fellows, over whom he was still leaning.

We increased the strength of our defences as much as possible, strengthening and raising our walls, putting sacks on the biscuit boxes, etc., and were removing the thatch from the roof of the commissariat store, to avoid being burnt out in case of another attack, when at about 7 a.m. a large body of the enemy (I believe the same who had attacked us) appeared on the hills to the south-west. I thought at the time that they were going to attack us, but from what I now know from Zulus, and also of the number we put hors de combat, I do not think so. I think that they came up on the high ground to observe Lord Chelmsford's advance; from there they could see the column long before it came in sight of us.

A frightened and fugitive [auxiliary] came in shortly before and I sent for Daniells the pontman, who could speak Zulu a little, to interview him. Daniells had armed himself with Spalding's sword, which he flourished in so wild and eccentric a manner that the poor wretch thought his last hour had come. He professed to be friendly and to have escaped from Isandhlwana, and I sent him with a note to the officer commanding at Helpmakaar, explaining our situation, and asking for help: for now, although the men were in excellent spirits, and each man had a good supply of ammunition in his pouches, we had only about a box and a half left besides, and at this time we had no definite knowledge of what had happened, and I myself did not know that the part of the column with Lord Chelmsford had taken any part in the action at Isandhlwana, or whether on the camp being taken he had fallen back on Helpmakaar.

The enemy remained on the hill, and still more of them appeared, when about 8 a.m. the column came in sight, and the enemy disappeared again. There were a great many of our Native Levies with the column, and the number of red-coats seemed so few that at first we had grave doubts that the force approaching was the enemy. We improvised a flag, and our signals were soon replied to from the column. The mounted men crossed the drift and galloped up to us, headed by Major Cecil Russell and Lieutenant Walsh, and were received by us with a hearty cheer. Lord Chelmsford, with his staff, shortly after rode up and thanked us all with much emotion for the defence we had made. The column arrived, crossing by the ponts, and we then had a busy time in making a strong position for the night.

I was glad to seize an opportunity to wash my face in a

muddy puddle, in company with Private Bush 24th, whose face was covered with blood from a wound in the nose caused by the bullet which had passed through and killed Private Cole 24th. With the politeness of a soldier, he lent me his towel, or, rather, a very dirty half of one, before using it himself, and I was very glad to accept it.

In wrecking the stores in my wagon, the Zulus had brought to light a forgotten bottle of beer, and Bromhead and I drank it with mutual congratulations on having come safely out of so much danger.

My wagon driver, a Cape (coloured) man, lost his courage on hearing the first firing around the hill. He let loose his mules and retreated, concealing himself in one of the caves of the Oscarberg. He saw the Zulus run by him and, to his horror, some of them entered the cave he was in, and lying down commenced firing at us. The poor wretch was crouching in the darkness, in the far depths of the cave, afraid to speak or move, and our bullets came into the cave, actually killing one of the Zulus. He did not know from whom he was in the most danger, friends or foes, and came down in the morning looking more dead than alive. The mules we recovered; they were quietly grazing by the riverside.

On my journey homewards, on arriving at the railway station, Durban, I asked a porter to get me some [Africans] to carry my bags to the hotel. He sent several, and the first to come running up was my vorlooper boy who had taken me up to Rorke's Drift. He stopped short and looked very frightened, and I believe at first thought he saw my ghost. I seized him to prevent his running away, and when he saw that I was flesh and blood he became reassured. He said he thought I had been killed, and upon my asking him how he thought I got away, he said (the solution of the mystery just striking him), 'I know you rode away on the other horse.' As far as I could learn and according to his own story, the boy had taken the horse I rode up from the river to the commissariat store, and, wild with terror, had ridden it to Pietermaritzburg without stopping, where he gave it over to the Transport people, but having no certificate to say who he was, they took the horse from him but would not give him any employment.

During the fight there were some very narrow escapes from the burning hospital. Private Waters, 24th Regiment, told me that he secreted himself in a cupboard in the room he was defending, and from it shot several Zulus inside the hospital. He was wounded in the arm, and he remained in the cupboard until the heat and smoke were so great that they threatened to suffocate him. Wrapping himself in a cloak, or skirt of a dress he found in the cupboard, he rushed out into the darkness and made his way into the cook-house. The Zulus were occupying this, and firing at us from the wall nearest us. It was too late to retreat, so he crept softly to the fireplace and, standing up in the chimney, blacked his face and hands with the soot. He remained there until the Zulus left. He was very nearly shot in coming out, one of our men at the wall raising his rifle to do so at the sight of his black face and strange costume, but Waters cried out just in time to save himself. He produced the bullet that wounded him, with pardonable pride, and was very amusing in his admiring description of Dr Reynolds's skill in extracting it.

Gunner Howard, RA, ran out of the burning hospital, through the enemy, and lay down on the upper side of the wall in front of our N parapet. The bodies of several horses that were killed early in the evening were lying here, and concealed by these and by Zulu bodies and the low grass and bushes, he remained unseen with the Zulus all around him until they left in the morning.

Private Beckett, 24th Regiment, escaped from the hospital in the same direction, he was badly wounded with assegais in running through the enemy. He managed to get away and conceal himself in the ditch of the garden, where we found him next morning. The poor fellow was so weak from loss of blood that he could not walk, and he died shortly afterwards.

Our mealie-bag walls were afterwards replaced by loop-holed walls of stone, the work making rapid progress upon the arrival of half the 5th Company RE with Lieutenant Porter. As soon as the Sappers arrived we put a fence around, and a rough wood cross over, the graves of our poor men who were killed. This was afterwards replaced by a neat stone monument and inscription by the 24th, who remained to garrison the place.

I have already, in my report, said how gallantly all behaved, from Lieutenant Bromhead downwards, and I also mentioned those whom I had particularly noticed to have distinguished themselves.

On the day following, we buried 351 bodies of the enemy in graves not far from the Commissariat Buildings – many bodies were since discovered and buried, and when I was sick at Ladysmith one of our sergeants, who came down there invalided from Rorke's Drift, where he had been employed in the construction of Fort Melvill, told me that many Zulu bodies were found in the caves and among the rocks, a long distance from the Mission house, when getting stone for that fort. As, in my report, I underestimated the number we killed, so I believe I also underestimated the number of the enemy that attacked us, and from what I have since learnt I believe the Zulus must have numbered at least 4,000.

*Why did the Zulus retreat? Since noon the previous day, they had covered fifteen miles of broken country, from the valley of the Ngwebeni, where Durnford's men had discovered them before Isandlwana, much of it at a run. Some of them had fought in the running battle down the Fugitives' Trail, and all had endured a further twelve hours of savage fighting at close quarters. They were tired and hungry; worse, Chard's force seemed just as secure behind the barricades of Rorke's Drift as it had done when the battle first began. Now, they could probably see the remnants of Chelmsford's force moving down towards the drift in the distance. It was too much. Hallam Parr (in a slightly longer account quoted in* Major General Sir Henry Hallam Parr: Recollections And Correspondence, *1917) understood something of their plight, and goes on to describe Chelmsford's dismal return to the point where he had launched his campaign, less than a fortnight before:*

The Zulu army began to disperse directly after Isandlwana, many returning straight from the field of battle with their booty to their kraals. This was contrary to orders, but the severe fighting and the amount of booty which had fallen into their hands had entirely disorganised the Zulu regiments.

The Undi (the royal corps) however, preserved its discipline, and after sullenly and unwillingly retreating from Rorke's Drift, marched straight to Ulundi. The king, according to custom, received them in the grand kraal. He had only as yet received the news that the white man's camp had been taken, and that 'Somtseu's' (Shepstone's) column had been eaten up. He had not heard of the repulse at Rorke's Drift, nor was he prepared for the terrible gaps made in his regiments. As the men began to file into the enclosure, he saw there had been very different fighting to that he had known in the Swasiland or against the Amatonga.

The Tulwana (the crack regiment of the royal corps, in whose ranks, as already stated, Cetewayo himself had fought in his young days, and to which he still nominally belonged) was the last regiment, and it filed in and saluted. 'Why don't the rest come in?' cried the king impatiently. But the rest of the brave Tulwana could not hear him, for they were lying outside the mealie bags and biscuit-boxes at Rorke's Drift.

We left No. 3 Column on the morning of the 23rd of January, about half-past eight, recrossing the Buffalo River. The crossing this time did not take long. Harness's four guns and wagons, and one mule wagon, which had carried the biscuit, comprised our wheeled vehicles.

By half-past nine, the remains of No. 3 Column had marched up to Rorke's Drift, and were getting their breakfasts round the shattered buildings and temporary parapet, which for twelve hours had sustained so desperate an attack. This over, all hands set to work in putting things to rights; while the Headquarters Staff, the mounted men, and Harness's four guns continued their march to Helpmakaar.

One of the most necessary duties to be undertaken was the burial of the dead and the cleansing of the ground. This had to be taken in hand without a moment's delay, as decomposition comes on quickly under the hot African sun. The superintendence of this work happened to be my duty.

'It's your turn now, comrade, now we've cleared this rubbish out of your way,' said a 24th man to a dead soldier, who was found with two or three Zulus stretched almost upon him. 'I'm main sorry to put you away, mate,' continued he, laying the end of a torn sack gently over the dead man's face, 'but you died well and had a soldier's end.'

Homely words, but what soldier could wish a better requiem?

The dead of the little garrison were buried where the colonist who gave his name to the drift lies, and the burial service was read over them by the chaplain.

For the first few days the men were rather miserable. We had lost everything at Isandlwana; blankets and great-coats, as well as everything else, had been swept off by the Zulus. We had some wet nights, which, as the men had to lie down on the ground with no shelter, and with nothing more on than they wore in the day, was trying enough.

However, tarpaulin shelter and blankets were obtained as soon as possible from Helpmakaar, a depot of stores on the line of communications, about twelve miles off, and we soon became comparatively comfortable. But Rorke's Drift at best was a rat's-hole of a place, and though vigorous efforts were made to clear and cleanse the ground, there always seemed to be the smell of the dead Zulus in one's nostrils; and this was not imagination when the wind blew from the quarter towards which the line of Zulu retreat had lain.

The first personal communication which I myself had with the outer world came from Sir Bartle. His note will show how all his thoughts were outside of himself.

P. Maritzburg, January 25, 1879.

My dear Parr,

Only just a line to say how thankful I am you are safe, and to tell you what a relief it was to see your handwriting.

I need not say how valuable your letters are.

Give us all the names you can of both lost and saved among our poor fellows, for you know how anxious hundreds are here and elsewhere for news.

God bless you, ever your affectionate,

H. B. E. Frere.

105

I had been lucky enough to waylay the first messenger who went down to Maritzburg with the news of the disaster, and was able to entrust him with a telegram which he was to give Littleton, Sir Bartle's private secretary. I knew Littleton would get it off for me in the Governor's bag, and calculated on all telegrams in the bag getting precedence of press telegrams. This was what actually took place, and my mother and sisters were safely in possession of the telegram telling them that I was safe when the mournful cries of the newsboys rang through the streets.

For the first few days we were waiting hoping to hear of more survivors of Isandlwana. We had heard of some having been seen fighting their way out of camp, and we hoped against hope they might have reached Helpmakaar, Utrecht, or some other point in safety; but none were heard of.

*The defence of Rorke's Drift provided Chelmsford with a single piece of cheering news of a very bad day. To many, it seemed that the little garrison had saved Natal from the horrors of a Zulu invasion. That the Zulu commander, Prince Dabulam-anzi, had exceeded his orders in crossing the border, that he could have simply ignored the post and raided into Natal if he'd wished, was irrelevant; Rorke's Drift reassured the British public that though their leaders might sometimes blunder, the rank and file of the army could still be relied upon to save the day. The Thin Red Line had held. In due course, no less than eleven of the defenders of Rorke's Drift were awarded the Victoria Cross, Chard amongst them.*

*Chelmsford, meanwhile, had to shore up his defences as best he could. He had to break the news of the disaster to a Home Government which had not sanctioned the war, and he had to reassure the civilian population of Natal, amongst whom the news spread panic like wildfire. Without ceremony, as Hamilton-Browne describes, Chelmsford left Rorke's Drift: 'He shook hands with me, said some very kind things about my services, mounted his horse, and rode away.' Hamilton-Browne at once disbanded his 1/3rd NNC, whose nerve had been shaken beyond repair, and the remainder of Glyn's column settled down to make the best of its position in the*

*cramped and insanitary camp at Rorke's Drift. The first fort-
night was spent in daily expectation of attack, and the nights
passed in a dreary routine of drenching rain and false alarms.
Even the recovery of the Queen's Colours in the receding waters
of the Mzinyathi scarcely boosted morale, according to
Hamilton-Browne:*

A few days afterwards the river went down and a party of my
officers started off to try and find the lost flag. I was awfully
disgusted, for just as I was mounting, Colonel Glyn called me
and told me I could not go as he wanted me.

The party left however under the command of Major Black.
They found the remains of poor Melville and Coghill and
buried them. Then Harford and a few of the officers entered
the river bed and found the colours some way lower down.

They returned to the laager and as Black handed the old
flag over to Colonel Glyn the excitement was tremendous, the
Tommies and everyone cheering like fiends. The following
day Colonel Glyn, Major Black and the colours were escorted
by the officers of the defunct 3rd NNC to Helpmaker where
they were handed over to the keeping of the two companies
of the first 24th stationed there.

The reason I had been unable to take a hand in the finding
of the colours was, that Lieutenant Chard, RE, had been taken
very ill, and as I was a bit of an engineer I was used to super-
intend the building of the fort. But shortly a company of the
RE turned up and I was once more able to be in the saddle
with my boys.

The rains now came on with fury – rain, hail, thunder and
lightning, such as is never seen in England, and we had on an
average about four heavy storms during the twenty-four hours.
There we were without tents, blankets or greatcoats and we
had just to grin and bear it. True, the storms only lasted a short
time and then the sun would shine out and dry as quickly, but
we usually had one storm at least during the night and then
as the sun was absent we had to lie wet through the remainder
of the night and shiver in the mud or sleep as best we could.
We did everything possible to keep the laager clean but notwithstanding all our efforts it got very muddy.

It was not so bad when you were once down in the mud but it was very nasty to have to get up and then lie down again as would be the case if we had a false alarm. Of these we had but few and that notwithstanding the awful strain to their nerves the men had suffered by the disaster at Isandlwana, yet it speaks volumes for the second 24th and my filibusters to be able to state that during the whole time we garrisoned Rourke's Drift not a single shot was fired in the way of a false alarm. The same cannot be said of the relieving forces when they reached the front, when disgraceful false alarms, such as at Fort Funk, became common. However I will now tell you of the great and only false alarm that took place at Rourke's Drift.

We had attached to us a civilian doctor, a very good fellow, who had seen much service and who had distinguished himself in the Russo-Turkish War. He however had had a bad go of fever and his nerves had gone all to pieces though he still did his duty. Well one night I was lying down fast asleep in the angle of the laager I was in charge of; the aforesaid angle, having been the ancient pig-kraal of the farm, was by no means a pleasant bedroom although airy enough, and we had just had our usual rain-storm, when I was suddenly woke up by the doctor who in an excited tone said, 'For God's sake, Commandant, get up, the Zulus are on us.' I was up in a second and the muttered order, 'Stand to your arms,' was answered by a rustle as the men rose from their mud beds and manned the parapet. The pig-kraal angle was the most exposed portion of the laager and being nearest the river was most likely to be attacked first. A sharp click as the breeches of the rifles were opened and shut, a sharper rattle as the 24th stood to arms and fixed bayonets and every man was at his post.

Not a further sound, not a word spoken.

I got into the most advanced spot and peered out into the darkness but could see nothing.

A bit of a moon and the stars gave a glimmer of light that would have flashed on the Zulu spears and given them away had they been there, but I saw not a spark nor flash.

I could see the white range marks that I had had put up and had any large body of men been between them and me they would have been obscured, so evidently my corner of the laager was not in danger of immediate attack.

Just then Colonel Glyn (the OC) came round. 'What is it, Commandant Browne?' he said to me. 'I don't see anything, sir,' I replied; 'there can be no large number of the enemy on this front.' 'Who gave you the alarm?' 'Doctor —' The Colonel turned sharply round. 'What is it, Dr —? Why did you give the alarm, sir?' 'Good God, don't you hear them, sir?' said the medico, excitedly. 'Hear them? Hear what, sir?' snorted the enraged Colonel. 'Why, the frogs, sir,' ejaculated the doctor. 'The Zulus are waking them up as they advance.'

A dead man could have heard the frogs. Anyone who has ever been in Natal or further north knows the diabolical row the frogs kick up, after rain, and the frogs round Rourke's Drift were like a strong-voiced crew at a chanty.

Curses not loud but very deep saluted the doctor from all sides and he retired in disgrace after an unpleasant tête-à-tête with the OC, while the rest of us sought our mud beds again in disgust and disappointment. Rome was saved by the cackling of geese and they received great kudos. But the frogs lost their chance of similar worship at Rourke's Drift owing to the absence of any enemy. Anyhow the only thing expended was cuss words and they, at Rourke's Drift, were too plentiful to be missed. No ammunition was wasted as would have been the case later on in the war.

And now my messmate Harford got into disgrace. He was a gallant officer, a splendid companion, but, and the but is a very big one, he was a mad naturalist. He caught bugs and beetles both in season and out of season. I told a tale about him before in this yarn, but the awful tale I am going to relate now is one that even after a period of thirty years makes my blood run cold. For he committed a sin that in comparison made the seven deadly sins look trivial beside it. The crime was this, but I must give a short prelude so that it may be understood in all its hideousness.

The 24th had a small amount of reserve mess stores at Rourke's Drift, we had nothing, and although there was plenty of Natal rum I could not face the filth; vile stuff it was and hot enough to burn the inside out of a graven image. This being so the 24th, like the rattling good fellows they were, always asked me over to their corner whenever they opened a bottle and I had my tot.

Well just about this time a Natal man rushed through a wagon load of stores and asked leave to sell them. I happened to have about £2 in my pocket at the time of the disaster and after buying two night-caps and some spoons and forks for Harford and myself, I asked the man if he had any liquor. He said he had a big square rigger of gin for his own use but not for trade. I offered all the money I had left and an equal-sized bottle of Natal rum for it and we traded. Well now there was corn in Egypt and I could, in a small way, return the hospitality of the 24th so I at once sent round to my friends to come to my corner, that evening after inspection, and partake of the plunder. They had run out of spirits and the news was joyful.

I handed the bottle over to my servant Quin and told him to guard it with his life, and he swore he would do so. I was called away and I left Quin on sentry go over that precious bottle; he placed it carefully between two sacks and sat down on it so I thought I thought it safe and attended to my duty. That afternoon we had our usual rain-storm and when it was over Harford came to me and asked me if he could have some gin. I was very busy at the time and said, 'Certainly, ask Quin for some.'

Now it struck me it was strange that Harford should ask for it as he never touched spirits, but I thought he might feel chill after the rain and want a tot to warm himself.

Well the retreat was blown, the men manned the parapet, the OC inspected, and the men fell away. In a few minutes round came my friends, anxious for the tot they fondly expected to be in store for them.

'Hoots, Maori, where's the drappie?' said Black. I turned to Quin, who was standing stiffly at attention, and at once saw the worthy man was disgusted, sulky, almost mutinous. 'Give me the bottle, Quin,' I said. 'Better ask Mr Harford for it, sir,' he answered, with a grin on his expressive mug like an over-tortured fiend. 'Harford,' said I, 'where is the gin?' and at once my heart darkened with apprehensions. 'Oh, Commandant,' quoth he, 'I have caught such a lot of beauties,' and he produced two large pickle bottles filled with scorpions, snakes and other foul creeping beasts and reptiles. 'Do look at them.' 'But the gin, Harford?' I murmured, so full of consternation that I could hardly articulate. 'I've preserved these with it,' said he, utterly oblivious to his horrid crime. 'What!' yelled I. 'Oh yes,' said he, 'this is a very rare and poisonous reptile indeed' – pointing to a loathsome beast and beginning to expatiate on its hideousness and reel off long Latin names. 'I don't care if it is a sucking devil,' groaned I, 'but where is the gin?' 'In these bottles,' said he, and so it was, every drop of it.

Ye Gods! The only bottle of gin or any other drop of decent drink within 100 miles of us had gone to preserve his infernal microbes, and a dozen disgusted officers, who were just beginning to grasp the awful situation, were cursing him and lamenting sadly, oh, so sadly, his pursuit of natural history, while dear old Black had to be supported back to his angle making remarks in Gaelic. He was such a good fellow he was soon forgiven, but I do not think the dear fellow ever quite understood what an awful sin he had committed or realised what a wicked waste of liquor he had perpetrated.

*Perhaps it was just as well that King Cetshwayo's army was in no real position to launch an attack. The warriors had dispersed to their homesteads to lick their wounds, and in any case the king was determined to hold his hand. This would prove a costly mistake: with each passing week, British confidence began to seep back, and with it the chance of a lasting Zulu victory slipped away. At Rorke's Drift, the remains of the Centre Column began to regain its fighting spirit, pushing patrols across the river, harrying Zulu civilians, and searching out intelligence. Hamilton-Browne was a zealous participant:*

One evening the OC sent for me to dine with him. I had sent him a pau (bustard) I had shot with my revolver and as he had also received some small stores from Helpmaker we fared sumptuously. After a tot and a smoke he looked at me and said quietly, 'Maori, do you think you could catch me a live Zulu?' I said, 'I don't know, but I will try, sir.' He said, 'Don't hurt him too much as I must question him. I am very anxious to obtain information on certain matters and it is the only way I can obtain it.' I said, 'Had I not better question him outside, sir?' He said, 'No, I'll have none of your Spanish Inquisition tricks. You bring him into camp, I will question him myself.' I was not at all sure the dear old man knew how to extract information out of a native but I always obey orders, that is, if my inclinations are not too strong the other way. So talking the matter over with Captains Duncombe and Develin we determined to cross the river during the night and lay in ambuscade for any man who might be travelling from kraal to kraal. This we did and hiding our horses among some bushes and rocks we lay dogo by a footpath and waited.

About 6 a.m. along came a native and we were on him before he could let a yell out. I had him by the throat and threw him. Duncombe had him by the arms and Develin tied them. In a few seconds we were mounted, a rheim was passed round the Zulu's neck so that he must run or hang and we were just starting when a lot more natives appeared. Duncombe had the prisoner, so at once cantered off while myself and Develin turned to cover his retreat. We were both dead shots and the party of the enemy were so surprised and astonished that they stood stock still. Crack, crack went our carbines and over rolled two of them. We loaded again. Both our horses were trained shooting horses and stood like rocks. We let rip and over went two more; again we fired and browned them, the MH bullets at 100 yards range would go through two or three men, so they let go a yell and bolted. So we turned our horses and cantered after Duncombe, who was riding as fast as he could get the prisoner to move. A little persuasion from the butt end of a carbine made him mend his pace so that we reached and crossed the river without being cut off and brought our capture to the laager in triumph.

Our prisoner turned out to be a seasoned warrior instead of a young man so Colonel Glyn could get nothing out of him and gave orders that he should be taken down to the drift and let go.

He was also unkind in his remarks to me and blamed me for bringing him such a man as if I could pick and choose, besides he had only requested me to catch him a [Zulu] and had not specified what sort of a one he wanted, but then this world is full of injustice and a scout must not be cast down if he gets his whack of it.

Now we had a picket on the top of the hill at the rear of the fort and they reported that they daily saw a Zulu at the top of another hill, overlooking the fort, who evidently took stock of everything that went on. After a few days this bounder, evidently thinking he was quite safe, began to send up smoke signals and this piece of cheek roused the bile of the OC. Several parties were sent out to catch him, but he could see them leave the camp and he would disappear into some very rough ground. One night the OC sent for me and said, 'Maori, I want you to put a stop to that fellow, it is simply disgraceful you have allowed this kind of thing to go on so long.' Here was more injustice; he had entrusted the suppression of the Johnnie to others and now blamed me, but I have found it sound policy never to argue with or point out his faults to a choleric or liverish senior so I wisely said nothing but accepted the rebuke and the contract with equanimity.

It was evident that the Zulu must cross the river somewhere and I had noticed while scouting down our side of it a spoor leading in the direction of the hill from which he carried on his observations. At this spot there was a large mealie field abutting on the rough ground on the bank of the river, then some open ground and then some small patches of mealies. I had noticed that the spoor ran from the big field to one of the small patches and I determined to try for him there. Taking my two officers, Captains Duncombe and Develin, with me, we left the laager a couple of hours before daybreak and rode down to the spot, hid our horses and lay dogo. As soon as it was light we observed carefully the far bank of the river, the near bank we could not see, and the open space between the big field of mealies and the patch. Develin looked after the bank, Duncombe watched the open ground and I let my glance wander everywhere. One of us, therefore, if he came, was bound to spot him. It had not long been daylight when Develin whispered to me, 'There he is.' There was no morning mist and I just spotted him slide down the far side of the river bank, where we lost sight of him. We could now all concentrate our attention on the open ground and presently Duncombe spotted him crawl from the mealies and start squirming towards one of the small patches for fresh cover. I must say he did it splendidly; his naked body blended with the colour of the ground and would have been unseen by an untrained eye. He was evidently paying most attention to his right flank on which side was the camp from whence he might expect danger but we were on his other side and well concealed. We could easily have shot him but I wanted to capture him alive. My last capture had not been a lucky one and I wanted to take a prisoner to the OC as I knew he was most anxious to obtain information. Well we watched our friend gain the small patch. We could hunt him out of that if he tried to hide there, so we mounted and went for him. He must have been well on the *qui vive* for we had not gained the open when he burst out of his cover and was running like a scared cat, for the big field, to try and regain the rough ground by the river bank, where he, at all events, would be safe from capture. But it was not to be. He ran well and was within thirty yards of his refuge, when my horse, the fastest of the three, overtook him and a tremendous smash, between the shoulders, from the butt of my carbine sent him rolling over and over like a shot rabbit. Before I could pull up my horse, the others were up to him and had tied his arms so that when I rode back to them he was sitting up looking very cheap. As he was still a bit sick I gave him some water and looked him over.

I was out of luck again, for instead of being a young fellow as I had hoped, he turned out to be a fine old war-dog, so it was good-bye to any chance of getting any information out of him. His field kit consisted of the usual Zulu outfit, one skin apron in front and one behind with the usual charm, etc., but there was one etc. he had no right to wear and that was a piece of turkey-red cloth bound round his head. This was the uniform of the Natal Native Contingent and on Duncombe demanding why he wore it, he answered, so as to deceive the red soldiers if he chanced to meet any. This was a fatal admission as it at once turned him into a spy.

I almost felt sorry for the poor chap, but a scout must have no feelings and years of savage warfare had blunted any I might have ever possessed, so as soon as he had recovered his wind a rheim was passed round his neck and we trotted back to camp. On our arrival there we handed over the prisoner to the main guard, which during the day used a wagon outside the laager for a guardroom, and I at once reported to the OC.

*The fate of this 'spy' was a grim one; like several other Zulus, who may or may not have been combatants, he was strung up from a makeshift gallows by the vengeful garrison. King Cetshwayo might perhaps have read a message in that, had he a mind to: his people would pay a high price for Isandlwana before the war was over.*

CHAPTER THREE

# The Siege And Relief Of Eshowe

I N the weeks before the ultimatum expired, a sprawling military camp sprang up on the Natal bank of the Thukela river
at the Lower Drift. A stout earthwork was erected on a knoll
which commanded the crossing, and named Fort Pearson, after
Colonel Charles Knight Pearson of the 3rd Regiment (the
Buffs), who was in command of this, the No. 1 or Right Flank
Column. Pearson's base was not far from the mouth of the
Thukela, and, after weeks of heavy summer rain, the river
flowed out to sea as a wide, deep expanse of smooth brown
water. It was impossible to cross on foot, but as the days ticked
by, Pearson's men fastened a hawser to the far bank, and a
flat-bottomed ferry was built to ship the column – which consisted of two battalions of infantry, one section from an artillery
battery, a Naval Brigade detachment, the 2nd Regiment NNC,
and mounted men from the Natal Volunteer Corps – into Zululand. The atmosphere on the sub-tropical coastal strip was
noticeably more humid than in the higher reaches inland, and
the advance promised to be a gruelling one. Pearson's first
objective was the deserted mission station at Eshowe, nearly
forty miles away across rising downland intersected by a succession of swollen rivers. The mission station, abandoned
when its occupants fled Zululand as the political tension
mounted before the war, had been selected as an advanced
supply depot, on the assumption that its buildings could be
pressed into service to protect a stockpile of stores. From
Eshowe Pearson would, in due course, move towards Ulundi,
coordinating his advance with Chelmsford and Wood.

With no word from King Cetshwayo, Pearson began the

laborious task of crossing the Thukela on 12th January 1879. Among those in his ranks was 'Harry O'Clery, of the Buffs', whose exact rank is uncertain, though he was clearly not an officer. O'Clery's account was included in *Told From The Ranks*, an anthology of accounts by ordinary soldiers of Victorian campaigns, published in 1901. His story is interesting, and not just because of what it says about the Zulu War; it clearly reflects the improving social conditions and educational level of the British Army in the 1870s. O'Clery describes the build up to the campaign, the start of the invasion, and his baptism of fire at the battle of Nyezane, when Zulu forces stationed near the coast moved down to try to block Pearson's advance. The battle took place on 22nd January – co-incidentally, the same day that Isandlwana was being fought. He tells of the column's arrival at Eshowe, and how the mission was prepared for a state of siege. His is also, incidentally, the only account which suggests that Zulu envoys might have tried to make contact before the ultimatum expired, but were driven off by British fire:

*

It was at Canterbury, in July 1877, that I joined Her Majesty's forces. I was led to that step by Recruiting-Sergeant Jack Gavigan, who had the credit, while stationed at St George's Barracks, of enlisting more men in one year than all the other recruiting-sergeants put together.

I was placed in the Depot M Company of the Buffs.

Having received a fairly good education, I soon afterwards sat for an examination, and having gained a second-class certificate – which was thought something of in those days, for men were not then up to the present standard of knowledge – I was appointed an assistant schoolmaster to the depot, with the remuneration of fourpence a day. It was my duty to take the two lower classes of the men; and I very frequently found myself in charge of the whole school, as the acting schoolmaster, a sergeant whose name I will not disclose, had frequently to repair to the mess for the purpose of refreshment.

About five months after enlisting, I learned that we were

ordered to join the regiment at Pietermaritzburg; and soon afterwards we proceeded to Southampton, where we embarked on the ship *American*, and found ourselves in company with a detachment of the 88th Regiment, known as 'The Old Fogs', or the 'Faugh-a-Ballagh Boys', from the war-cry of the corps; 'Fag-an-Bealoch' meaning 'Clear the way'.

During the voyage to the Cape we heard this war-cry on several occasions, and the monotony of the voyage was varied by occasional fights between men of the two regiments, who probably considered that, as they were going out to fight, there could be no objection to a little practice beforehand; and I can speak from experience in saying that most of my countrymen enjoy nothing better than a lively argument, and a free fight to wind up with.

We encountered a gale off Cape Finisterre, and had to be battened down below; but at this time I was afflicted with sea-sickness, from which I did not recover for seven days. The rest of the voyage was most pleasant and enjoyable.

We disembarked at Cape Town, and after a few days sailed from thence to East London, where we remained about a week, and then proceeded to Durban on HMS *Himalaya*. Owing to the roll of the sea here, we had to land in surf boats. It was anything but a pleasant experience. Fifteen or twenty men would go down the ship's side into the boat, and a canvas would be stretched over her to keep out the water. Then, in the dark, we found ourselves jerked and jolted, one against another, for some considerable time, until the boat was hauled to the beach, where we landed more dead than alive, for the rolling and pitching of a whole sea voyage was crammed into that brief trip in a surf boat.

After a short stay at Durban, we marched up the country to Pietermaritzburg, a distance of upwards of fifty miles, which we accomplished in four days, being cheered towards our journey's end by meeting the band of the regiment, which played us into the town to the tune of a then popular comic song. On joining the regiment I was drafted into the B Company.

While staying in the town we turned out to welcome the 24th Regiment, passing through on their way up the country.

They stayed about a week, and I made the acquaintance of two brothers, Fred and George Conboy, both in the band.

Soon we learned that Cetewayo, the Zulu king, had been called upon to pay a fine of a certain number of bullocks, for some filibustering expedition which some of his young warriors had made into Natal; and the date of payment was fixed for the 12th January, which was about twelve months after we had left England.

On and before that particular day we were encamped upon the southern bank of the Tugela River, upon which the Royal Engineers, assisted by the soldiers told off for the work, were busily constructing a floating raft, or bridge, by the aid of which we were, if needful, to cross over into the enemy's country.

We numbered in the camp between two and three thousand men, consisting of the Buffs, the 99th Regiment, Mounted Infantry, Naval Brigade, Royal Artillery, a native contingent, and some mounted volunteers from Stanger and Victoria (two small towns on the coast of Natal) who evidently thought they were out for a picnic, and brought with them several waggon-loads of bedding, tinned meats, comforts and luxuries, of which I shall say a word or two in the course of my yarn.

The river was very full, and some half a mile wide, and there were plenty of crocodiles in its waters. Two or three poor fellows, while at work on the raft, were snapped up on falling overboard, and seen no more. One was a friend of mine belonging to HMS *Active*.

It was the day before the final pay-day, and away in the distance we could plainly see a body of natives, who were by many in the camp believed to be the people whose arrival we were awaiting. But the commanding officers, I suppose, thought differently, and sent a shell bursting among them to tell them we were there.

The next day we crossed the river, and then war began. The crossing of the river was accomplished this way: two companies, of about one hundred men each, marched on to the raft, and it was then hauled across by the Naval Brigade. As soon as the men landed on the opposite side, the empty raft was drawn back again for a fresh freight; and so, as it was a tedious job, the whole day was taken up. From what I could learn of the plan, the British force was to invade the country in four columns. No. 1, nearest the sea, was under the command of Brigadier-General Pearson, numbered 4,200, and was to advance along the coast. No. 2 consisted of 3,000 natives, commanded by European officers under Colonel Durnford, RE, who was to cross the Tugela at Middle Drift and march up the left side of the river to Rorke's Drift. No. 3, commanded by Colonel Glyn, was about 3,000 strong, and contained the first and second battalions of the 24th Regiment, numbering about 1,000 bayonets. And No. 4, under Colonel Evelyn Wood, also about 3,000 strong, was to operate from Utrecht, in conjunction with Colonel Glyn's column.

We, in No. 1 column, learned now and then of the movements of the others, by the native runners, who were sent from one column to another with despatches. Poor chaps, they risked their lives for very slight remuneration, and it was dangerous work to play the spy as they did; for the Zulus, when it became known that we were marching on their capital, determined to make a stand for it.

We were marched up country, and terribly wet weather it was, no mistake, for the first week or so. Not a single shot was fired by any of our skirmishers, who were on in front of us. The natives retired before us, keeping, as they went, a watchful eye upon our movements, but taking care to keep out of range. As a proof of their nearness, however, we found, upon coming to their camping-grounds, that the embers of their fires were still smouldering.

Every night we camped in *laager*. This consists of drawing the waggons into a circle and digging a slight trench all round it, the earth taken from the trench being thrown up on the outer side to form a breastwork.

Our first laager was formed near the farm of an English settler named John Dunne, who had, I think, married a native woman, and suited himself to the customs of the country. He knew his way about the country, and some little while before we crossed the Tugela he joined our column, bringing with him his family and a large number of followers.

Another stopping-place was upon the banks of a river, and

after that at another river. Crossing this at a shallow part, we continued our march, and noticed that traces of the enemy were becoming more and more frequent. This gave us hope of a brush with them.

We were halted to prepare breakfast at a place called Inyezane, when we heard firing in front, and found that our skirmishers were engaged with a Zulu 'impi'. On pushing forward to the brow of a hill, we found ourselves under fire. Puffs of smoke were appearing in all directions from the bush away in front of us, and we therefore lay down, and fired at every spot from which a puff appeared.

It was my first appearance on a battlefield. We were told by our officers to keep ourselves cool and steady, and fire low; and I tried not to get carried away by the excitement, but it's not so easy, when you know that each puff *may* mean a dose of death to you or the man next you.

We had with us a naval brigade of two hundred and seventy bluejackets and marines from the *Tenedos* and *Active*, and these had charge of the waggons and two Gatlings. The Zulus came on in fine style, but the steady fire we kept up prevented them coming to close quarters. They, however, attempted a flanking movement; but Colonel Parnell led a spirited charge, and cleared the heights, and the enemy were driven off, leaving about nine hundred killed and wounded upon the battlefield. I think we lost in the action seven killed, and about twenty-seven wounded. These we took with us, but left the enemy where they fell.

We had had no breakfast before the fight, and as we had to reach a certain distance each day, we had no refreshment till 9 p.m.

Next day we were overtaken by a native runner, who was taken to the General, and in consequence of the news he brought we were hurried forward with as little delay as possible. These runners are strange individuals; they take to running when they are tired of walking, and I noticed they seemed to get their breath better by so doing. On the following morning, eleven days after the invasion of the country, we arrived at the village of Ekowe, about forty miles due north of the river Tugela, where there was a mission-station; and here we set to work to build a fort around the church, which was intended to be used as an hospital if required.

We formed a laager, into which we went for safety during the night, the day being occupied in building a fort. Here, upon its completion, we took up our position.

This was how we built the fort. The church tower in the centre was a look-out post for our best marksmen; and around the church, at a considerable distance, we dug a trench, some ten or twelve feet deep, and about twenty feet wide, and into this trench we planted stakes pointed at both ends. The earth from the trench formed a high breastwork, with steps formed on the inner side of the fort; and outside, beyond the trench, we dug small holes, at regular distances apart, into which we drove sharpened stakes, upon which we stretched wire to entangle the legs of the enemy who might venture within the maze.

Our position being considered very secure, the native contingent, with the mounted volunteer picnic-party, were, to the surprise of many of us, sent back, as they could be of no service and would make a considerable difference in our commissariat department.

The mystery of the runner's message was soon cleared up. It turned out that he was the bearer of bad news. A British force had been attacked in camp at Isandlwhana, and literally cut to pieces. In confirmation of the terrible message we happened to capture about this time a Zulu soldier, belonging to the Kandampemvu Regiment, who was wearing a jacket and carrying a rifle which had belonged to a man of the 24th Regiment.

We questioned him about the battle, and the account he gave was that the soldiers and volunteers retired, fighting all the way, and as they got into the camp the Zulus intermingled with them. One party of soldiers came out from among the tents, and formed up a little above the waggons. They held their ground until their ammunition failed, when they were nearly all assegaied.

As I said before, what a private soldier knows about the plan of campaign is what he picks up from hearsay.

It soon leaked out that our fort was itself surrounded by

Zulus, in such numbers that there was no possibility of leaving the place, either to go backward or forward, until reinforcements arrived. We were therefore put on short rations, and the small allowance of meat and flour which was doled out to us we cooked in various ways. For drinking purposes we had a small quantity of either tea, coffee, or lime juice; but we were altogether short of vegetables and tobacco.

I kept a diary while in Ekowe, and took note of the prices realised when the luxuries left behind by the mounted volunteers were put under the hammer, on the 22nd February 1879. Most of the goods were purchased by the officers, as prices were high:

| | £ | s | d |
|---|---|---|---|
| 1½ lbs. tobacco | 1 | 9 | 0 |
| 1 small bottle of curry | 0 | 14 | 0 |
| 1 large    do. | 1 | 7 | 0 |
| 7 cigars | 0 | 9 | 0 |
| 1 tin of condensed milk | 0 | 14 | 6 |
| 1        do. | 0 | 15 | 6 |
| 1        do. | 0 | 18 | 0 |
| 1        do. | 1 | 0 | 0 |
| 1 tin of lobster | 0 | 13 | 6 |
| 1 small bottle of pickles | 1 | 6 | 0 |
| 1 small bottle of sauce | 1 | 1 | 0 |
| 1 pint of ketchup | 0 | 15 | 6 |
| 1 box of sardines | 0 | 11 | 0 |
| 1 bottle of ink | 0 | 7 | 0 |
| 1 pot salmon | 0 | 15 | 6 |
| 1 pot herrings | 0 | 13 | 6 |
| 1 lb. dubbin | 0 | 9 | 6 |
| 1 small packet of cocoa | 0 | 11 | 0 |
| 1 ham (12 lbs.) | 6 | 5 | 0 |

The last item, I remember, was knocked down to an officer of the 99th Regiment, who invited the Colonel to dine with him in the evening; but at the appointed time the feast was given up, for some person or persons unknown had stolen the joint!

We were now compelled to keep within the fort, except that occasionally we made raids in search of vegetables. Several times we visited native kraals, from which a few natives would fly on our approach, and here we sometimes found growing maize or pumpkins, which on our return we cooked and ate with much relish. But these raids were not unattended with danger, for frequently the Zulus would fire at us from the bush, and then there would be one or more wounded men to bring back, and place in the hospital tent. Each day, also, some of us were told off to guard the cattle outside the fort, and bring them back in safety at nightfall.

Doleful days were these; the rain used to come down in torrents, and we made our beds beneath the waggons, upon the damp ground, while creeping things crawled and ran over us as we slept. The officers used to sleep inside the waggons, and were, so far, a little more comfortable than the rank and file, but even they were roughing it.

We made the best of our time, now and then having an open-air concert, with choruses by all hands, at which times a few natives might be seen in the distance listening to our melodies; and now and then our marksmen would have a shot at them, for our rifles could reach them while theirs could not carry to us.

Sometimes the tables were turned, and frequently our mounted outposts would be attacked by Zulus, who crept up to them under cover of the long grass. One poor fellow rode back to the fort with more than a dozen wounds. How he managed to keep his seat and fight his way through the enemy I cannot tell. Those who fell into the hands of the Zulus were terribly mutilated, and left on the open ground to be found by their comrades on the following day, and carried back to the fort for burial.

That word 'burial' reminds me of the funerals which so frequently took place, for typhoid fever came among us, and, despite the efforts of the doctors, carried off a good number of the men. The Rev Mr Ritchie, our chaplain, was a splendid man, and always hopeful and light-hearted. He attended all the funerals, none of which were very ceremonious; we simply wrapped the dead men in their blankets, and laid them in their graves without a parting volley, as ammunition was precious and we had no blank cartridges.

Time dragged wearily on, and there seemed no prospect of

relief. Lieutenant Rowden, of the 99th Regiment, made several exploring expeditions, and ascertained the whereabouts of the Zulus; and on two or three occasions we captured from neighbouring kraals a considerable quantity of cattle, which were a welcome addition to our commissariat department.

*Also shut up in the cramped and insanitary fort was Captain C. R. St Leger Shervington. Shervington was serving with the 2nd NNC, but when the NNC were sent back to the Thukela, Shervington attached himself to the column's scratch mounted infantry force. In his letters and diaries, quoted in* The Shervingtons: Soldiers of Fortune, *published in 1899, Shervington describes the hardships suffered by the garrison as the Zulu net drew tighter, and the constant skirmishing between Pearson's outposts and the Zulu patrols:*

There is a great deal of sickness among the men, and we have made a sanatorium of bushes on a hill opposite the fort, 400 yards off. A guard is posted there, and the sick are carried out for fresh air every morning.

The real cause of sickness is the constant exposure, one day to the sun and the next day to the rain, then turning in dripping wet, with the rain or a cold wind beating in underneath the wagons. We all sleep under wagons, as no tents are pitched. The covers are stretched out on either side, something like two verandahs.

We grind down the Indian corn into meal, and it makes excellent porridge, but it is hard work and we all do our share, so as to relieve our servants, who have their own interests to look after as well as their masters'. Pumpkin-pie is very nice with lime-juice and sugar added, but we have to save our ration of sugar for several days before such a luxury can be decently hinted at. At a sale milk fetches £1 a tin, curry powder £1 3s. a bottle, 12 lbs. of ham £6 5s., and other things in proportion. It is wonderful how everybody keeps up their spirits, the blue-jackets especially. Many a time have I seen the water rushing through their shed, carrying away blankets, boots, and every-thing movable, but this only makes Jack Tar sing the louder.

A wet day is always a regular field-day for Captain Cotton,

99th, at our tobacco. We have scraped together a few dirty mouldy cakes, which we mix with the better ones to make our scanty stock hold out. Cotton has manufactured a tobacco-cutter, and spends his wet mornings in chopping up the tobacco – a most tedious process with his clumsy but invaluable machine.

The only difference between Sundays and other days is Church parade at 6.30 a.m. so as not to interfere with the day's work. At first Moody and Sankey's hymn 'Hold the Fort,' was always played by the band. The bands of the Buffs and 99th play alternately every afternoon, since the work about the fort began to slacken – before that the bandsmen had to take their regular turn of duty with the others. We were glad when our baggage was restored to us and sods put in its place.

The sickness is increasing, and medicine running short. Our ration of bread has been reduced to 6 ozs. of flour and two biscuits a day, but the want of tobacco is felt far more than the short rations.

The excitement of the whole camp may be imagined when they first signalled to us from Tugela by looking-glass.

We had been three weeks without any news from the outer world, when one Sunday a bright flash was seen in the direction of the Tugela. We knew what it was at once, for we had often talked about it. It took us two days before we could make out clearly what they said, but after that we improved rapidly, and at the end of a week had manufactured a signalling machine for ourselves out of a looking-glass and an ammunition box, and began asking questions.

Our first message from the Tugela was that Colonel Law would advance to our assistance on March 13th, with 1,000 troops and 1,000 natives, when we were to be prepared to sally out with what troops we could spare and meet him.

We immediately set to work to cut a more direct road to Inyezane, and while occupied on it, had several skirmishes with the enemy, who came down in such force one morning that we had to retire, and they always followed us up in the evening when we knocked off work. We got rather sick of this, so one evening the engineers put down 18 ozs of dynamite at the point where we had left off working, and a friction tube

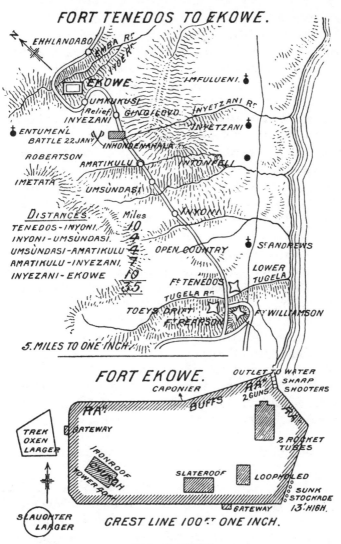

MAP OF EKOWE.

connected with a pole stuck in the ground. We had hardly left it when about 30 Zulus came down, saw the pole with 'Torpedo' written on it, and at once tried to pull it up. It took three or four to do it, and up it came, blowing about six Zulus to pieces and frightening the others out of their wits. The moral effect was excellent, and they never interfered with our work again.

About the same time the Zulus began annoying our outposts, and one morning about fifteen of them jumped up out of the long grass, and fired a volley into one of the men, Carson of the 99th. He was wounded in five places and his horse assegaied, but he managed to get away, and rode into camp. He had two fingers shot away, a bullet through the wrist, another through both thighs, and his back lacerated by a ball which glanced off his carbine. The doctors pronounced his wounds severe, but not dangerous.

I was at breakfast one morning when I heard shots in the direction of No. 4 vidette post. I rushed out and found a man galloping in, who told me Private Kent, 99th, was shot. I took his horse from him and rode out to the post, and saw Kent's horse walking in covered with blood; no one had seen him fall. I galloped to the spot where the shots came from, but could see nothing. I was joined by some videttes from another post. We found Kent's body lying in the grass with sixteen assegai wounds all in front. He must have fallen off when his horse was shot and got up and run, but finding the Zulus ran faster, turned round and tried to defend himself. He was a very good man, and we were all sorry for him.

*As the siege dragged on throughout March, the isolation began to take its toll. It became more and more difficult to send runners through the Zulu cordon to Fort Pearson, Chelmsford's nearest outpost. Pearson's men had no signalling equipment with them, and without news of the outside world, morale began to flag. With remarkable ingenuity, the column's Engineers tried to improvise some means of contacting the Thukela garrison; they tried small small hot-air balloons, a paper screen erected on a hill-side near the fort, and, at last, someone succeeded in constructing a makeshift heliograph using a mirror and a length of piping taken from the mission roof. Harry O'Clery describes how Pearson's men learned of their impending relief:*

Several of the Engineers who were with us manufactured a home-made heliograph, and were continually flashing signals to inform Lord Chelmsford of the desperate position we were in. For a long time these signals appeared to be unnoticed, but at last we learned that some reinforcements had arrived from St Helena in HMS *Shah*; and these, with a number of sailors forming part of the ship's crew, and others from HMS *Boadicea*, together with 3,300 whites, 1,600 natives, and a small body of cavalry numbering about 160, with rocket tubes and nine-pounders, were marching to our relief under Lord Chelmsford.

To this encouraging information our men replied, cautioning the advancing army that a force of Zulus, estimated at about 35,000, were prepared to bar their progress.

*What had been happening in Natal? Since the disaster at Isandlwana, Chelmsford had been re-organising his forces. However reluctant the Home Government might have been to embark on the war, they were not prepared to see British prestige dragged though the mud, and honour would have to be satisfied before peace was restored. In response to Chelmsford's modest request for troops to make up his losses, he was offered a veritable shower of military riches: no less than six infantry battalions, two cavalry regiments and two artillery batteries were sent out from Britain and the Empire, together with four major-generals to fill places on Chelmsford's staff, and detachments of Engineers, Army Service Corps, Commissariat and Transport Department and medical facilities. By the time the final drafts had arrived in Africa in the middle of April, Chelmsford would have received a total of 418 officers, 9,996 men, 1,868 horses, and 238 wagons as reinforcements.*

*Obviously, the Zulu victory at Isandlwana had scotched his original invasion plan. When it became clear in February that the Zulus were not following up with a major incursion across the Thukela, Chelmsford began to re-think his entire strategy. Before he could consider mounting a fresh invasion, however, he had to look to his two remaining columns. Wood, in the north, had remained on the offensive – as we shall see – by raiding local Zulu chiefdoms, but it was clearly impossible to leave Pearson's men holed up in Eshowe. As the first re-inforcements began to arrive in Durban, they were marched up to the front and gathered at the Lower Drift, in readiness for a dash to relieve the beleaguered garrison.*

*Throughout March bad weather and supply problems forced Chelmsford to postpone the start of the expedition several times, but finally, on the 27th, he crossed the Thukela with the 57th and 91st Regiments, six companies of the 3/60th Rifles – all newcomers – and two companies of the Buffs. They were sup-ported by a Naval Brigade armed with Gatling machine-guns and heavy 24-pdr rocket tubes, two battalions of the NNC, and members of the Natal Volunteers. Supplies were carried in 122 wagons, but there were no tents, and the troops could look forward to miserable nights in the incessant rain, lying on the ground without shelter.*

*The story of the Eshowe relief expedition is best told by Cap-tain W. C. F. Molyneux, one of Chelmsford's staff, in his* Cam-paigning in South Africa and Egypt *(1896). Molyneux gives a vivid impression of the hardships of the march, of the appalling conditions, and of that extraordinary character, King Cetsh-wayo's former adviser, the 'White Zulu' John Dunn:*

From March 25th to the 29th we were hard at work all day and half the night ferrying the force over the Tugela by the pont. The Naval Brigade worked the machine and where quite in their element. It would take only one waggon and its team at a time, so that more than a hundred trips over and back were required for the transport alone; and as the river when high in about half a mile wide, it will be understood that the Blue-jackets had no light task. A fort, called Tenedos, had been constructed on the Zulu side, while Fort Pearson, 180 feet above the water, covered the ferry on our side. By the night of the 28th the whole force was across, and bivouacked on the left bank in a terrific storm of rain, which put out all the fires and turned the ground into a swamp.

On Saturday, March 29th, the leading Brigade advanced at

daybreak, hoping to reach the Inyoni River only nine miles off. Reach it we did, for the oxen were fresh, but the tail of the column had only got half-way by noon, and that night the waggon-drivers, who had had no practice in laagering, got so out of hand that the laager was made anyhow, and would only hold one third of our oxen. So much for our first trek and our first laager.[1]

The next morning was so wet and foggy that the oxen could not be turned out to graze till five o'clock, and no start was possible before eight. However, in spite of one shocking bad drift, over which only one waggon could be got at a time, we were all laagered and entrenched on the Amatikulu River by half-past five that afternoon. This was better than the previous day's work: we had done seven miles in seven hours, and the laager this time was large enough and fairly well made; but the performance was not good enough for the critical eye of John Dunn.

John Dunn was the son of a Scotchman who had settled at Port Elizabeth in Cape Colony. Being of an adventurous frame of mind he had come to Natal about 1850, had been made interpreter to the Governor of Durban, and somehow got mixed up in the Zulu civil war of 1856, when Cetewayo defeated his brother Umbulazi on the Tugela. Though Dunn had been on that occasion with the losing side, he seems later on to have become most friendly with Cetewayo, and with his brother Dabulamanzi, whom he taught to ride and shoot with a rifle. The king gave him land near the Lower Tugela and wives, and he was now a chief over a tribe. He had warned Cetewayo against fighting us; but when at the beginning of

---

[1] When I returned from Natal in 1879, a friend asked me to give him some notes on laagers for use in a text-book on field-fortification which he had been commissioned to draw up. I did so, but as towards the end of 1880 his book had not yet appeared, and as affairs between ourselves and the Boers of the Transvaal were very much strained, I got his leave to send a copy of my notes to the secretary of the Royal United Service Institution. They were accepted for the journal and published in vol. xxiv., p. 806, just in time, as it happened, for the Boers revolted in December, and those who wanted to know what a laager meant, and how it was to be made, were not without the information.

1879 he saw war was imminent, he went over with his tribe into Natal and remained neutral.

The General had asked him to come with us to Echowe as guide, for he knew every path and every bit of bush on the way. He would not promise, but when we had started he set off after us, and of course all the fighting men of his tribe followed their chief. We welcomed them warmly, gave each a red handkerchief for his head, and employed them as scouts. John Dunn was a handsome powerful man of about forty years of age, a perfect rider and rifle-shot, rode an excellent *jagd paard* (shooting-horse) on all occasions, had the best of saddlery, breeches, boots, and other clothes (which he always got from England, though he had never been there), and but for his large wideawake hat and tanned face might have been taken for an English country gentleman.

Familiarity with the Zulus had not bred contempt in him. Almost the first thing he said to me on the 29th, when a bad drift had temporarily lengthened our column, was, 'We shall have to do better than this if we are to beat Cetewayo's impi.' On the 30th, when Zulu scouts were observed on our left flank, he was much relieved to find that practice had got our heterogeneous set of conductors and foreloopers into some sort of order, able at least to understand and to obey. With waggons and teams each of forty yards in length one mistake may upset the whole column; for each vehicle takes such an enormous space to turn in that unless a laager-master is regularly told off, and given an assistant to catch each conductor as he comes up, a block is almost a certainty.

That night it rained in torrents again, and there lay the Amatikulu right in front of us. Anywhere except in South Africa, if you were told that a river was 'down' you would understand that it was lower; but in Natal or Zululand the term means exactly the reverse, and that the water is 'down from the mountains'. The Amatikulu was down with a vengeance; it was forty yards wide and four feet deep; in that depth an ox has no power, and the current was running like a mill-stream. Every single waggon would have to be double-spanned (thirty-six oxen instead of eighteen), and it was clear that the passage alone would be as much as we could do that day. The Chief therefore decided that our next camp should be only a mile and a half on, where the river, reaching a sharp bend just above the drift, runs nearly north and south, so that the left flank of the column would be partially protected by it after crossing. Barrow's mounted men and Dunn's scouts began the passage; then followed the first brigade, and then the convoy of waggons and carts. The brigade took two hours to cross, the waggons six, losing an ox or two, but on the whole making the passage in fine style. The second brigade brought up the rear, wading up to their arm-pits, rifles and pouches on their heads. The whole column was in camp before five, after nearly eleven hours' hard work, everybody as wet as a sponge.

The enemy's scouts on our left were more numerous this day, and the laager at night, though better, was not perfect. It was decided, therefore, after due consultation, that for the future the laager should be an exact square of one hundred and thirty yards (thirty waggons and carts to a side), and that the shelter-trench should be fifteen yards in front of the sides. This would hold about two thousand men in close order two deep; and as we had just over three thousand all told, this arrangement gave us one thousand for outposts, reserve, mounted men, and casualties. I was told off for laager-master next day, and John Dunn promised to show me a good camping-ground.

Next day accordingly, April 1st, Dunn and I, with my four mounted orderlies, cantered on ahead of the column to an open space near Ginghilovo kraal, five miles from our late camp and one mile short of the Inyezane River; it was only slightly commanded on the south side, with regular glacis-like slopes on the three others. I at once placed my four mounted points: the column soon appeared; and the laager was finished and the shelter-trench marked out in no time. The distances worked out beautifully; we had guns, rockets, or gatlings, at the angles of the trench; an opening in the middle of each face to let the horses and cattle in and out, with four waggons ready to run in and close it at any moment. The men then went to their dinners before digging the trench.

Barrow's scouts (who had done beautiful work this day) had reported that there were small but organised bodies behind the Umisi Hill to the west of us, and Dunn had an idea that there would be some to our left front up the valley of the Inyezane; so, when the laager was finished, he asked me to come out with him and reconnoitre. I got leave, was told to take care of myself, and off we rode. Now the man came out: 'I am sure that is not all mist; there is smoke with it; I want to keep along the stream, cross it at a place I know, leaving you with the horses and see what is over the rise on the other side. Now you know we are in for a dangerous job, and as I have never been out with English officers before, I should like to be certain, before I start across, that our ideas are the same. In Africa a white man must stand by a fellow while there is life in him; if his friend is dead, then he may save himself. Do you agree?' I managed to satisfy my companion on this score, and then we took to the soft low ground near the bush and rode on in file silently, for Zulus have eyes like vultures and ears like watchdogs.

The rain began to fall again in perfect torrents, which was all the better for us, as any scouts about would be likely to crawl back to their fires. After a couple of miles Dunn turned off into the bush, pushed through it to the Inyezane, and stopped to listen. Not a sound was to be heard but the patter of the rain-drops and the roar of the river. Beckoning me up to hold his horse, he stripped, tied his clothes up in a bundle which he gave to me, took his rifle, swung himself into the torrent and, holding on to the branches of a tree that had fallen across it, landed on the other bank and disappeared. The good old horses stood like lambs; but a Kafir crane found me out on his peregrinations in search of a dinner, and made off with rather more noise than I thought necessary. It was rather uncomfortable work as the dusk began to fall, and I was not sorry to see my naked friend wriggling down through the grass on the farther bank. I don't know how he managed to get back, for the river had risen ten feet in the hour, and the trunk of the tree was submerged; but he swung himself across somehow, landing blue with cold. We were soon on the march again, he drying his rifle and changing the cartridge as we made our way through the bush, and as soon as we reached the open, away we went at a gallop for the laager. As we rode he told me that he had seen an impi and a lot of bivouac-fires, that he had been nearly discovered by one of their scouts who, when the clattering crane rose, had advanced to within a few yards of where he lay, that he had been obliged to lie low till the fellow was satisfied and went back, and that he wanted a gallop now to warm himself.

When we reached the laager the trench was completed but full of water in places, and the state of the ground inside it defies description. When five thousand human beings, two thousand oxen, and three hundred horses have been churning up five acres of very sodden ground for two or three hours, it makes a compost neither pretty to look at, easy to move about in, nor nice to smell. There were unpleasant reptiles about also, for two puff-adders had just been killed close to our waggon. Dunn's report, combined with Barrow's, told us pretty well what we might expect on the morrow. As it was clear that the ground would not permit the waggons to be moved for at least a day, it was decided that the oxen should be kept at home next morning, and that our two native battalions should be sent out to attack the enemy at daybreak, with orders to fall back behind the laager when the Zulus were well stirred up, so that the latter might come on at our shelter-trench, manned, as it would be, two deep, shoulder to shoulder, by British soldiers and sailors.

The morning of April 2nd broke over Ginghilovo laager in quite a cheery way; it was not raining, and a white mist presaged a hot day. The Zulus did not need much stirring up, for at six a.m., just as our natives were being let out to do it, the outposts began to fire and fall back. Soon the mist cleared a bit, and we could see black bodies of men across the Inyezane River and on the top of the Umisi Hill, opposite our front and left faces. 'Stand to your arms – saddle up – no independent firing – volleys by companies when they are within three hundred yards,' were almost the only orders. From a waggon I could see the Zulus advancing in the usual formation: two encircling 'horns' and a 'chest', with the 'chest' hanging back at first. We were in luck: there could be no doubt about the day now; but what had induced them to leave us alone on the march and attack us now, when we had all our oxen safe inside and all our fighting men ready outside, passed my comprehension. I suppose they had watched us, seen that the oxen were let out to graze before the march, expected we should do it to-day, and laid their plans accordingly; for, if the oxen are captured, the column is ruined; that must always be your weak point when fighting with an enemy who has no transport but women and boys, who in fact always fights *en l'air*.

Not a shot was fired except by the outposts as they hurried back; but when our front was clear the petty officer in charge of the Gatling gun at the left-front angle implored Ernest Buller to let him have one turn at a body of Zulus that had formed in full view half a mile away. 'Beg your pardon, sir,' he said, 'last night I stepped the distance to that bush where those blacks are, and it's just eight hundred yards. This "no firing" seems like throwing a chance away. I've got her laid true for them; may I just give her half a turn of the handle?' The Chief, who was close by, did not object to the range being tested, providing he stopped at once. A final sight, and, I am sure, quite two turns of the handle was the response, and there was a clear lane cut right through the body of men. The effect of the fire of a machine-gun is awful if it is served by a cool hand; the gun has no nerves, and, provided the man is steady and the cartridges do not jamb, nothing can live in front of it. The captain of this gun was a veteran, and afterwards during the fight his exhortations to his crew would have made, when carefully expurgated, an admirable essay on behaviour under fire.

The first attack came from the north on the front face of the square, and the extreme left horn swinging round attacked part of our right face a moment later. The other horn from the Umisi Hill was a little behind in attacking the left and rear faces of our trench; but the attack was fairly simultaneous, and the shouts of the Zulus could be heard even amid the roar of the volleys.

It was hot work on our right front angle. Some rocket-tubes were there, and from our saddles we could see the Zulus' behaviour in the long grass. Rockets look awful instruments of destruction; but they do none at all except when used to frighten horses or to set tents on fire. The Zulus evidently thought them living devils, for I saw many men fire at them as they passed over their heads. As one went skimming just above the grass, and the Zulus in that direction fell back a bit from its flaming tail, the General told Barrow to take out the Mounted Infantry on the right face and keep them on the run. But the Zulus, quickly recovering from their panic, and showing no fear of the horsemen, and the attack, which had come on our left and rear, extending round to our right face, the Chief, fearing Barrow might be cut off, ordered me out to recall him. It was done only just in time, for we had to fight our way back. One fellow missed me at close quarters, and paid the penalty by a revolver bullet in his forehead, but another shot straighter; the bullet entered poor old Lampas just below the seat of the saddle; he carried me over the trench and then succumbed, sending me headlong into the miry mess. Barrow and two of his men were wounded; three horses were killed and three wounded.

It is a curious sensation when a horse going at a gallop under you gets a mortal wound. He falters in front, picks himself up and drops behind, gets his hind-legs under him once more, makes one supreme effort, and then turns a complete somersault; it is much the same sensation as trying to sit the mechanical horse when bucking, an exhibition that I had visited in London in my youth. My poor brute lay still but alive; so I gave him his quietus, cleared him of saddle and bridle, and saw under the saddle on the opposite side to the wound a lump like a warble; one touch of a knife and the bullet dropped out, a very badly cast spherical thing, half hollow, with the waste lead still left on it.

With my load I staggered through the mud, round the laager to the left face where my man and other horse were. Noot was sitting on the top of the waggon alongside John Dunn, loading for him and beaming with joy. 'Here's about the first man killed on our side,' he said as he got down. 'It's our forelooper; he went and lay under the waggon in a fright; I told him to come out as it was all luck, and that minute a bullet hit him in the head. And there's the first drunk man,' he added, pointing to one of the Native Contingent who lay under a

137

commissariat-waggon breathing stertorously. A Martini bullet had pierced a cask of rum, and the nose of a native had detected the well-loved smell even amidst the 'villainous salt-petre'; he had caught the stream in his mouth and was, when discovered, quite insensible. 'I tell you that gentleman is a fine shot,' my man went on; 'he never misses them; he has his own and my rifle; he shoots, I load.' 'Well, get on with the other horse, and clear as much of the filth off the saddle as you can,' I said, and mounted up alongside Dunn. 'I've picked out an induna or two,' was his only remark, as I took Noot's place as loader. The Zulus were now on their stomachs in the long grass, rising to their knees to fire. The men in the trenches could not see them, and had ceased firing, kneeling at the ready in case of a rush; but up above we had a clear view and could fire over the soldiers, and many a Zulu fell to Dunn's rifle that day.

When Poll Evil was saddled I went out to look for the General. The 57th were hotly engaged now, they volleys ringing out as clear as if they were at Aldershot. If every regiment had possessed such seasoned men as those, we could have walked to Echowe and back without having to burrow into the ground like ant-bears. The Native Contingent were squatting on their hams between the waggons and the trenches; some of them, I am afraid, occasionally getting rather roughly handled by their officers. They had been ordered to keep their muzzles pointing to the sky and not to fire at any price, their white officers being in front of and facing them; but they are an excitable race, and gun after gun was let off in the air, some-times at no very great elevation. Then came bad words and hard boots; cracks on the head are no good; you might as well hit a cocoa-nut.

I found the General, reported myself as dirty but not hurt, and that Barrow's men were all back. Crealock was the only one of the staff hit, luckily not severely. As they were mounted and outside the waggon-square during the whole engagement, it is a miracle that they escaped so well. Just as I reached them at the front face, Lieutenant-Colonel Northey, of the Rifles, was hit in the shoulder by a Martini bullet. I thought it was slight, for he told the next senior and walked away to the ambulance-waggons; but though the bullet was extracted, the shock was too much, and four days later he was dead.

An hour and a half of this work had pretty nearly convinced our foes that there was no chance for them this day. They were now evidently wavering; so the General sent Barrow at them again, and ordered the Native Contingent out to pursue. The Zulus gave the mounted men a few shots and then turned and fled; the Native Contingent followed, and the foe that threw away his arms when overtaken by the horses found short shrift at the hands of our allies. It is a very common trick with savages to feint a retreat, and then turn on you in the disorder of the pursuit. The strictest orders had accordingly been given that neither soldiers nor sailors were to leave the trenches. The Commodore had been impressing on his Blue-jackets the awful things he should be obliged to do to them if one of them moved; but this was too much for him. 'Come along!' he said to his flag-lieutenant, and away they went hacking and slashing on foot, while the tars, who obeyed orders and never stirred, yelled with delight. 'Go it, Admiral!' they would shout. 'Now you've got 'em! Look out, sir, there's one to the right in the grass!' till every one was roaring with laughter. Sailors are the best of comrades in rough times; nothing puts them out; I suppose because the ship is their home, and a run on shore is always and in any circumstances a holiday to them.

There was one warrior who would not fly, but set his back to a thorn bush and defied his foes. 'Leave him to me,' said a sergeant of the Greys who was instructor in the Mounted Infantry. A ring was formed and at it they went, sword mounted against assegai and shield dismounted. The soldier was the more skilful, but the Zulu was in better condition. Cutting was tried at first, but it was turned by the shield invariably; at last a point went through shield and man, and the hero found the death he courted.

The loss on our side was returned at nine men killed, six officers and forty-six men wounded, twelve horses and thirty-four oxen killed or wounded; and from five to six rounds a man had been expended. The Zulus were calculated to have lost about twelve hundred killed. Upwards of four hundred guns and rifles was picked up, some of them Martinis with the stamp of the 24th regiment on them; and in the dead Zulus' pouches and bags were found stationery captured at Isandhlwana, which they had been using as wadding for their smooth-bores, ration-returns, letters, English newspapers, and all sorts of odds and ends. From off one Zulu an English officer's sword was taken and brought to the Chief. Crealock's clerk, who had been an assistant in the orderly-room of the battalion annihilated at Isandhlwana, at once recognised it as having belonged to Lieutenant Porteous of the 24th; it was accordingly preserved and sent to his friends. The total number of Zulus engaged was ascertained to have been about ten thousand. Somapo was in command, with Dabulamanzi, Cetewayo's brother, next under him.

The garrison from Echowe now flashed us their congratulations, to which the Chief replied, and we all felt very pleased with ourselves.

This was my first experience of these savages, and I was certainly astonished at their pluck. Before an impi marches to battle, every warrior is given an emetic and then some witch-doctor's stuff. This would not raise the courage of a white man, who prefers to fight on a good breakfast; but it seemed to act well with them; there could be no question of their pluck, and they were as active as cats.

After the fight we let out the oxen and set to work to reduce the laager to one hundred yards square, leaving out the carts that were to accompany us onward the next day. The trenches had to be levelled first, then the oxen inspanned, and the left and rear faces of the waggons moved in thirty yards. While we were all hard at work the most appalling yells were suddenly heard, and thinking the foe might be mustering for a fresh attack, every one stood to their arms, not without an anxious thought for the grazing oxen. It turned out, however, that one of our native battalions had come across a crowd of wounded Zulus in a patch of bush, and with the chivalry peculiar to the nature of the semi-civilised, were killing them in cold blood and celebrating the heroic deed by a war-song. Employing natives was a horrible necessity in Zululand; their behaviour at a crisis was contemptible; at other times they were cruel,

140

and their white officers could not be everywhere to guard against it.

Next morning the Chief started at eight a.m. with the 57th, the 60th Rifles, the 91st, part of the Naval Brigade, the Mounted Infantry, Dunn's scouts, and fifty-eight carts, to march the fifteen miles to Echowe; leaving two companies of the Buffs, five of the 99th, part of the Naval Brigade, and two battalions of the Native Contingent, besides details, to defend Ginghilovo laager.

Four miles from Echowe Colonel Pearson came out with part of his force to give us a helping hand in case there was any fighting; but as our scouts could find no enemy, the General told him to send the troops back. The staff stayed with us, showed us a short cut, and gave us a concise history of the seventy days. I think the universal cry was want of tobacco, tea-leaves and coffee-grounds being carefully preserved, dried, and smoked; otherwise they were not in actual want, but coast-fever and typhoid had claimed many victims, while rough fare, watchfulness, and anxiety had set their mark on all.

We reached Echowe at half-past seven, but the rear of the column was not in till midnight. To add to the fame of the British army and navy not one man fell out that day, though they had been sixteen hours on their legs, and, according to my pocket-aneroid, had climbed 1,400 feet in the fifteen miles. This sounds perhaps no very hard day's work to those who climb in the cool air of Europe; but in a semi-tropical climate the fatigue of getting a convoy over it must be felt to be believed. None of the regiments had their bands on this expedition; but the 91st had their pipers, who played their best as they marched past Fort Echowe to their bivouac amidst thundering cheers from both relieved and relievers.

*In Eshowe, Harry O'Clery described the joy which greeted the arrival of Chelmsford's column:*

Though we could hear the fighting, we made no sortie, but simply waited until the relief came, and I shall never forget that relief as long as I retain my wits. It *was* good to grasp the hands of men who had risked their lives for us, and how we did

141

enjoy a 'square meal' and a smoke. Our friends had brought provisions, but had carefully avoided overloading themselves. Early the next morning we made a successful raid on the kraal of a chief named Dabulamanzi, situated a few miles from Ekowe, and having procured some provisions, with payment in lead, we set out on our return journey to the Tugela.

*Chelmsford had no intention of holding Eshowe, and intended to pull back to a safer post closer to the Thukela. Before doing so, however, he organised an expedition to attack the personal homestead of Prince Dabulamanzi, which lay only a few miles from Eshowe. Dabulamanzi had achieved a fearsome reputation amongst the British, who knew him as the Zulu commander at Rorke's Drift, and imagined him to be the most daring and resolute of their enemies; the attack on his homestead was a gesture of defiance, a reminder that the British would be back. John Dunn took part in the foray, and it was just as well that he harboured no illusions that his former friendship with the Zulu Royal House might yet be salvaged, as Molyneux describes:*

Fort Echowe was to be evacuated on the 5th, for it was evident that a better route to Ulundi could be found nearer the coast, by way of St Paul's, than by keeping to the track through Echowe. That morning we inspected the fort. It was an irregular hexagon of weak trace but strong profile, and if all its ditches had been flanked could have defied the whole Zulu army. They had been too wise to run their heads against it, even as it was; and there is no doubt that its continued occupation had so impressed them that it prevented them from invading Natal.

From some spies it was discovered that after the fight at Ginghilovo, Dabulamanzi had returned to his kraal at Esulwini, which was only about six miles north of Echowe. The General determined to show the king's brother that he too had a long arm to strike with; so about eleven that morning all the mounted men were sent off at a gallop to try and surprise him, the staff going with them to see the fun, Dunn, of course, as it was supposed, making one of the party. But as I was on the point of starting I came across Dunn sitting on the ground in the middle of an *umkumbi* (circle) of his men. Apologising for the interruption, I told him that the General had just started. 'He did not ask me and my men to come,' was the answer, and it was evident that the chief and his men were highly indignant. I told him that a notice had been sent round the camp, and that orders had been given to show it to him; that he knew of it was obvious, from the fact of his being offended. 'Of course the General wants you to come with him,' I said. 'I'll gallop on and get the invitation from him direct if you won't believe me.' He relented, was on his horse (with his 'after-rider' close behind him) in a moment, and away we went while the men stood up, raised their right hands to the sky, groaned *Inkos*, and raced after us. It is necessary to be most particular in your behaviour to a Zulu chief; and Dunn, while amongst his men, could not afford to waive any portion of his dignity. He had by this time, more-over, assimilated many of his people's habits and modes of feeling; and I fancy they would all have thought it more correct if the General had sat upon his hams every morning with an umkumbi of all the heads of departments round him, hearing their reports, and deciding on the day's operations.

We soon overtook the staff; a few words put all to rights, and then it was a race to the Entumeni Mountain and Esulwini.

There is a high kraantz at the back of Esulwini kraal from which the Zulus must have kept a pretty good look-out, for when we reached the place, fat Dabulamanzi was on the top out of danger, though there were some men still climbing who shouted their war-cry in defiance at us. We killed two loiterers, took one prisoner, and set fire to the huts. There must have been many loaded guns left in them, for the explosions became so frequent that we all moved some distance off, and were standing in a group when, noticing that Martini bullets were dropping around us with great regularity, we became aware that the fellows on the kraantz 1,200 yards off were making some uncommonly good practice at us. They were just on the skyline; Milne had a naval telescope and Dunn the best of eyes; he plainly recognised Dabulamanzi, and then commenced a duel with Martinis. Dunn shot better than his former pupils: with the glass we could see them duck as the shots reached them; but as there was nothing to be gained by this sport, we destroyed the mealie-fields and made our way back to Echowe.

Pearson had marched on the 4th with his garrison four miles towards the Inyezane and laagered. On the 5th we followed him, reached his camp at eight, and halted till ten to let his rear proceed. But the road was worse than ever, and at last the General told him to take command of his old column and move it by its original route straight to Fort Pearson, while the relief column struck off to the left and made a road for itself towards Ginghilovo laager.

This was a most trying day from the heat, the long grass, and scarcity of water. The men, too, now that the excitement was over, were falling out every moment. There was no shamming: they did their best; but as one old soldier said to me. 'Now those chaps are relieved you seem to begin to feel yourself, and I'm just as if I had no heart left at all and no legs.' It was plain that we could not reach the laager by night-fall, so Crealock and Dunn went ahead and chose a place near the Inyezane for a camp. The column was all in by half-past six, when we entrenched in a rectangle and lay down for the night.

The entrenchment was guarded by pickets from each regiment three or four hundred yards in advance of it, and Dunn's scouts were sent to occupy some mealie-fields just beyond them. We had kept the tents lent us by Pearson, and after getting our dinner, Dunn and I turned in to one of them, and using our saddles as pillows were soon asleep. Early the next morning some outlying man fired a shot by accident, when the scouts and one of the pickets began to fall back, the latter soon making 'a strategic movement to the rear' at full speed, leaving its officer standing alone. The men in the trench opposite them fixed their bayonets and, unable to distinguish friends from foes in the dark, met them with the point, the result being that five soldiers were wounded, and of Dunn's men two killed and eight wounded. At the sound of the shot we were up; at the sound of the rush we were outside the tent and on our way to the trench. It was heart-rending to hear the wild appeals of those outside to those within to keep cool.

144

The poor scouts were the worst off, their only distinguishing mark from the enemy being the red cloth round their heads. They had been drilled by Dunn to answer 'Friend'; the best they could manage was 'Flend', and shrieks of 'Flend' were heard above all the din, yet they were stabbed unmercifully. Dunn was mad. 'They are killing my people! Are the men fools? Can't they hear them calling out? Oh, my children!' he cried as he ran towards the trench; and then the soldiers recovered their wits, and we did what we could for the wretched victims of funk.

No one can account for the madness which seizes upon bodies of men at times. It is no use saying it is only young soldiers that are thus affected; old ones may be less liable, but they are not impervious to it. One has only to read Froissart's account of the siege of Tournay in 1340, where one night, 'Four thousand Flemings, lying in their tents asleep, suddenly felt such a fear in their hearts that they rose, beat down their tents and fled, not abiding for one another, without keeping of any right way;' or to read Napier's account of the panic that seized the Light Division one night in a cork wood during the Peninsular War; or, if those be considered too ancient examples, Sir William Russell's account of the last bivouac at Old Fort in the first year of the Crimean War, where 'The picquets fell back tumultuously at the sight of a few Cossacks, and later on fell back firing and wounding each other when there were no Cossacks at all.' The history of war is full of such examples; and, as he is the best general who makes fewest mistakes, so we may call that the best army which has the fewest panics.

Before we marched we could see Echowe in flames, so there had been no long delay in avenging Dabulamanzi's burned kraal. We reached Ginghilovo laager at half-past eleven; but the air and water were so contaminated by the still unburied bodies of men and horses, that the General moved a mile and a half further on, and gave Colonel Pemberton, who was to be left in command here, orders to move his laager to new ground next day.

That afternoon a general court-martial administered five years' penal servitude to one of the runaways of the morning;

but the proceedings were subsequently quashed at home for some unexplained reason. It was supposed afterwards, when a worse runaway was suffered to go unpunished, that this man could not in justice be brought to book. Others said that it had been forgotten to send out a warrant to South Africa empowering the officer commanding the forces to assemble general and district courts-martial. Few know the truth to this day.

On the 7th the headquarter staff left for Fort Pearson en route for Durban, for the transports with troops were arriving there daily, and it was then the busiest place in South Africa. We made an early start, and riding rather nearer the coast so as to pass Dunn's house between the Inyoni and the Tugela, reached Fort Pearson at noon.

Dunn's house (or rather houses) was a sorry sight. Everything had been looted or pitched outside: some things had been burned; but what vexed him most was the destruction of all his journals. He took it very stoically, merely observing, 'I have not done with the Zulus yet.' I only saw John Dunn once again, at Durban; and though invited, I never had a chance of visiting him at his home. Rough things have often been said against one who has 'turned Zulu'; but the account I have given of him will show, I hope, that he was a genuine man, brave, generous, warm-hearted, and to us on this expedition certainly a host in himself.

*The harrowing scare that night on the road from Eshowe was a grim reminder that Gingindlovu had not seen off the spectre of the Zulu bogeyman, his spear still red with the blood of the victims of Isandlwana, which lingered in the darker corners of the minds of Chelmsford's soldiers. They were a long way from the industrial slums and quiet country lanes of Britain, and in the soft African night, every strange rustle in the undergrowth, every startled cry from a disturbed bird or animal, was transformed into a terrifying mirage of lurking savages. And there were many more sleepless nights to come.*

CHAPTER FOUR

# WOOD'S COLUMN: HLOBANE AND KHAMBULA

C HELMSFORD had always intended that Evelyn Wood's column, operating in northern Zululand, should be the most free to use its initiative. Wood had served under Chelmsford in the Cape Frontier War, and Chelmsford knew him to be a dynamic and flexible commander with a flair for African warfare. What's more, Wood's column was operating a long way from any central control. The area he had to traverse, a rolling upland, broken by chains of rugged flat-topped mountains, was the heart of the 'disputed territory' between the Zulu kingdom and the Transvaal, and it had bred a frontier outlook in both communities.

There were a number of powerful Zulu groups in the area who owed nominal allegiance to the Zulu king, but over whom Cetshwayo had only varying degrees of control. The largest of these was the abaQulusi, who were not a clan as such, but the descendants of an ibutho quartered in the area by Shaka. When, in due course, the warriors dispersed and married, they settled in the area, and came to dominate it. They were outside the normal regimental system, but considered themselves a royal section, and were fiercely loyal to the king. Although they lived in family homesteads across the region, in times of trouble they retreated to a chain of three linked table-topped plateaux, known as Zungwini, Hlobane and Ityenka. The summit of each was largely sealed off by a line of cliffs, broken here and there by steep paths which the abaQulusi sealed off with walls of boulders.

Further north, in the steep Phongolo and Ntombe river valleys, lived the infamous Mbilini kaMswati. Mbilini was a Swazi

147

prince who, after an unsuccessful attempt to seize the throne of his people, had fled south and pledged allegiance to Cetshwayo, Cetshwayo had allowed him to settle in the remote border regions, but Mbilini was largely beyond his control, and raided both black and white homesteads alike in an attempt to rebuild his fortunes. Mbilini had a good relationship with the abaQulusi chiefs and, indeed, had a second homestead on the southern flanks of the Hlobane mountain. Mbilini's prime motivation was self-interest, but the coming war would give him ample opportunity to prove his skills as a raider in the Zulu cause.

Scattered across this wild country were a number of European farms and settlements. The largest of these was the Transvaal Border town of Utrecht, about fifteen miles from the border, but even more vulnerable was Luneburg, a hamlet built by hard-working German settlers in the very heart of the disputed territory. King Cetshwayo had particular resented the claims of the Luneburg settlers, and had established a small royal homestead nearby to assert his authority. Furthermore, Luneburg was only five miles or so from Mbilini's principal stronghold, the Tafelberg mountain, which overlooked Myer's Drift on the Ntombe. Most of the other European farms in the area were owned by the descendants of Republican Boers who had moved out of Natal to escape British rule in the 1840s. Evelyn Wood made a serious effort to recruit them to fight against their traditional enemies, the Zulus, but the Boers hated the English just as much, and their temper had not been improved by the annexation of the Transvaal. In the event, only one Boer leader of consequence, Piet Uys, joined the British, bringing with him his sons and followers. The rest were content to sit back and, with a certain amount of glee, watch their two most despised neighbours tear one another to shreds. Some, indeed, were later implicated in abetting Zulu raids around Luneburg.

Wood's objectives, therefore, were not only to co-ordinate his advance with Chelmsford, but also to suppress any activity by local Zulus, whilst at the same time protecting the frontier communities. As the start of the campaign drew near, Wood himself was a bundle of energy, bustling about with his staff, seeking intelligence for himself, interviewing farmers, brow-beating chiefs, and arranging transport and supplies for his men. It was not always work best suited to a commanding officer, as the countryside was rough, and maps practically non-existent. He had one or two scrapes, as he described in his autobiography, *From Midshipman to Field Marshal* (1906):

*

At 4.30 p.m. I started, with my orderly officer, Lieutenant Harry Lysons.[1] The Cape cart had 27 miles to go, but Lysons knew a short cut, and a ford across the Buffalo River, just south of where it is joined by the Incandu and Ingagane Rivers. We cantered to the Buffalo, 12 miles, without drawing rein, well under two hours, including a stop at a Fingoe's kraal, from whom I hoped to buy mealies. He was a prosperous settler from the Cape Colony, speaking English well. The day was now closing in, and after we were across the river, Lysons hesitated. He had guided me as straight as a line drawn on the map hitherto, but the ground on the right bank of the Buffalo is difficult to understand, and there is no doubt that, having crossed the main stream once, we kept too far to our right, and came back to it. We now realised we were wrong; but after turning northwards, darkness came over us, and 'our rest' became, not 'stones', but puddles. Vainly attempting to read my compass, for it was now quite dark, we plodded on at a walk. Light rain fell incessantly, and a black cloud, the precursor of heavy storms, blotted out every star, and compelled us to dismount and feel for footpaths, which crossed and recrossed each other in the most bewildering manner.

About eight o'clock we came to a river, the whirling waters of which we could just distinguish lying below us, with steep banks on either side. After wandering up and down for twenty minutes, our horses jumping round every few minutes, when the flashes of lightning were more than usually vivid, I found a place where oxen had descended, and holding the horses I sent Lysons down to explore, as on the far bank we thought we saw a light. He slipped twice going down, and when he

---

[1] Son of my friend, General Sir Daniel Lysons.

reached the water being nervous he might be drowned, I called to him to take off his waterproof coat, adding that, as I should probably not hear him, I would sing loudly until his return. I waited an hour, the horses turning round and sliding about, endeavouring to get their faces away from the rain, and after the first quarter of an hour I sang 'Far Away' till I was tired of the tone of my voice, but could not hear a sound. I began to calculate the chances of my ever getting 'War Game' and Lysons' pony down the bank, and came to the conclusion that I should either lose my orderly officer or my horse, who constantly rested his nose on my shoulder. When the heavy rain came on about five o'clock, I had shifted my unread English letters from my pocket to my wallets; but now, thinking I ought to try and find Lysons, even though I lost my horse, I put the letters back in my pockets, fearing, however, to find them in a shapeless pulp in the morning. Just then Lysons greeted me so cheerily from the opposite bank, I thought he must have a [African] with him, but when, having again waded across the river, he rejoined me, he said he could not find the lights, and he believed he had wandered in a circle. As he reported very badly of the descent, we led the horses up stream for 300 yards, but the banks being more unfavourable we returned. So far as I could make out from my watch, it was about eleven p.m. A heavy storm, obscuring everything, obliged us to stand still, and I sat down and slept for ten minutes, but a loud peal of thunder frightening 'War-Game', made him jump so violently as to hurt my arm, which I had passed through the reins. I then decided to try and descend step by step, utilising the lightning for a light. I went down the bank, 'War-Game' following me like a dog. It was nervous work walking exactly in front of him, but unless I did so he would not advance a foot! When he reached the water I rewarded him with a piece of sugar, which I generally carried for my horses.

We got across the river about midnight, and after wandering for about an hour in and out of small ravines, another storm compelled us to halt. We lay down as close to each other as we could for warmth; but as 'War-Game' jumped at every vivid flash of lightning, and pulled at my arms, I could not sleep.

Lysons slept, not soundly, but still he did sleep. I stood up from about 12.30 a.m. till 4 a.m. wondering occasionally which of the two shivered most, master or horse. I felt nervously at my letters every five minutes to see whether they were still dry. About 4 a.m. the water was so deep under Lysons I made him get up, and he presently heard a cock crow, towards which we led our horses. After walking for ten minutes I asked, 'Do you hear him now?' 'No, not at all. Shall I challenge?' He then screamed such a cock-a-doodle-do that my horse jumped into the air, and nearly knocked Lysons over; but his challenge was immediately answered, and ten minutes' walk brought us to a kraal. After much shouting we got a [Zulu] out, and I let off my only Zulu sentence, asking the way to Newcastle. I could not say 'Come and show us', but a half-crown in my left hand, and a grip of his neck with my right, indicated what I wanted, and the [Zulu] trotted off, bringing us to the bank of a river, through which we waded with some difficulty. The water came in over the top of my boots, Lysons on his pony going in up to his waist. When we got to the far side, being now sure of the track, I threw the half-crown to the astonished [Zulu], who probably never earned one so easily before, and we cantered into Newcastle.

After an hour's sleep, and having had some breakfast, we drove northwards, but the jolting of the Cape cart was intolerable. Presently, looking back, I observed a farmer following us in a 'Spider'.[1] I knew him as a man who had ox-waggons for sale, and suggested he should take me into his carriage. This he did, and in a four hours' drive I learnt a good deal with Colonial life. While we sheltered in one of his farms, occupied by a Dutchman, who would not speak a word of English, but who made some tea for us, frying beef and eggs together in one pan, we escaped one of the heaviest storms I ever saw. I have often read with incredulity travellers' stories of hailstones being as large as walnuts, and can scarcely, therefore, hope my readers will believe my statements when I say that I have seen many such under the Drakensberg range of mountains. I bought a span of oxen during the storm, and then

[1] A light four-wheeled American carriage.

151

started again at three o'clock. The farmer was to have taken us a short cut, but what was generally a little rivulet was now a whirling river, and we had to go round by the ordinary track.

We stopped that night at Meek's farm, 30 miles north of Newcastle, and next morning, rising at daybreak, got the loan of the Spider and two of Mr Meek's ponies. The ground was heavy, and neither animal would pull, so we started in a somewhat undignified fashion, my orderly officer pushed the cart behind, while Paliso, the interpreter, and I hauled on the shafts until we got up the hill, and could start with the advantage of the downward incline.

When we reached the farm of Andries Pretorius, there were twenty of his kindred awaiting my arrival. They were all surly, and although it is customary in that part of the country for the host and his family to come out and assist in unharnessing a guest's horse, nobody offered to help, except Pretorius. He apologised for his kindred, explaining they detested the sight of an Englishman. He was careful to impress on me, however, that were I not his guest he would be equally discourteous. He had a remarkable face, hard, resolute, and unyielding. When we went in – Mr Meek interpreting – I explained the object of my visit. 'I know,' I said, 'there is a strong feeling against the Imperial Government, but you have many relatives on the border, and their farms, now valueless, will be very valuable when we settle the question.' Pretorius replied: 'We have sworn an oath to be true to Messrs Kruger and Joubert, who went to England to see your Government, and we will not move till we hear the answer to the deputation, and we will not help you till the Transvaal is given back to us.' 'I shall not, then, have the pleasure of your assistance.'

We talked for two hours as 'friends'. Pretorius argued on the Annexation question, and, as I thought, got the worst of it. He said, 'You came into my house, saying "How dirty it is; turn out." And now you cannot clean one little room named Sekukuni! And what a small broom you have got, to try and sweep up Cetewayo! He will destroy that broom.' I observed, 'Well, your house was dirty, and tumbling down; moreover, it had just then taken fire. My house was next yours, and as you could not put out your fire, I was obliged to try to do it. It is true that the broom was not large enough to sweep up Seku-kuni, and it may be destroyed in sweeping up Cetewayo, but my Queen can send out 45 Regiments instead of the 5 stationed here, and if the little broom is destroyed you will soon see more brooms.' 'But why do you light a big fire before you put out a little?' 'We hope when he put out the big fire, that the little one will go out of itself.' 'Then,' said he, 'tell me honestly – do you prefer to have with you your own soldiers, or Dutchmen, when fighting Natives?' 'For shooting Natives and taking cattle, I prefer Dutchmen. In the Perie Bush, in Kaffraria, I had 300 Dutchmen in my command, but when I had a pos-ition to carry, and the [Xhosa] were standing up to us, I took soldiers. In four months I never had a Dutchman killed in action.' Although this honest opinion was not appreciated by Pretorius or by his family, we had much conversation, and finally, when I left the farm, all the Dutchmen came out and expressed the hope that personally I might come safely out of the Zulu War.

*Despite the reluctance of the Boers to join him, Wood was not slow in opening the campaign. In the first week of January, he established an advanced base at Bemba's Kop on the Zulu side of the Ncome (Blood) River, and as soon as the ultimatum expired, he began harrying the Zulus. His force was a strong one: it consisted of the 1/13th and 90th Light Infantry, an artillery battery, six troops of mounted irregulars, and two battalions of locally recruited black auxiliaries, known as Wood's Irregulars. The mounted men were under the com-mand of Lt-Colonel Redvers Buller, Wood's right-hand man, who was courageous, resourceful, and ideally suited to the type of guerilla warfare which soon developed in the region. Wood described his early moves, the skirmishing which marked the beginning of the campaign, and life amongst a hetero-geneous force:*

Being uneasy concerning Zulus to the north of our left flank, I directed Colonel Buller to send there the Frontier Light Horse under Captain Barton, who took between 500 and 600 head of cattle, clearing the Pemvane and lower Bevane Rivers, while the column was moving forward slowly, much impeded by heavy rain, to the Umvolosi.

I had obtained the General's approval to my going in a north-easterly direction to clear the Ityenteka Range, including the Inhlobane mountain, of Zulus under Umsebe and Umbeline, hoping to be back before the General was ready to advance with No. 3 column. Having reached the Umvolosi River on the 19th, we built a fort at Tinta's Kraal, which, humanly speaking, should have been impregnable if held by two companies, and off-loading seventy waggons I sent them in the afternoon back towards Balte Spruit, escorted by Captain Wilson's company of the 90th, with orders to fill up the waggons and return to Tinta's Kraal, where I intended to leave him, and a company of the 13th.

About 7 o'clock in the evening I got a note from Colonel Buller, saying that he had been engaged for some hours on the Zunguin mountain with several hundred of the Makulusi tribe, who were pressing him back, and, as he was writing at sunset, had crossed in small numbers to the right bank of the Umvolosi. This disturbed me considerably, for they were now within a few miles of our empty waggons, and it was not only the chance of the loss of the company and £21,000 worth of property, but it would have been difficult to replace the waggons. I knew that the convoy was not more than three or four miles off, for there was a muddy ravine which could only be passed with difficulty, and that Captain Wilson intended to begin to cross it at daylight.

Captain Woodgate, seeing I was perturbed, asked me the reason, and on reading to him Colonel Buller's note, at once went to the company, although we were just going to have something to eat. He had the oxen inspanned at once, the drivers and foreloupers on learning the news being anxious to get away to a place of safety. His unconsciousness of danger was shown by handing his horse to a Zulu when he dismounted to help the waggons across the ravine, with the result that he never saw it again for three days. Nothing of importance, however, occurred, for Colonel Buller, by showing a bold front to the Makulusi, held them on the river, and they retired after dark to their stronghold on the highest part of the mountain.

On the night of the 20–21st we made a long night march with the 90th Light Infantry, two guns and the mounted men starting at 11 p.m., and at daylight climbed the western end of the Zunguin mountain, along which we advanced during the day, taking some cattle and driving 1,000 Zulus off it, they retiring to the Nek connecting it with the Inhlobane. Looking down from the eastern extremity, we saw about 4,000 Zulus drilling under the Ityenteka Nek; they formed in succession a circle, triangle, and square, with a partition about eight men thick in the centre.

We descended at night for water, and rejoined the 13th, the 90th Light Infantry having been nineteen hours out of the twenty-four under arms, and having covered a considerable distance. In mileage, however, it was not so great as the distance covered by Wilson's company escorting the waggons, which filled up at once and returned to the Umvolosi, marching 34 miles in twenty-six hours.

We heard the guns[1] fired at Isandwhlana, 50 miles off, that evening as we sat round a camp fire.

There was thick mist on the morning of the 24th which delayed our advance, but when it cleared we moved forward and came under fire from Zulus hidden in the rocks under the south-western point of the Inhlobane. Leaving the 90th and two guns to follow the waggon track with the baggage, I went to the right with the 13th Light Infantry, Piet Uys and his troop of 40 Burghers, with whom I was disappointed, as it was necessary for Piet and myself to ride in front to induce his men to go on to cover the advance of the guns. When we reached the rocks from whence the fire had come it was clear we could not hope to get the guns down, so after driving back a few Zulus who were in broken ground I turned northwards, and went to a

---

[1] These were fired by Lord Chelmsford's troops returning from Sirayo's district to the wrecked camp. Our senior officers asked my opinion, what was the probable cause, and I said guns fired after dark indicated, I apprehended, an unfavourable situation.

hill under which I had ordered the 90th to halt with the wag-gons and outspan. When I got there the oxen had just been loosened from the Trek-tow, but to my great vexation they were without any guard, and the 90th, which ought to have been with them, was three-quarters of a mile in front, advanc-ing rapidly in line, without any supports, against some 4,000 Zulus.[1]

I looked up the ravine, which farther to the southward had stopped my onward progress with the 13th Light Infantry and guns, and was concerned to see about 200 Zulus coming down it towards the 90th's Ammunition carts, which had been left with some bugler boys, who had no firearms. I had just told an orderly to call Colonel Buller, when I was accosted by a [African] who had ridden 48 miles from Utrecht bringing a note from Captain Gardner, recounting the disas-ter of Isandwhlana, of which he had been an eye-witness. Buller came to me at once, and telling him in one sentence of the misfortune which had befallen No. 3 column, I sent him up the ravine to drive back the Zulus, while I galloped to the 90th and expressed a strong opinion to the senior officer (not belonging to the regiment) who had contravened my orders. The Zulus in front of them made no stand. The young soldiers were very steady, and expended less than two rounds of ammunition per man; but the Zulus fled from the sight of the advancing line, and went ten paces to one covered by our men. The Frontier Light Horse and the Dutchmen pursued them until they climbed the Inhlobane mountain, and then after a halt of two hours I ordered the column to fall in, and, against the advice of some of the senior officers, read to the men the note I had received.

We moved back as far as our camp of the previous day, and

---

[1] It appeared later I had greatly under-estimated the Zulu force, imagining it was the Makulusi regiment only, but the High Commissioner learnt from his agent and reported to the Secretary of State, not only was the Makulusi routed and dispersed, but that the Nodwengu and Udloko regiments shared in their fate. Later, Sir Bartle Frere wrote: 'The Zulus are greatly impressed with the skill with which this force (Colonel Wood's) has been handled, and are afraid it may push on to the Inhlazatze, and threaten the Royal Kraal.'

156

next morning returned to our fort on the Umvolosi River. I was now in some difficulty. I did not want to abandon supplies, and I had 70 loads for which I had no waggons. The Dutchmen, who were well provided with waggons, and were themselves wonderful drivers of oxen, came to my aid. Piet Uys and his men, who had only about 1,000 lbs weight in each waggon, loaded up to 8,000 lbs, and then we moved slowly westwards, halting on the 28th at Venter's Drift, where I was within reach of firewood, our greatest want in that part of the country. There were trees growing in the ravines south of the Ngaba Ka Hawane Mountain.

Here I received a considerate note from Lord Chelmsford, giving me a brief account of the disaster at Isandwhlana, and telling me I had a free hand to go anywhere or adopt any measures I might think best, ending: 'You must now be pre-pared to have the whole of the Zulu Army on your hands any day .... No. 3 Column, when re-equipped, is to subordinate its movements to your column. Let me know how it can assist you.' I replied to Lord Chelmsford on the 31st January that I was in a position on Kambula Hill which I anticipated being able to hold even against the whole of the Zulu Army. I under-stood he did not wish me to incur risk by advancing, and I would not move unless it became necessary to do so in order to save Natal.

In spite of the carriage for stores lent to us by the Dutchmen, we had some trouble before we succeeded in finding a good military and sanitary position, and even to men who did not feel much compassion for oxen, to make them pull 8,000 lbs through the swamps is trying to their feelings as well as to the oxen's hides. It has often been a wonder to soldiers in South Africa how the Dutch, under Pretorius and other leaders forty years earlier, took waggons up and down mountains which appear to us impracticable for wheel traffic, but the maximum weight in a waggon on commando was 1,500 lbs, five adults being allowed a waggon between them, which of course made a great difference on a bad track. The difficulties of transport caused me to halt every second or third day, as I was obliged to make two journeys with my loads, and I soon had warning that I could not remain in the valley of the Umvolosi, by the loss of horses and oxen, followed by that of a man of the 90th, who died of very rapid enteric fever.

The military situation, although I tried to conceal the fact, affected my health. I never slept more than two or three hours at a time, going round the sentries for the next three months at least twice every night. We shifted camp five times before we finally took up the position in which the greater part of the Zulu Army attacked us on the 29th March, and as we constructed slight entrenchments in every camp, and improved the formation of the encampment so as to obtain the greatest amount of fire from all sides, the men were kept employed, and gained valuable experience. We worked on Sundays, saying our prayers in a practical manner, for I had Divine Service parade on ground immediately adjoining the spot where two companies were at work throwing up redoubts, and let the men put down their picks and shovels and join in the service, which, during the sixteen months in which I either read it myself or caused one of the staff officers to do so, never kept the men standing more than ten minutes, and I have never seen soldiers so attentive.

From December 1878 I had native scouts 20 miles in front of our force, and patrols six miles out an hour before daylight, but in the afternoon we amused ourselves, although the early morning was a period of anxiety. My spies informed me of impending attacks, which were predicted for each new and full moon, which periods are held by the Zulus to be auspicious. Mounted men were stationed six miles in front by day, and two companies beyond our cattle at grass. The arrangements for security during night were peculiar. It rained regularly when the sun went down, throughout the months of February and March, which added to our difficulty of ensuring security without impairing the health of the soldiers. To save them, the outlying pickets were allowed tents pitched in a circle, 200 yards outside the laager. Groups of eight men were placed 100 yards farther out, six lying down under blanket shelters, while two watched and listened. Beyond on the paths most convenient for the enemy's approach, under a British officer, were small parties of Zulus,[1] whose marvellous hearing by night, and sight by day, enhanced the value of our precautions. After the disaster on the Intombe these men asked to speak to me, and said: 'We want to go home to our families, for you are going to be attacked by the whole of the Zulu Army.' 'Well, that is just the reason why you should stop with me; I have been paying you all these months, and you have never yet been in danger.' 'Oh, we are not nervous about ourselves, you are sure to repulse the attack, but some of the Cetewayo's men will sweep round in raiding parties on both flanks, and kill our women and children, who are near Luneberg.' 'I promise you I will insure your wives and your cattle if any harm comes to them while you are with me,' on which they saluted and went back to the kitchen fires quite content.

It is interesting that at some athletic sports on the 19th February, in the country pastime of throwing the assegai, the Zulus, who since Chaka's time had been taught not to throw long distances, but to rush on their foe and stab him with the short assegai, were easily beaten, the first prize being won by a Hottentot about 5 foot in height, who propelled an assegai 70 yards, the second man being a Colonial born Englishman, while no Zulu threw an assegai farther than 50 yards.

Our team in the tug-of-war, which had only been once defeated, was thoroughly beaten by Piet Uys and his Dutchmen. In 1872, when we were at Aldershot, I wished the battalion to enter a team for Divisional Athletic sports. I could get no volunteers, the battalion had never pulled in a tug-of-war, and showed no inclination to begin; eventually I had to appeal to the sergeant-major, who practically coerced the

---

[1] They were drawn from the Border Zulus I enlisted at Luneberg in November, and attached to battalions, six to each company; their powers of hearing were extraordinary; they could see farther than we could with field glasses, – their vision was surpassed only by the telescope. They lived near the battalion cooking fires, and were the cause of considerable difficulty with respect to their clothing. I could not buy soldiers' greatcoats in Africa, but it was the dumping ground of cast-off full dress uniforms of the British Army, and I obtained from Maritzburg old cavalry tunics, those of the Heavy Dragoon Guards being the only ones into which the Zulus could squeeze their bodies, and in these it was only the top buttons that would meet.

colour sergeants into producing one man a company. When I looked at them, selecting a man who seemed to be about my own size, I said: 'I do not think you will be much good for this job, – I doubt whether you can pull me over.' 'I can do that, sir, and without much trouble.' Taking up a rope, I told him to try. He gave one look at me, and then pulled me off my feet; and although I sacrificed my spurs by digging them into the ground, he took me across the parade ground without any apparent effort. My judgment was decidedly faulty; although he was not more than a stone heavier than I was, his arms and back were abnormally powerful. I was much interested in training the team, which beat in succession every battalion at Aldershot, the Garrison Artillery at Portsmouth, every regiment of the Guards, a brigade team of the Guards, a team from HMS *Excellent* at Portsmouth, and a team of the Royal Marines. We sent it about to different garrisons, and it was never beaten until it met the 96th Regiment, which had an equally well trained team, each man being about half a stone heavier in weight, the effect of which was decisive.

When we were marching up from King William's Town to Natal, our men vanquished the Frontier Light Horse, composed of fine men, as they did when at Utrecht, and again at Kambula Hill, but they could not make the Dutchmen take their pipes out of their mouths. I said to Piet Uys, 'I do not think your pipe will be alight in a quarter of an hour.' He laughed, and at the end of the quarter of an hour the laugh was against me, for the Dutchmen, averaging 14 or 15 stone, with enormous knotted arms, and hands like iron, waited until the 90th were exhausted, and then without an effort pulled them over.

In each camp we occupied I made a lawn-tennis ground, playing it, and polo on alternate afternoons, when I was not out on reconnoitring expeditions.

*It was not all fun and games in Wood's command, however. In the aftermath of Isandlwana, Chelmsford reorganised his forces. The disaster had prompted republican stirrings in the Transvaal, and Colonel Hugh Rowlands, who commanded the stationary column further north, was sent to Pretoria to reassert imperial control. His troops were placed under Wood's command, and a garrison of the 80th was moved down to Luneburg, where Mbilini's followers had been raiding outlying farms. This garrison was under the command of Major Charles Tucker, and was still supplied by wagon convoys making the long haul from the Transvaal town of Derby in the north. These were particularly vulnerable, since the road wound through the Ntombe valley, and crossed the river at Myer's drift, which, although only a few miles from Luneburg, lay under the very eye of Mbilini's Tafelberg stronghold.*

*At the beginning of March one such convoy started out, and was plagued from the first by appalling weather, which flooded the rivers, and turned the road into a quagmire. For Mbilini, the temptation proved too much, as Tucker wrote in a letter from Luneburg dated 19th March 1879 (first printed in* The Journal of the Society for Army Historical Research, *no. 22, 1943, and reprinted in Frank Emery's* The Red Soldier*):*

Long before this reaches you, by telegram you will have heard that some of the 80th have been cut to pieces not far from here, and doubtless you will be anxious to hear all about it from me. Some waggons were coming from Derby to this place loaded with ammunition, flour, and Indian corn (mealies they are called here). There was an escort with the waggons. On the 5th, when they were, owing to the troubled state of the roads and rivers, broken down at various intervals some eight or nine miles from here fearing an attack here that night from Umbeleni, I sent out to the escort to say they were to be in here that night at any cost. This order they carried out to the very letter, for at ten o'clock Anderson and his escort turned up, leaving the waggons as I tell you anywhere. They certainly had passed a fearful day, having been wet thro' ever since eleven a.m., and during the whole day they were pulling waggons out of mud holes and thro' rivers.

They managed to get six waggons as far as the Intombi River, but trying to get one thro' the drift it stuck fast, and then broke, so those behind couldn't come on. Six waggons they left stuck fast three miles farther on at the Little Intombi River; these were in a very nasty place, high hills occupied by the enemy

161

on either side, and they contained, so Anderson told me, ammunition. I could do nothing that night, but the following day I sent a party of men to the Intombi River, about six miles from here, to try and get these waggons with ammunition into Luneberg.

On arriving at the river they found it impassable, but they managed to unload the waggon stuck in the drift, and to pull it out. At night they returned to camp. The rain had been fearful all that day. The next morning, the 7th, I sent off Captain Moriarty with a hundred men and a waggon loaded with beams and barrels to make a raft, and ordered him to get the ammunition waggons out of their difficulties and bring them on to the other bank of the Intombi and laager them with the waggons already there and to wait there until the river went down. I went out there myself that day and saw the raft constructed, but it was bad.

I started some oxen and men to get out the waggons at the Little Intombi River. Seeing the rain was coming, I rode home, but before starting I ordered the men to pitch three tents on this side of the Intombi to put their things in if the rain came on. When about half-way home rain came down in torrents – harder, if possible, than we had had before – and although I had a waterproof I hadn't a dry stitch upon me when I reached Luneberg.

On the 8th we had a very wet day and still worse night. On the 9th the rain continued. On the 10th it was fine for an hour or two, but at ten a.m. on it came again and continued until daybreak. I cannot describe to you the fearful misery the poor men were in. Everything belonging to them had been wet thro' for days, and the difficulties they experienced in getting their food cooked in the open air were almost insurmountable. With joy we hailed the morning of the 11th March fine, and later on, the sun coming out, we very soon had all our wet things dry, and our clothes once more washed, but the ground around the tents was still a sea of mud.

After lunch I went out to the Intombi River to see what poor Moriarty had done, and found that they had been in a worse plight than ourselves, as the river had risen so very high as to come half-way up his laager, but during the morning it had gone down considerably. You will see by the enclosed rough sketch that the men were divided, thirty-five being on this bank and seventy with the waggon laager on the opposite side. On this side the bank all along is very steep and high, but on the other where the laager was the ground slopes gradually to the edge of the water.

When I reached them on the 11th the river was still very high and the stream rapid. I went across on the raft and it was as much as I could do to keep my feet dry; the other three officers with me all got wet. I didn't at all like the construction of the laager, first because the base did not quite rest upon the river, and secondly the desselbooms (poles) of the waggons were not run under one another or outside the waggon in front of it, as I always have laagered my waggons, but the desselbooms were tied to the wheels of the waggon in front, and up against the desselbooms were placed bags of mealies, thus leaving a low gap about two to three feet high between the waggons. I cannot consider this any protection whatever in the event of the Zulus attacking in numbers, as they are sure to do; they can very easily pull themselves over this.

They had all the cattle, about 250, inside the laager at night, and you will see the spot where two waggons of ammunition containing 90,000 rounds were placed. In such a position that, the attack once commenced, no one could possibly get to them on account of the quantity of cattle; but there is every excuse for the laager not being properly constructed. He was short of oxen, and in the fearful weather he had experienced it was almost impossible for the men to have placed them properly, and when they made the laager the water was up to its base, which under ordinary circumstances would have been a very good defence. I also thought the men being divided was wrong, but this turned out to be the salvation of forty-four lives; but for their being there not one single soul could possibly have escaped, for all those who got away from the far side had to throw away their arms in the river.

Harward was the subaltern with Moriarty, and the afternoon I was there, hearing some cattle had strayed, I ordered some men to go out and see if they could find them. It appears they went away into the hills, killed a couple of [Africans], took

163

some rifles and a few goats. Coming back to camp late, Harward was very tired and, his blankets being in Moriarty's tent, he lay down to sleep; when the latter said to him, 'You must get over to the other side to sleep,' Harward remonstrated, but Moriarty said, 'You must go; it's the Major's orders.' Now I have no recollection of having ever alluded to the matter, but that makes no difference; Harward went, and to this he owes his life.

On the morning of the 12th about six thirty a.m. I was awoke by a fearful voice saying 'Major! Major!' I was up in an instant, and there, at my tent door on his knees, the picture of death, was Harward. He gasped out, 'The camp is in the hands of the enemy; they are all slaughtered, and I have galloped in for my life.' He then fell on to my bed in a faint. I gave him some water, got him round, and he then told me as follows. All the men's statements are pretty much the same. About half past three in the morning of the 12th – it was then raining and misty – a shot was fired not far from the camp. The alarm was given and the men turned out; but Moriarty, thinking it was nothing, told the men to turn it again, but cautioned the sentries to be on the alert. On his side he had two sentries right and left of his tent, about fifteen to twenty yards off. There was a small rise in front of them, so that they couldn't see fifty yards. On this side there was but one sentry, but if the morning had been clear he would have had a very good view right over the laager below him.

About five o'clock the mist began to clear and the sentry from this side saw the [Zulus] quite close to the camp and almost round it; he at once fired his rifle and gave the alarm. The sentries on the other side did the same. Of course, the men were up in a moment, some men sleeping under the waggons and some in the tents; but before the men were in their positions, the Zulus had fired a volley, thrown down their guns – these were taken up by the reserve, a very large body, they tell me, well in rear of the advance party – and were around the waggons and on the top of them, and even inside with the cattle, almost instantly. So quickly did they come, there was really no defence on the part of our men; it was simply each man fighting for his life, and in a very few minutes

164

all was over, our men being simply slaughtered. The cattle were all driven out of the laager in a few seconds, and our men from this side fired volley after volley into the mass of Zulus and white men; but seeing about 200 of the enemy were crossing the river in a body rather high up, evidently with a view to get behind them, and the fighting being virtually over, these men very wisely retired; and not at all too soon, as the Zulus were coming from a hill in their rear to prevent their going into Luneberg. Most of these men kept together, pursued by the Zulus for at least three and a half miles. When they showed symptoms of closing, the men under a Sergeant [Booth] halted and gave them a volley, which frightened the Zulus. Four men left this retreating party and took a short cut under a hill; they were met by some Zulus and all killed. The moment Harward saw the Zulus coming across the river he saddled up the horse of another man and galloped into the camp. Only twelve men out of seventy from the far side escaped alive. One man who couldn't swim was well out in the river; a Zulu passed him without an assegai; he caught hold of the enemy, who swam with him to the opposite bank. Another man and a Zulu were trying to drown one another when up came one of our men with his rifle and hit the Zulu with his butt. At this moment a man from this bank fired and killed the Zulu and our two men escaped. The sight in the river, they tell me, was frightful – Zulus and white men all mixed up together, yelling, howling and screeching.

I had all the horses I could raise at once saddled and, ordering 150 men to follow, started for the Intombi. About a mile from the scene we were on high ground and could see from there and from miles away to our right dense masses of Zulus extending for at least two miles under the hills, and the last Zulus were then leaving the laager for the hills eastward. They were all trotting off as fast as they could, evidently expecting we should soon be there from Luneberg.

As we approached the Intombi Drift a fearful and horrible sight presented itself, and the stillness of the spot was awful; there were our men lying all about the place, some naked and some only half clad. On the opposite side of the drift I need not attempt to describe to you what I saw; all the bodies were full of assegai wounds and nearly all were disembowelled. This is the custom of the Zulus, arising from a superstition that unless they do so their own stomach will swell and burst. I saw but one body that I could call unmutilated. As soon as we got to the Intombi, I shouted at the top of my voice so that any man wounded might know we were at hand. Instantly out of the earth came one of our men and two [Africans]; our man was some considerable way down stream. I went to him and found he was slightly wounded in the head from an assegai, and his hand cut between thumb and finger. The story is as follows. He was sleeping in a tent when he heard a shot and the sentry shout, 'Guard, turn out!' He had his arms by him and his accoutrements on him, and being at the tent door he was first out.

The Zulus were then in the act of getting on to the waggons, and a second later they were inside the laager and began to drive out the cattle; they are most extraordinary hands at handling cattle. He does not know how he got thro' the laager to the river, but being there, and not able to swim, he thought he might as well drown as be killed by the Zulus, so into the water he went and fired several rounds from there; but going in still farther, the water at least reached his neck and the stream took him off his legs. He threw away his rifle and down the river he went; presently his foot touched the ground, but being under water and thinking he was being drowned, he undid his waist-belt and up he came to the surface close to the opposite bank. He laid hold of some grass, but it gave way with him and on he went. A second time the grass was near him and he held it, finally getting to the top of the bank; but being exhausted, having swallowed a lot of water, he rested on his hands and knees. While in this position a Zulu came at him with an assegai; our man caught hold of his assegai and they struggled. The stick broke, leaving the blade in our man's hand, who at once killed the Zulu. The effort was too much for him; he fell back into the river, but again caught the .grass, and, hearing the Zulus all about, he let his body go under water and covered his head well up with grass. Here he remained some time, but presently he heard from the opposite bank voices shouting, 'Come out, Jack; they have all gone.

Come out, you fool!' in very fair English. He was on the very point of coming out, but seeing a [African] with a shield on the opposite bank he thought all was not quite right and so remained where he was. At the same time he saw right opposite to him a [African] hiding like himself under the grass, and he remained watching this fellow until our arrival, when the [African] turned out to be one of the escaped waggon drivers. He was watching our man, but feared to move for fear he should be taken for a Zulu and shot.

The 150 men soon arrived and we set to work at once to collect the dead and dig an enormous trench in which to bury them; this took us nearly all day. About five p.m. I read the burial service over the dead; we fired three volleys and then returned to camp with what little the Zulus had left in the waggons. Nearly everything had been broken or torn to pieces, the tents being in shreds and the ammunition boxes broken to atoms, the mealies and flour thrown all about the place. They had killed all the dogs save one, and that we found with an assegai wound right through its neck. We have it in camp and it is going on all right. We found one Zulu wounded at the laager; he was a very handsome man. A bullet had hit him in the shin, broken both the bones, and nearly cut his leg off. He told us his friends were in a great hurry to get off for fear we should come from Luneberg; they took with them a man next to him with a body wound because he could walk; they told him that there were many killed and wounded. This man has since died; he would not have his leg cut off.

You will see where Moriarty's tent was pitched outside the laager. I hear that the Zulus surrounded this place, that Moriarty was seen coming out of his tent and immediately had an assegai into his back; he was then getting into the laager over a deselboom when he was shot. Falling onto his knees, he said, 'I am done; fire away, boys.' We found him lying on his face inside the laager, quite naked; he wasn't disembowelled. He was a fine big man with quite white hair, and seems to have been known, for we have since heard from a woman that has come in from Manyeoba that the white captain himself killed three of Manyanyoba's sons. We brought into Luneberg the bodies of Moriarty and Dr Cobbin, who was also killed there, and they were buried the following day. Coming in from the Intombi, our men searched all the mealies and long grass, and about three miles from the river they found a Zulu with a bullet wound which went in under his chin and came out at his right side, thro' his lungs. He says he was stooping down when he was shot. Another bullet has made a clean cut on his cheek and taken off the lobe of his ear; this man is going on all right. Close to him in a stream they found the dead bodies of the men who took the short cut; these we brought into Luneberg, and at nine p.m. we buried them by torchlight.

On the 13th I sent some mounted men to search all over the ground for the twenty men we then had missing. They rode over a large extent of country, but saw no trace of anyone. The river was still very high, but going down. On the 14th I found the river was very considerably lower, so on the 15th I sent out some men with oxen to try and get the waggons (twenty-one) into Luneberg; they succeeded in bringing all the waggons over the river on this side and brought in here ten waggons; they found three bodies in the river and a rifle or two. On the 16th I sent out for the remaining waggons; they again found three more bodies and one rifle in the river, and brought into Luneberg the eleven waggons. On the 18th I rode out there and the river was so high that I had to kneel right up on my saddle to keep my legs dry.

We have found about the scene of this misfortune the bodies of thirty Zulus; no doubt they must have taken some away and nearly all their wounded. Our loss [in the 80th Regt] out of 105 all told is sixty dead and missing; one officer dead, four we buried here, forty-one at the Intombi River, and fifteen are still missing. No doubt the latter are in the river, and we may recover some more bodies when the stream subsides.

Redvers Buller, Moysey, Engineers, and Hamilton, 90th, have been over here from Kambula Camp to inquire into the misfortune; they went out with me on the 18th to see the spot. The first night they slept here our natives were all on the scare. Just as we had finished dinner, some [African] waggon-drivers came running in from the hill at our rear, where they generally go at night to sleep, saying they had come across an *impi* of Zulus. Our men got hold of this and altho' I assured them that these [Africans] had only seen some friendly [blacks] and that the enemy could not possibly get on to the hill without our knowing it, their minds were still very uneasy, and about eight-thirty off went a couple of rifles and all went into laager and fort; the nights are very dark and no doubt they fired off at imaginary Zulus. Posted again, but about two hours later off went a couple more rifles and in they all came to the fort, and there I kept them for the night, and the rain I am sure well cooled down the excited ones by daybreak. These young soldiers are more bother than they are worth. A fellow nearly let off his rifle last night at a log of wood, but an officer happened to visit him at the moment he was challenging it for the third time and so saved an alarm. This finishes, I hope, the affair at the Intombi River, and I trust this may be the last time I have to write about it.

*In due course, Booth was promoted colour-sergeant, and awarded the VC. Lieutenant Harward was court-martialled for deserting his men in the face of the enemy. The court accepted his argument that he had done what he could for them, and then ridden for help, and found him not guilty. This verdict was greeted with astonishment by the military establishment, however, and comments condemning his behaviour were ordered to be read at the head of every regiment in the British army.*

*Wood clearly could not let the Ntombe affair pass without retaliation. Buller led a raid into the valley, burning homesteads and scattering any warriors he came across, but Mbilini himself had slipped away south, and taken refuge with his abaQulusi friends on Hlobane. It was becoming increasingly obvious that if he was to suppress local resistance, Wood would have to deprive the Zulus of their Hlobane retreat. Whilst he was pondering his course of action, however, he scored a notable diplomatic success. On 10th March Prince Hamu kaNzibe came into the Khambula camp and surrendered.*

*Hamu was Cetshwayo's half-brother, and was known to have been jealous of his rise to power. Before the war, British propaganda had painted Cetshwayo as a ruthless despot whose subjects were eagerly awaiting the opportunity to throw him over, and it was part of Chelmsford's plan, therefore, that his commanders should attempt to prise leading Zulus from their allegiance to the king as the columns advanced. Wood had been particularly diligent in this regard, but most of the local chiefs had preferred to sit on the fence publicly, whilst surreptitiously supporting Mbilini's raids. Hamu, however, had responded favourably, if cautiously, as Wood relates:*

Uhamu, a brother of Cetewayo's, came into our camp[1] in the Cape cart which I sent for him, he being so enormously bulky that it was difficult to find a horse to carry him. He had made many appointments, but in the procrastinating Zulu fashion had failed for various reasons to keep them, until Colonel Buller had ceased to believe in his being willing to come over to us. Finally he went to my assistant political agent, Norman Macleod, in Swaziland. He was no sooner in our camp than he asked me if I would be good enough to go after his wives. 'How many are there, Uhamu?' 'I don't know but about 300,' he replied vaguely. 'But you have got two now with you,' I urged, 'These are only slaves – I should like to have the others.' 'I am not willing to take the responsibility of escorting all your wives unless you will come with me.' 'Oh, in such a case, Great Commander, I would sooner do without them.'

Uhamu's head place was in a rugged country, 45 miles from our camp, between the Black Umvolosi and Mkusi Rivers, and Ulundi being within 40 miles of the kraal, there was the possibility of our return being cut off if either of Uhamu's men let it be known, by Cetewayo's adherents, they were collecting the women in anticipation of our arrival.

Looking, however, to the political effect of getting out the tribe, I decided to go down, and on the 14th March started with 360 mounted men under Buller, and 200 of Uhamu's men, many of whom had fought against No. 3 Column at Isandwhlana. Some of my officers objected to my leaving

---

[1] Sir Bartle Frere eulogised my agent, Captain Macleod, and me for our 'temper, judgment, and patience' in getting Uhamu over from his brother; and a Zulu agent told Bishop Colenso, and Sir Bartle later, that Cetewayo's altered tone was due to the defection of Uhamu.

Buller and the white men and accompanying Uhamu's people, by a short cut over the Zunguin Mountain, which would save three hours' travelling. I argued that there was absolutely no danger while their chief was located in my camp, especially as the men looked forward to bringing their wives and children back with them.

I took with me Captain Woodgate,[1] Mr Llewellyn Lloyd,[2] my interpreter, Lieutenants Bigge,[3] Bright[2], and Lysons.[4] We joined Colonel Buller under the Inhlobane, down the slopes of which some aggressive Zulus came, and fired at us at long ranges. I allowed two or three men to return the fire, and then had two shots myself, and the bullets falling amongst the Makulusi – for they occupied the mountain, silenced their fire.

About 2 p.m. we saw a few cattle to the south of us, and Piet Uys despatched his two boys, aged fifteen and thirteen, with half a dozen men to drive them to us. Master Dirks Uys shot a Zulu. When the father heard the firing he tried to look unconcerned, and was too proud to ask me (for his eyes were not as good as mine) if I could see what the lad was doing. Lysons told me later that he kept on repeating, 'Are they coming back yet?' The men brought back about 100 head of cattle, and I said to my friend Piet, 'I am glad the lad has come back. I saw that you were nervous.' 'Yes,' he said, 'I am always nervous if I am not there myself,' a feeling which I understood. Nevertheless he risked them in every skirmish, though the warmth of his affection for his youngest born – Piet was a widower – was evident. In an argument, he said something which I thought unworthy of the bigness of his character, and I remarked, 'Why, you risk Dirks for us, you should not talk of farms and property'; and he replied, his eyes filling, 'You are quite right, I would not give Dirks for all Zululand!' An hour or two later Piet called out that he saw Zulus, and galloped off with his two boys, but on this occasion nothing happened, for the Zulus he

---

[1] General Woodgate, mortally wounded at Spion Kop.
[2] Both killed in action a fortnight later.
[3] Now Colonel Sir Arthur Bigge.
[4] Lately colonel commanding a battalion of the Bedfordshire Regiment; now on staff in India.

171

had sighted were some of Uhamu's men, who, taking advantage of our presence, were coming to join us.

We marched steadily till sunset, when we off-saddled for an hour, to let the horses graze, and, moving off again at dusk, at 9.30 p.m. reached the spot I had arranged with Uhamu, having taken three hours to pass over the last seven miles. We descended a mountain by a goat path, and all the Europeans dismounted; but I, being tired from having been touched by the sun in the forenoon, threw the reins on my pony's neck and let him choose, or rather feel, the path – it was too dark to see, and we got down without accident.

At sunset Uhamu's 200 men who accompanied me had asked me to stop, declaring they were tired. This I refused, and when we got down they had nearly cooked their food, having passed down by a still steeper but shorter path. Before I went to sleep I had some of the women for whom I came brought out of a cave three miles off, as I foresaw there would be delay next morning, and every hour added to the chance of our being caught by some of Cetewayo's regiments. During the night I sent six miles away to some caves where I heard there were more women, being unable to sleep soundly, although greatly fatigued, for one troop of the Frontier Light Horse, linked[1] in line, nearly walked over me, after they had eaten all the grass within reach. Buller came and pulled them away; indeed, every time I awoke in the night I saw him walking up and down, but he felt we were in a precarious position.

At daylight we shook ourselves, and began to start – a long stream of humanity. The refugees numbered between 900 and 1000, men, women, and children. Many of the latter, although only five years old, walked from 6.30 a.m. till 9.30 p.m., when they had covered 30 miles. I sent Captain Barton on in front, while Colonel Buller and I remained behind. At 8.30 we were assured by Messrs Calverley and Rorke – two traders who had often been in the district – that we had got the whole of the women and children. My engagement was that I would remain

---

[1] Horses are linked by a headrope being passed through the head collar, and then through that of the next horse.

till daylight, that is, six o'clock. At 8.30 Colonel Buller marched, a small rear guard, remaining with me till 10.30, as even then stragglers were coming in, the last few being shot at, and two assegaied in our sight but too far off for us to save them. My friend Buller had stoutly declared that he would have nothing to do with the verminous children, nevertheless during the march I more than once saw him with six little black bodies in front of and behind his saddle, children under five years of age.

As we passed under the Inhlobane, the Makulusi tribe, which had been reinforced by one of Cetewayo's regiments from Ulundi, fired a few shots at us without any effect, and we bivouacked at nightfall on a small effluent of the White Umvolosi, where Vryheid now stands.

Next morning I started the procession at daylight, remaining myself on the top of the Zunguin range to see the rear guard into camp. I had sent in for all mule waggons available, to save the children a farther walk of ten miles, and was waiting at the top of the pass, up which we had climbed on the 22nd January, for a dozen women who were loitering half up the mountain. It was past noon when I desired Piet Uys to descend and hurry them up, holding his horse for him, for it was too steep to ride down. When he returned he said, in his curious mixture of Dutch, German, and English, 'Kurnall, die vrow sie sagt now too sick, presently have baby, then come quick.' 'Piet,' I exclaimed, 'oughtn't we to send some of these women back to see after her?' 'Not necessary, Kurnall, she come.' Calling Mr Llewellyn Lloyd, my interpreter, I apprised him of the situation, and said, 'You are not to go into camp until that woman gets there.' Finally, waiting for the waggons longer than I expected, I did not reach camp till 5 p.m., and, having had nothing to eat or drink since our morning cocoa at daylight, I was annoyed to see Lloyd sitting in his tent with a cup of tea, and observed in a somewhat irritable tone, 'I thought I told you not to come into camp until the woman who was about to bring a baby into the world had arrived.' 'Yes, quite so,' he replied, 'but she has been in camp a long time. Half an hour after you told me, she passed me like one of Waukenphast's pictures, doing five miles an hour easily, and I, suspecting that she had left her baby in the rocks, made her angry by insisting on seeing it, but she had it right enough under her arm.'

*In the event, any hopes that Hamu's defection might have precipitated the collapse of the Zulu kingdom proved false. No other important Zulu leaders defected to the British until the very last stages of the war, and in fact Hamu's defection merely stimulated the resolve of loyalist Zulus to fight harder. Nevertheless, the incident had a good effect of morale in Wood's camp, and many of Hamu's warriors declared themselves ready to fight for the British. Accordingly, when Chelmsford sent Wood a message towards the end of March, asking him to make a diversionary attack to support the advance of the Eshowe relief column, Wood judged it an appropriate moment to launch the overdue attack on Hlobane. Unfortunately, the moment proved far from appropriate: King Cetshwayo was also planning to embark on a new campaign.*

*Cetshwayo had called up his army in the middle of March, once it had recovered from the shock of Isandlwana. The king had taken the diplomatic initiative, sending messages to Natal in the hope of restoring peace, but this overture had been rebuffed, as neither Frere nor Chelmsford was prepared to countenance an end to hostilities before Isandlwana had been avenged. With British forces mustering on the border once more, therefore, Cetshwayo resolved to launch another major strike. He had been bombarded with messages from Mbilini and the abaQulusi chiefs demanding help against Wood's depredations, and it was obvious that the northern column was the most serious remaining threat. The same amabutho that had triumphed at Isandlwana would be sent into the field again; despite the losses they had suffered, they remained convinced that the British were no match for them. Cetshwayo gave them careful instructions not to attack defended positions, but to feint towards the border settlements, and thereby try to draw the British into the open. In the event, Colonel Wood tells us, the last week of March brought surprises and heartache for both himself and King Cetshwayo:*

In the forenoon of the 27th March, the two columns which were to attack the Inhlobane at daylight next morning marched; I followed in the evening, intending to lie down 5 miles under the western edge of the Inhlobane. The more important part of the operation was intrusted to Colonel Buller, under whose orders I placed the two battalions of Wood's regiment. The 1st battalion, under Major Leet, bivouacking near the White Umvolosi, where Vryheid now stands, was intended to ascend the Western end of the mountain; both columns were to get as high up as they could before daylight on the 28th. In the orders I stated that, as Cetewayo was said to be advancing with his whole army, scouts were to be sent to the south and south-west, to watch the avenues of approach from Ulundi.

I took with me Mr Lloyd, assistant political agent and interpreter, Captain the Honourable Ronald Campbell, Coldstream Guards, and Lieutenant Lysons, 90th Light Infantry, orderly officer, my personal escort, eight mounted men of the battalion, and seven mounted Zulus under Umtonga, a half-brother of Cetewayo's, whom the father, Umpande, had originally designated to succeed him. Before I went to sleep I had a long talk with Piet Uys, who was to accompany Colonel Buller, and had stayed behind to see me, while the Colonel had bivouacked five miles farther to the east. Mr Potter, a captain in the 1st Battalion, Wood's Irregulars, also came to me. Both men knew the Inhlobane, and Potter had often been up on it.

I asked whether, if we should have the bad luck after taking the mountain to see Cetewayo's army advancing, we could get down on the north side, and Mr Potter assured me that we could, by leading our horses. Piet Uys was confident that Colonel Buller would get up, without serious loss, and we agreed that, except in the probable contingency of the Zulu main army coming in sight, our operation ought to be a success; then Piet turning to me, said, 'Kurnall, if you are killed I will take care of your children, and if I am killed you do the same for mine.' We had heard, indeed, for several days that Kambula was to be attacked, but were informed that the Zulu Army could not leave till the 27th, as there had been a delay in 'doctoring' one of the largest regiments. This was inaccurate. It had started on the 25th March.

At 3 a.m. on the 28th I rode eastward, with the staff officers and escort. Captain Campbell and I were silent, but the two younger men chattered till I wondered whether their voices could reach the Zulus on the Inhlobane. When Ronald Campbell spoke on Lloyd's challenge for his thoughts, he replied, 'I am hoping my wife is well and happy.' Lloyd and Lysons, jubilant at the prospect of a fight, remarking on my silence, asked, 'Are you doubtful, sir, of our getting up to the top of the mountain?' 'Oh no, we shall get up.' 'Then, of what are you thinking?' 'Well, which of you will be writing to my wife tonight, or about which of you young men I shall be writing to parents or wife?'

Colonel Buller, to avoid risk of being surprised, had shifted bivouac twice during the night, but at daylight we struck his track and followed it. We met a squadron of his force coming westwards, the commandant having lost his way the previous night, and I directed him to move to the sound of the firing, which was now audible on the north-east face of the mountain, where we could just discern the rear of Colonel Buller's column mounting the summit. I followed the squadron, but when it came under fire, as it did not advance rapidly, I passed to the front, the track at first being easy to follow, from worn grass and dead horses of Colonel Buller's command lying on it. Hard rock now replaced the beaten down grass, and as we came under fire I unconsciously, by leading directly towards the rocks whence the bullets came, missed the easier gradient, up which Buller's men had ridden, losing only one officer. The ground was now steep and very rugged, so we dismounted and put the horses of my white and black escort in a cattle kraal, the walls of which were 2½ feet high. Campbell invited me to leave my horse. I said, 'No; I am a bad walker,' and pulled it after me, Mr Lloyd being close on my left hand. Half a dozen of the foremost of the Irregulars had dismounted sooner, and followed me until Lloyd and I were within 100 feet of the crest of the mountain, and we came under well-directed fire in our front, and from both flanks, the enemy being concealed behind huge boulders of rock.

The men of the squadron 200 yards behind us now opened fire, and Mr Lloyd said, 'I am glad of that, for it will make the Zulus shoot badly.' He had scarcely spoken these words when a Zulu rose up from behind a rock 50 yards above us, and, touching Lloyd with my elbow, I observed, 'He won't hit us in the face,' for he laid his gun directly at my waistbelt. He fired, and Lloyd fell back, exclaiming, 'I am hit!' 'Badly?' 'Yes, very badly; my back's broken!' I tried to lift him on my shoulders, but he was taller than I, and the ground being steep I stumbled, when Captain Campbell climbing up said, 'Let me lift him,' and carried him on his shoulder 50 yards down to where the horses were standing in the cattle kraal, under the walls of which the escort were sheltering. I climbed a few yards higher, when a Zulu fired at me from underneath a rock, 20 yards distant. The charge struck my horse immediately in front of the girth, killing it instantaneously, and as it fell, striking my shoulder with its head, knocked me down. I heard an exclamation from my comrades, and scrambling up called, 'No, I am not hit!' and as they began climbing the hill, added, 'Please stop where you are. I am coming down, for it's too steep to get on any farther, in this place.' When I got down to the kraal, I saw Mr Lloyd was dying. He could no longer speak; obtaining some brandy from Lysons, I tried to pour a little down his throat, but his teeth were already set.

I told Captain Campbell to order the Irregular horsemen, who were taking cover under rocks below us, to clear the caves from whence the firing had come which killed my horse. He found much difficulty in inducing the men to advance, as they alleged the position was unassailable; and eventually, leading four of my personal escort, with Lieutenant Lysons, he climbed up, Bugler Walkinshaw going with him. I called Walkinshaw back before he was out of sight, for I wanted help for Mr Lloyd; and thus he, one of the bravest men in the Army, missed the chance of gaining the Victoria Cross. In a few moments one of the men told me that the cave was cleared, but that Ronald Campbell was dead. He had led the small party of three or four men, passing up a narrow passage only two feet wide between rocks 12 feet high for several yards, and was looking down into the cave, when a Zulu fired, almost touching him, and he fell dead. Lieutenant Lysons and Private Fowler,[1] 90th Light Infantry, undauntedly passing over the body, fired into the cave, and the few Zulus in it disappeared through another opening.

By the time the men brought Ronald Campbell's body down, Mr Lloyd was dead. Telling Walkinshaw to put his ear down to his heart, he made sure, and then I tried to put the bodies up on my baggage animal. The fire from the rocks on all sides was fairly accurate, killing many out of the 21 ponies we had with us. As bullets were striking all round me on the stones, my pony moved every time I got Campbell's body on my shoulder. Walkinshaw, who was entirely unconcerned at the bullets, said, 'If you will hold it, sir, I will put the bodies up'; and this he did.

It then occurred to me that in the wallets of the saddle under my horse, which was lying with all four feet in the air, was Campbell's wife's prayer book, a small one I had borrowed before starting from Kambula, as my own was a large Church Service, and I said to Walkinshaw, 'Climb up the hill, and get the prayer book in my wallets; while I do not want you to get shot for the saddle, you are to take all risks for the sake of the prayer book.' He climbed up in a leisurely fashion, and, pulling the saddle from underneath the horse brought it safely down on his head. We then moved down the mountain 300 yards, to find a spot on soil clear of rocks.

The operation of digging a grave was laborious, as our only implements were the assegais of the native escort, and when it had been completed to about four feet in depth, the men got flurried by the approach of some 300 Zulus from the Ityenteka Nek, and, lifting the bodies, placed them in the grave. It was not long enough, and although I realised the possibility of our having trouble with the approaching Zulus, yet as they were still 600 yards off and were most of them bad shots at that range, I had the bodies lifted out, and the grave made a proper length to receive them without the lower limbs being

[1] They both received the Victoria Cross.

doubled up. When I was satisfied, I read an abridged form of
the burial service from Mrs Campbell's prayer book. We were
now assisted by the fire of some of Colonel Buller's men, who,
seeing our difficulty, opened on the advancing Zulus, and,
being above them, checked their approach. The officer commanding the Irregulars asked permission to move down the
hill to regain Colonel Buller's track, and by it he finally reached
the summit without further casualties. He had lost only 6 men
dead, and 7 wounded, up to this hour.

As all firing on top of the mountain had now ceased, I decided
to move back, and see how the other column had fared. Passing
one of the Irregulars who had been shot in the thigh, I put him
up on one of the dead men's horses, and as there was no apparent hurry, Umtonga's men drove with us a flock of sheep and
goats. We stopped occasionally to give the wounded man stimu-
lants, being unconscious that the main Zulu Army was moving
on our left, across, and towards our path. When we were under
the centre of the mountain, Umtonga, whom I had sent out to a
ridge on our danger flank, gesticulated excitedly, explaining by
signs that there was a large army near us. Cantering up, I had a
good view of the force, which was marching in five columns,
with the flanks advanced, and a dense centre – the normal Zulu
attack formation.

I sent Lieutenant Lysons to the officer commanding the
western party with the following order:

*Below the Inhlobane. 10.30 a.m. 28/3/79*
There is a large army coming this way from the south.
Get into position on the Zunguin Nek. E.W.

The plateau which Colonel Buller's force had cleared was
150 feet fighter than the lower plateau on which the western
column stood, but both parties saw the Zulu Army a considerable time before I did, as I was 1,000 feet below them. Buller
had seen it at 9 a.m., and the western force had seen it rather
earlier, Buller being engaged in covering a party of 25 of
the Frontier Light Horse under Captain Barton, Coldstream
Guards, who were descending the eastern slope to bury one
or two men killed in the assault.

Sending word to Captain Barton to retire, Buller fell back

to the western end of the mountain, and forming some selected men into a rear guard, he took them down the almost precipitous edge of the upper plateau. The path was down the apex of a salient angle, with long sides, and the head of the descent was well suited for defence. Buller's men had previously collected a great number of cattle, which had been driven down towards the Zunguin Nek at 7 a.m. Colonel Buller and all his party would have got safely away had not the Makulusi, and the men of the Regular regiment with it, taking courage at the advance of the Zulu Army, emerged from their caves and harassed the retreat, during which some valuable lives were lost. Colonel Buller came down, practically the last man, and was at the foot of the descent from the upper plateau, when, seeing men nearly surrounded by Zulus, he went back on two occasions, and brought out a succession two on his horse. Piet Uys came down with him, until he saw one of his sons having difficulty with his horse, and going back, was assegaied by a Zulu crouching behind him.[1]

---

[1] The death of Piet Uys was a great loss to us, and Lord Chelmsford supported the earnest representations I made in his favour, as did also Sir Bartle Frere, who knew a great deal about him. He was intensely patriotic, and had done not only good service to No. 4 column, but to South Africa, for although he had opposed the Annexation, the justice of which he denied as regards his countrymen, he admitted its necessity in the interests of the country at large and he lent all his great influence, in opposition to many of his oldest and dearest friends, in pressing on the attention of his countrymen their duty in combating our savage foes. He had armed, equipped, mounted, and provisioned his numerous family at his own expense bringing all his sons into the field. He had persistently refused to accept pay for himself, or for any of his relatives, who, after his death, declined to accept the arrears of pay which I offered. He constantly acted as arbitrator in compensation cases for damage done in the operations to the property of Dutchmen, and no decision was ever questioned by the sufferers, or by myself, who had to decide on the claim. When one of his own farms was accidentally damaged, he would not allow it to be reported. I asked for 36,000 acres of Government land to be set apart for his nine children, and was supported in my request by the High Commissioner, whose last official letter before leaving Natal some months later was to urge on the Colonial Office the importance of giving effect to my recommendation; but I doubt if it would ever have been carried into effect had I not been afforded the opportunity of stating the case personally to Her Gracious Majesty the Queen, who ensured the provision being made.

About 80 of the First Battalion of Wood's Irregulars were overtaken and killed, and with them, to my great regret, Captain Potter, and Lieutenant Williams[1] of the 58th regiment.

The main Zulu Army being exhausted by their march, halted near where Vryheid now stands, but some of their mounted men came on, and a few of the more active and younger footmen. Before leaving camp I had given orders for a barricade of planks, 5 feet high, to be erected, and securely bolted into the ground with supporting struts, to run between the redoubt and the south end of the cattle laager, to stop a rush from the ravine on to the fort. To those who objected that the Zulus would charge and knock it down by the weight of their bodies, I replied it would cause a delay of several minutes, during which 300 or 400 rifles, at 250 yards range, ought to make an additional barricade of human bodies, and I now sent an order to the senior officer in camp, to chain up the waggons, and to continue the strengthening of the barricade. I wrote I had seen between 20,000 and 25,000 Zulus, and remained on the Zunguin Mountain till 7 p.m., hoping to cover the retreat of any more of our men who might come up, being particularly anxious about Captain Barton,[2] of whom we had had no news since he descended the eastern end of the mountain.

[1] When the latter joined me, not very long before, I had a very favourable report of him from the assistant military secretary, Colonel North Crealock, and my experience during the few days in which he worked under my command fully justified it.

[2] I tell now the manner of Robert Barton's noble end, although it was fourteen months later that I obtained the details. He had shown not only distinguished courage, but in actions great humanity, and in the previous January nearly lost his life in trying to take a Zulu prisoner, the man firing his gun so close to Barton as to burn the skin of his face.

When, on receipt of Colonel Buller's warning, he descended the mountain, he trotted on westward, followed by the men of the Irregular squadron who had been with me at the eastern end, and who, before I returned, had gained the summit without further loss. As they reached the western base of the mountain, some of the Ngobamakosi regiment headed them, and they tried to cut their way through, but, after losing some men, retraced their steps eastwards, and, though many fell, Barton got safely down over the Ityenteka Nek.

When I was with Her Imperial Majesty the Empress Eugénie, in May 1880, on the Ityatosi River, I asked Sirayo's son, Melokazulo, (reported as having

I never knew until that day the depth of regard which Buller felt for me. I was sitting on the summit of the Zunguin range when he climbed up it, and, seeing me suddenly, uttered so fervent a 'Thank God!' that I asked for what he was thankful, and he explained that he thought I had been cut off at the eastern end of the mountain. It rained heavily on the evening of the 28th. All the mounted men had been on the move day and night since the 23rd, when we went to Luneberg; but at 9 p.m., when a straggler came in to say that there were some Europeans coming back by Potter's Store, Redvers Buller immediately saddled up, and, taking out led horses, brought in seven men, who were, as we believed, the sole survivors of the parties at the east end of the mountain.

So far as I know, the only officer who get down the western end of the Inhlobane on horseback was Major Leet, who commanded the 1st battalion Wood's Irregulars. Six weeks earlier, at the athletic sports, we had a tug-of-war between the officers of the 13th and 90th Light Infantry, captained by Leet and

---

been killed in Bambaata's rebellion, 1906) who was a mounted officer of the Ngobomakosi tribe, if he could tell me whether any of his men had killed my friend, whose body had never been found. He said, 'No; for I followed you, although you were not aware of it, and, when failing to overtake you, I turned back, I was too late to overtake those who were going eastward, and the pursuit was taken up by mounted men of the Umcityu regiment. I know a man named Chicheeli, who was a mounted officer of the Umcityu, and I believe saw what took place.' I said, 'Send for him,' to which he replied, 'He won't come unless you send for him. He will believe Lakuni,' (This was my name among the Zulus. The word describes the hard wood of which Zulus make their knobkerries, or bludgeons.) Chicheeli came, and talked quite frankly, giving me a still higher opinion of the powers of observation of the savage than I already had. After describing the coat and other clothes that Barton wore, he said, 'The white man was slightly pitted by smallpox.' Now I had lived at Aldershot for two years in daily intercourse with Robert Barton, and at once said, 'then it is not the man I mean.' Chicheeli, however, declined to be shaken from his statement, and repeated that the marks on his face were slight, but that there was no doubt that he had had smallpox. Opening my portmanteau, I took out a cabinet-sized photograph and a magnifier, and, examining the face closely, I then perceived that what I had for two years taken to be roughness of skin was really the marks of smallpox, which Chicheeli had noticed as he stood over the dead body.

myself, and as the 90th pulled over the 13th Leet wrenched his knee out of joint, and I had told him to remain in camp on the 27th. This, however, he did not do, and as he could only hobble, he tried, and successfully, to ride down the mountain. I believe he got down before the counter attack; but while on the lower plateau, and being followed up closely by the enemy, he showed distinguished courage in going back to help a dismounted officer, for which he received the Victoria Cross.

On the night of the 28th March, as I sat at dinner, I could not keep my mind off Ronald Campbell, who had sat opposite me for three months, and had anticipated every want with the utmost devotion, and I cannot write now, even after the lapse of a quarter of a century, without pain of the loss the army sustained when my friend fell. As I visited the outposts at least

---

Chicheeli told me that on the Ityenteka Nek he followed several white men and killed them, one man, as he approached, turning his carbine and shooting himself. When he, with several others, got down on the plain, seven miles from the mountain, he overtook Captain Barton, who had taken Lieutenant Poole up on his horse. He fired at them, and when the horse, being exhausted, could no longer struggle under the double weight, the riders dismounted and separated. Chicheeli first shot Lieutenant Poole, and was going up towards Barton, when the latter pulled the trigger of his revolver, which did not go off. Chicheeli then put down his gun and assegai, and made signs to Barton to surrender. I asked, 'Did you really want to spare him?' 'Yes,' he replied; 'Cetewayo had ordered us to bring one or two Indunas down to Ulundi, and I had already killed seven men.' Barton lifted his hat, and the men were close together when a Zulu fired at him, and he fell mortally wounded; and then, said Chicheeli, 'I could not let anyone else kill him, so I ran up and assegaied him.' I said, 'Do you think you can find the body?' 'Yes, certainly,' he said; 'but you must lend me a horse, for it is a day and a half' – equal to 60 miles. I sent Trooper Brown, VC with him next day, and, with the marvellous instinct of a savage, he rode to within 300 yards of the spot where fourteen months previously he had killed my friend, and then said, 'Now we can off-saddle, for we are close to the spot,' and, casting round like a harrier, came in less than five minutes upon Barton's body, which had apparently never been disturbed by any beast or bird of prey. The clothes and boots were rotten and ant-eaten, and tumbled to pieces on being touched. Brown cut off some buttons from the breeches, and took a squadron pay book from the pocket filled with Barton's writing, and then buried the remains, placing over them a small wooden cross painted black, on which is cut 'Robert Barton, killed in action, 28th March 1879,' and then he and Chicheeli buried the body of Lieutenant Poole.

twice every night from the date of Isandwhana till after Ulundi, 4th July, my clothes were nearly always damp from walking through the long grass, which, when not wet from the heavy rain which fell constantly through the months of February and March, was soaked with dew, and I had forbidden either of the staff accompanying me, because, as we slept in our boots and clothes, anyone who walked round the sentries got saturated up to the waistbelt. I had, however, once or twice suspected that I was being followed, and one night, turning suddenly in the darkness, I knocked against a man, and then recognised Campbell's voice, as he answered my challenge. I said sharply, 'Why are you disobeying orders? What are you doing here?' 'I have always the fear, sir,' he replied, 'that one night you won't hear the challenge of one of the sentries, and you will be shot.' On two occasions on which I was in bed with fever for three days, he nursed me as tenderly as could a woman, and I never saw anyone play a more heroic part than he did on the morning of the 28th March 1879.

I went round the sentries twice during the night, although I did not anticipate an attack until daylight, feeling sure the large masses of Zulus I had seen could not make a combined movement in the dark. When the night was past, the mist was so thick that we could not see more than a hundred yards. Captain Maude, who had temporarily replaced Ronald Campbell, asked me if the wood-cutting party of two companies was to go out as usual. Our practice was that they should not start till the front was reported clear for 10 miles, but until the sun came out there was no chance of the mist clearing off, and after thinking over the matter I decided the party should go, because we had never been able to get up reserve of fuel, and it was possible the Zulus might not attack that day. Our men would certainly fight better in two or three days' time if they had cooked food, and so I accepted the risk, but ordered two subalterns to keep ponies saddled to recall the companies in good time. Fortunately, though five miles away, the place was behind the camp.

All the mounted men had been continuously in the saddle since daylight on the 23rd, and it was difficult to get a trot out of the horses;[1] but Commandant Raaf went out with 20 men to the edge of the Zunguin plateau, and when the mist lifted, about 10 a.m., reported the Zulu Army was cooking on the Umvolosi and a tributary stream.[2] He remained out himself to warn me when they advanced.

All our arrangements in camp were perfected, with the exception of the barricade, to which we had added some strengthening pieces.

The Dutchmen came to see me early in the day, to say that, as Piet Uys was dead they wished to go home, and, except half a dozen who had hired waggons to us, they departed. Great pressure had been brought on my gallant friend Piet to induce him to withdraw from the column. His friends told him he was a traitor to their cause, but Uys always replied that although he disliked our policy, he thought it was the duty of a white man to stand up with those who were fighting the Zulus.[3]

Between 80 and 100 of Uhamu's men, who held on to the cattle they had driven from the Inhlobane, were overtaken and killed near the Zunguin Mountain on the 28th, but in the battalion which had gone out with Colonel Buller there were very few casualties. Nevertheless, Zulu-like after a reverse, the two battalions of Wood's Irregulars, about 2,000 strong, dispersed.

I spent the forenoon, after saying good-bye to the Uys detachment, in writing a report on the previous day's reconnaissance, and letters to the bereaved relatives of those who had fallen.

At 11 o'clock Raaf reported that the Zulu Army was advancing, and I sent the officers to recall the wood-cutting parties, and had all the Trek oxen driven in, except about 200 which had strayed away from the drivers, whose duty it was to herd them. We got the two companies back in time for the men

[1] One of my ponies had carried me 94 miles in fifty-four hours, without corn, getting only the grass he could find when knee-haltered.
[2] Where Vryheid now stands.
[3] When in December 1878 I was endeavouring to get Dutchmen to join, some queried my impartiality as arbitrator in deciding claims for captured cattle – the South African form of prize money – and I rejoined, 'I'll not take any for my personal use.' I gave my share towards erecting a memorial to Piet Uys in Utrecht and all the soldiers of the column contributed.

to have a hasty dinner before the attack actually began. The commanding officers asked if the battalions might not be told to hurry their dinners, but I said, 'No; there is plenty of time', for by the system enforced in the column during daylight, as Lord Chelmsford saw five weeks later, our tents could be struck, and the men be in position in the laager, within seventy seconds from the last sound of the 'Alert'.

At 1.30 p.m. Colonel Buller suggested he should go out and harry the Zulus into a premature attack, and this he did admirably.

We had shifted camp several times for sanitary reasons. My friends the Dutchmen could never be persuaded to use the latrines, although I had one dug specially for them; moreover, Wood's Irregulars and the oxen had so fouled the ground as to induce fever, unless the camp was often shifted. The position in which we received the attack was on a ridge running in a southwesterly direction, an under feature of the Ngaba-ka-Hwane Mountain.

The waggons of the 13th Light Infantry formed the right front and flank, four guns were in front of the centre, and the 90th Light Infantry on the left. The Horse lines were in the middle, and the rear face of the laager was held by the Irregular Horse; 280 yards in front, on ground 20 feet higher than the laager, was a redoubt, its main lines of fire being in a northerly and southerly direction, while 150 yards to the right front of the main laager was a cattle laager, into which we crammed upwards of 2,000 oxen. The outer side of it stood on the edge of a deep ravine, into which the laager drained. The wheels of the waggons were securely chained together, and the space between the forepart of one and the rear of the other was rendered difficult of ingress by the poles (or dyssel-booms), being lashed across the intervals.

Two guns under Lieutenant Nicholson were placed *en bar-bette*,[1] at the front end of the redoubt. The other four guns came into action under Lieutenant A. Bigge[2] and Lieutenant Slade,[3] by sections on the ridge, connecting the redoubt with

---

[1] Gun placed on raised ground, thus firing over the parapet.
[2] Now Colonel Sir Arthur Bigge, KCB.
[3] General F. Slade, CB, lately Inspector-General, Royal Artillery.

the main laager. The men belonged to garrison companies, but I have never known a battery so exceptionally fortunate in its subalterns. Lieutenant Nicholson, standing on the gun platform, fought his guns with the unmoved stoical courage habitual to his nature.

Major Tremlett was renowned as a fearless sportsman, and both Bigge and Slade were unsurpassable; they with their gunners stood up in the open from 1.30 p.m. till the Zulus retreated at 5.30 p.m., and by utilising the ridge were enabled to find excellent targets with cover during the first attack on the southern slope, and later on the northern slope, and suffered but little loss.

The direction of the Zulu advance was, speaking generally, from south-east, but when they came in sight they stretched over the horizon from north-east to south-west, covering all approaches from the Inhlobane to Bemba's Kop. When still three miles distant, 5,000 men moved round to our left and attacked the side held by the 90th Light Infantry, prior to the remainder of the Zulu Army coming into action. This fortunate circumstance was due to Colonel Buller's skilful tactical handling of the mounted men, whom he took out and dismounted half a mile from the Zulus. The Umbonambi regiment suffered a galling fire for some time, and then, losing patience, rushed forward to attack, when the horsemen, remounting, retired 400 yards, and, repeating their tactics, eventually brought on a determined attack from the Zulu right flank. The Umbonambi followed up the horsemen until they were within 300 yards of the laager, when their further advance was checked by the accurate firing of the 90th Light Infantry, greatly assisted by the enfilading fire poured in from the northern face of the redoubt. I saw a fine tall chief running on well in front of his men, until, hit in the leg, he fell to the ground. Two men endeavoured to help him back as he limped on one foot. One was immediately shot, but was replaced by another, and eventually all three were killed.

We now sent the Artillery horses back into the laager, keeping the guns in the open, on the ridge between the redoubt and the main laager. I had instructed the officer commanding to serve his guns till the last moment, and then, if necessary, leaving them in the open, take his men back to the laager, which was within 188 yards.

The attack on our left had so slackened as to give me no further anxiety, when at 2.15 p.m. heavy masses attacked our right front and right rear, having passed under cover up the deep ravine, on the edge of which the cattle laager stood.

Some 40 Zulus, using Martini-Henry rifles which they had taken at Isandwhlana, occupied ground between the edge of the ravine and the rear of the laager, from the fire of which they were partly covered by the refuse from the Horse lines which had been there deposited, for, with the extraordinary fertility of South Africa, induced by copious rains and burning midday sun, a patch of mealies four feet high afforded cover to men lying down, and it was from thence that our serious losses occurred somewhat later. The Zulu fire induced me to withdraw a company of the 13th, posted at the right rear of the cattle laager, although the front was held by another half company for some time longer.

I could see from where I stood on the ridge of land just outside the fort, leaning against the barricade, which reached down to the cattle laager, that there were large bodies in the ravine, the Ngobamakosi in front, and 30 men (leaders) showed over the edge, endeavouring to encourage the regiment to leave the shelter, and charge. I, in consequence, sent Captain Maude to order out two companies of the 90th, under Major Hackett, with instructions to double over the slope down to the ravine with fixed bayonets, and to fall back at once when they had driven the Zulus below the crest.

A 13th man coming away late from the cattle laager, not having heard the order to retire, was shot by the Zulus lying in the refuse heap, and followed by four from the cattle laager. I was running out to pick him up, when Captain Maude exclaimed, 'Really it isn't your place to pick up single men,' and went out himself, followed by Lieutenants Lysons and Smith, 90th Light Infantry; they were bringing the man in, who was shot in the leg, when, as they were raising the stretcher, Smith was shot through the arm. I was firing at the time at a leader of the Ngobamakosi, who, with a red flag, was urging

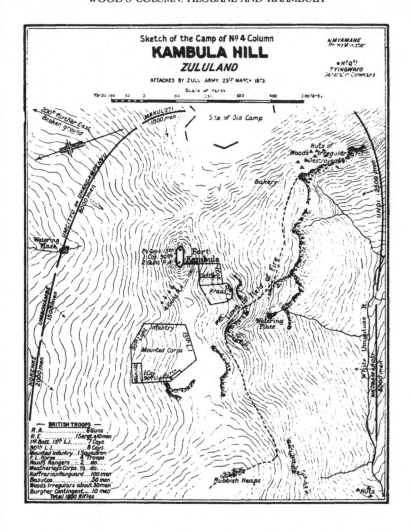

Sketch of the Camp of Nº 4 Column
# KAMBULA HILL
### ZULULAND
ATTACKED BY ZULU ARMY 23ᴿᴰ MARCH 1879.

his comrades to come up out of the ravine, and assault the laager. Private Fowler, one of my personal escort, who was lying in the ditch of the fort, had asked me, 'Would you kindly take a shot at that chief, sir? It's a quarter of an hour I am shooting him, and cannot hit him at all.' He handed me his Swinburne-Henry carbine, and looking at the sight, which was at 250 yards, I threw the rifle into my shoulder, and as I pressed it into the hollow, the barrel being very hot, I pulled the trigger before I was ready – indeed, as I was bringing up the muzzle from the Zulu's feet. Hit in the pit of the stomach, he fell over backwards: another leader at once took his place, cheering his comrades on. At him I was obliged to fire, unpleasantly close to the line of our officers leading the counter attack. I saw the bullet strike some few yards over the man's shoulder, and, laying the carbine next time at the Zulu's feet, the bullet struck him on the breast-bone. As he reeled lifeless backward, another leader seized and waved the flag, but he knelt only, though he continued to cheer. The fourth shot struck the ground just over his shoulder, and then, thinking the carbine was over-sighted,[1] I aimed on the ground two yards short, and the fifth bullet struck him on the chest in the same place as his predecessor had been hit.

This and the counter attack so damped the ardour of the leaders that no further attempt was made in that direction, although several brave charges were made to the south of the cattle laager, against the right flank of the redoubt. While I was firing at the leaders of the Ngobamakosi Regiment, who, from the ground falling away towards the ravine, were out of sight of the main laager, the two companies 90th Light Infantry came out at a steady 'Double,' Major Hackett leading, guided by Captain Woodgate, who knew exactly where I wished the companies to go, and how far the offensive movement was to be carried out. Lieutenant Strong, who had recently joined us, ran well in front of his company, sword in hand, and the Zulus retired into the ravine. The companies, however, were fired on heavily from the refuse heaps, at 350 yards range, and Major Hackett was shot through the head; Arthur Bright fell mortally wounded, and the colour-sergeant of Bright's company, Allen,

[1] We paced it afterwards – 195 yards.

a clever young man, not twenty-three years of age, who had been wounded in the first attack, and, having had his arm dressed, rejoined his company as it charged, was killed.

The Umcityu and Unkandampenvu had charged so determinedly over the open on our left front, as had part of the Ngobamakosi up the slope to the redoubt, from the south side of the cattle laager, that I did not at first realise the full effect of Hackett's counter attack, and apprehended the mass still crouching below the crest would rush the right face of the laager. They would have had some 200 yards to pass over from the edge of the ravine to the waggons, but, owing to the ground falling rapidly, would have been under fire from the laager for 100 yards only. I therefore went into the main laager, being met by Colonel Buller, who asked me cheerily for what I had come, and I replied, 'Because I think you are just going to have a rough and tumble'; but Hackett's charge had done even more than I had hoped, and having looked round I went back to my position just outside the fort.

At 5.30 p.m., when the vigour of the attack was lessening, I sent Captain Thurlow and Waddy's companies of the 13th Light Infantry to the right rear of the cattle laager, to turn out some Zulus who were amongst the oxen, which they had however, been unable to remove; and I took Captain Laye's[1] company to the edge of the krantz on the right front of the laager, where they did great execution with the bayonet amongst the Undi Regiment, who were now falling back. I then sent a note to Buller, asking him to take out the mounted men, which he did, pursuing from 5.30 p.m. till dark, and killing, as it happened, chiefly the Makulusi tribe, who had been his foes on the previous day.

When the enemy fell back in the direction in which they had come, they were so thick as to blot out all signs of grass on the hillside, which was covered by their black bodies, and for perhaps the only time in anyone's experience it was sound to say, 'Don't wait to aim, fire into the black of them.'

At 3 a.m. on the 30th, one or two shots from the outpost line roused the camp, and the Colonial corps opened a rapid fire to the front, immediately over the heads of the two line

[1] Now General Laye, CB.

191

battalions and artillery, who stood perfectly steady. Rain was falling, so, while Maude was ascertaining the cause of the firing, which was a Zulu who, having concealed himself till then, jumped up close to one of our sentries, I sat in an ambulance near the battery until the Colonials having put three bullets into the top of it, I thought it would be better to get wet than be shot by our own men. After five minutes the firing was stopped. The scare was excusable, for the nerves of the mounted men had been highly strung for some hours, a fourth of those who had ridden up the Inhlobane having been killed.

In the next few days we buried 785 men within 300 yards of our laager, which we were afterwards obliged to shift on account of the number of bodies which lay unseen in the hollows. We learnt after the battle that when the Zulus saw our tents go down they thought it was in preparation for flight, and that unsteadied their right wing.[1] They never fought again with the same vigour and determination.

The Line battalions were very steady, expending in four hours on an average 33 rounds a man; though that evening I heard that some of them had thought the possibility of resisting such overwhelming numbers of brave savages, 13 or 14 to one man, was more than doubtful. I had no doubt, and lost all sense of personal danger, except momentarily, when, as on five occasions, a plank of the hoarding on which I leant was struck. This jarred my head, and reminded me that the Zulus firing from the refuse heap in the right rear of the laager were fair shots. A few had been employed as hunters, and understood the use of the Martini rifles taken at Isandwhana.

Besides the men killed, we had 70 wounded, and amongst them my friend Robert Hackett. Born in King's County, Ireland, he was one of several soldier brothers. He was decidedly old-fashioned, and I have now before me an indignant letter, written four years before his terrible wound, urging me to use my influence to stop what he regarded as the craze for examining officers like himself, nearly forty years of age. He pointed out

[1] Zulu chiefs told me in 1880, when they saw our tents struck at 1.15 p.m., they made certain of victory, believing we were about to retreat, and they were greatly depressed by our stubborn resistance.

the injustice of expecting old dogs to learn these new tricks, and argued that as he had bought his commission without any liability to be examined for promotion, it was unjust to exact any such test from him now; and added that, as no staff appointment would tempt him to leave the battalion, and it was generally admitted that he was efficient in all regimental duties, all he wanted was to be left alone, and not troubled with books.

He was, indeed, a good regimental officer; he managed the mess, the canteen, and the sports club, and, indeed, was a pillar of the regiment. He kept a horse, but seldom, or never, rode, putting it generally at the disposal of the subaltern of his company. He played no games, and lived for nothing but the welfare of the men of his company, and the reputation of the regiment.

At Aldershot, in 1873, he gave me a lesson which I have never forgotten. I was senior major, being in temporary command of the regiment, and spoke to him about three young officers who did not pay their mess bills when due, and when the delay recurred the third time, I said, 'Unless these bills are paid to-morrow morning, you will put the three officers under arrest.' The commanding officer being away, I was in the orderly-room when he reported, 'The bills you spoke of have been paid, sir.' 'You see,' I remarked, 'it only required a little firmness on our part to get the Queen's Regulations obeyed.' He saluted, but said nothing, and when I saw him in the afternoon I said, 'Hackett, I do not quite understand your reticence. Why don't you help me in making these young officers pay their bills by the proper time? Why do they delay?' 'Oh, it's not wilful, sir,' he replied – 'only impecuniosity.' 'Oh, that can't be the case,' I argued, 'because when they had to pay, they paid.' He only answered 'Yes'; but something in his tone made me say, 'If you are right, can you explain how they got the money at such short notice?' 'That's quite simple, sir,' he answered; 'I paid the bills myself.' After this I thought less of the effect of my firmness!

When I visited him in the hospital the morning after the action, he was a piteous sight, for a bullet had passed from one temple to another, and, without actually hitting the eyes, had protruded the eyeballs, injuring the brain. He was unconscious of the terrible nature of his wounds, possibly from pressure on the brain, and observed to me, 'Your Commissariat officers are very stingy in not lighting up this hospital tent; the place is in absolute darkness.' We were all so fond of him that nobody ventured to tell him the truth, and it was not until he was in Maritzburg that the doctors begged a lady, who was a constant visitor at the hospital, to break the news to him.

When we received, on the 4th January 1879, the Gazette of the Promotions and Honours for the suppression of the Gaika outbreak, I addressed the military secretary as follows: 'Lord Chelmsford writes to me a kind letter about the omission of my name when honours were being served out, but I am not likely to trouble you on my own account, especially as one commanding officer rewarded has never been within 500 miles of bloodshed, but I confess Brevet Major Hackett might have attracted your, or His Royal Highness', favourable eye. A man of long service, old enough to be father of the junior captains, he has, I believe, been for many years the bed-rock of the 90th Light Infantry. An excellent regimental officer, ever ready to counsel or aid those of his brothers whose follies, or scanty purses, brought them into trouble. He has successfully neutralised the bad points of two commanding officers.'

When in the hospital at the close of the action, I did not speak to Arthur Bright, who was dozing, but after we had had something to eat I sent Maude over to see how he was going on. Maude came back saying that he was sensible, but very depressed, although the doctors said a bullet which had passed through his thigh had not touched any artery or bone. The two doctors had more than they could do, and may therefore be readily excused for not having noticed that the other thigh bone had been shattered; and Bright died, happily without pain, before morning. Over six feet in height, and very handsome, he exercised, through his high moral tone, great influence amongst the subalterns. He had been captain of a boat at Eton, was our boldest and best polo player, and was a gifted draughtsman, possessing also a beautiful tenor voice. He had only fifteen months' service when he took command of the company of which Maude was the captain. This company had been unfortunate, for Stevens, its captain, was dangerously wounded on the 30th April 1878, when Saltmarshe was killed; and now, in one day it had lost its only duty officer, Bright, and the gallant Colour-Sergeant Allen.

For two or three days after our victory I had some anxiety on account of our convoy of wounded men, which Buller escorted to the Blood River. My battalion was unfortunate, for, in addition to the two officers of the 90th whom we buried, we sent away three wounded in the convoy. I was obliged to keep Maude to help me, in spite of his company being without an officer.

Lieutenant Smith, whose arm was badly hit, was invalided to England. After seeing his family, he went to stay with Lady Wood, and, while he was giving his account of the fight in the drawing-room, his soldier servant was telling my wife's servants about it in the kitchen; and, alluding to the time when I walked across the open to the laager, he said, 'We saw three Zulus following him, and we knew he couldn't hear 'em, so we turned our faces away that we might not see him assegaied!' 'Ah,' the cook said, with deep emotion, 'that would have been a sad day for his wife and children!' when the soldier observed cheerfully, 'Oh, we weren't thinking of them, or of him either, for the matter of that, but what would have become of *us* if 'e'd been killed?'

I heard from Lord Chelmsford, who said he observed in my official report of my attack on the Inhlobane that I had made no reference to his having induced it; and, while thanking him for his generosity, I replied that I considered I was bound to help him, and that the operation I undertook was, moreover, feasible, and would have been carried out without any serious loss except for the coincidence of the approach of the Zulu main army.

*30th March.* Although nearly all of Wood's Irregulars had deserted the previous evening, we still had the Zulus attached to the companies, as well as the drivers and foreloupers of the waggons, and, knowing it was hopeless to expect them to bring in, without reward, any Zulus as prisoners, I made it known I would give a 'stick' of tobacco for any wounded or unwounded Zulu who was brought into camp. During the fight it was difficult to spare wounded Zulus who could sit up, for, when I took out a company from the redoubt for a counter attack at

5.30, an officer shouted, 'Look out for that wounded Zulu behind you.' He fired immediately, killing a soldier who followed me. When all resistance was over, I was anxious, not only for the sake of humanity, but in order to make an accurate report, to ascertain what regiments had attacked us. So I instructed our men to bring me, if possible, a representative of every Zulu regiment engaged.

Next morning, 15 or 20 grand specimens of savage humanity stood in front of me, while the interpreter took down their names and the names of the officers commanding the regiment to which they belonged, and we learnt that the Zulu army had numbered over 23,000 men. When I had obtained all the information I required, I said, 'Before Isandwhlana, we treated all your wounded men in our hospital, but when you attacked our camp, your brethren, our black patients, rose and helped to kill those who had been attending on them. Can any of you advance any reason why I should not kill you?' One of the younger men, with an intelligent face, asked, 'May I speak?' 'Yes.' 'There is a very good reason why you should not kill us. We kill you because it is the custom of the black men, but it isn't the white men's custom!' So, putting them in charge of an officer and a couple of Colonel Buller's men, I had them sent past our Outposts, as far as the Zunguin mountain.

We got in a considerable number of wounded Zulus, and as our hospital establishment was not capable of dealing with our own cases, I was obliged to hand them over to their countrymen attached to the companies of infantry; and to ensure the wounded men being well treated, I promised our Zulus an ox to eat at the end of the week. There was, however, but little animosity when once the fight was over, because all the border Zulus were so intermarried that we had cases of men fighting in Cetewayo's regiments against brothers in Wood's Irregulars.

It is not often that the narratives of victors and vanquished agree, so it is interesting to note that the Governor of Natal, in reporting to the High Commissioner on the 21st April, wrote:

The whole of the Zulu border population have returned to their homes. In conversation with our Natives, they give accounts of the two days' fighting with Colonel Wood, which agree with the published accounts in every respect. The Zulu losses on the first day are stated to have been severe. The Europeans who fell selling their lives dearly.

I had heard many stories of the gallantry shown by Colonel Buller in the retreat from the western end of the Inhlobane, but I had some difficulty in arriving at anything definite, because he guarded closely all the mounted men from receiving orders except through him, and I knew from his character that he would repudiate the notion of having done anything more than his duty.

A few days after the fight he went out with a troop of the Frontier Light Horse to endeavour to find Captain Barton's body, but could not reach the spot, as he was opposed by Zulus in force, making a raid in the direction of Luneberg, carrying off cattle, and killing men, women, and children. While he was out I received written statements from Lieutenants D'Arcy and Everitt and trooper Rundall, whom he had rescued at the risk of his life, and their reports were verified by those of other officers who were present. This enabled me to put forward a strong recommendation that his name should be considered for the Victoria Cross. A day or two later, on his return from another raid, in which he had been unsuccessful, I said, as he was leaving the tent after making his report, 'I think you may be interested in something I have written,' and I handed him the letter-book. He was very tired, and observed somewhat ungraciously, 'Some nonsense, I suppose!' to which I replied, 'Yes, I think I have been rather eulogistic.' When he handed me back the book his face was a study.

*The battle of Khambula was to prove the decisive one of the campaign. The Zulus had gone into it with their high courage and an optimism born of victory at Isandlwana, but they had suffered terribly in the face of Wood's concentrated firepower. Despite Wood's careful show of clemency, the mounted pursuit, in particular, had been very severe. The irregulars were in no mood to be merciful after their experience at Hlobane. Perhaps as many as 2,000 warriors had died in all, and as the army*

197

*streamed back towards Hlobane, sheltered by the falling night, all semblance of order collapsed. They refused the urging of their leaders to return to Ulundi, and most simply drifted back to their homes.*

*They would not take to the field in the same spirit again.*

*For the British, there was a curious postscript to Hlobane. The story is told in the Hon Gerald French's* Lord Chelmsford And The Zulu War *(1939):*

On April 15th a Frenchman named Grandier, belonging to the Border House, who was believed to have perished with Colonel Weatherley on March 28th, appeared in the camp at Kambula dressed in an old corduroy coat much slashed with assegai cuts, a pair of old regimental trousers cut off at the knees, and wrappings of cloth on his feet.

He had an extraordinary story to tell. Indeed, his experiences as related by him to Colonel Wood might well have provided material for one of Rider Haggard's thrilling novels.

His statement was as follows:

'On the 28th March, we were descending the Hlobane, when we met a large force of Zulus about the place where we had met Colonel Wood in the morning. We fell back, Colonel Weatherley giving orders to fire volleys. We crossed the Ityenka Nek, being assailed on all sides by the enemy. The horses were much exhausted. I was nearly the last and had put a comrade on my horse, I running alongside, when a Zulu caught hold of me by the leg. They did not attempt to assegai me, but took me to Umbeline's kraal which is on the south side of the Hlobane and about half-way up. Umbeline asked where Shepstone was and who was the leader of this commando. I was kept tied to a tree during the night.

'The next day Umbeline with two or three followers took me into the middle of a large impi, who threatened to kill me. Inzanane, a large stout man and a great chief, interfered and said he would send me to Cetywayo.

'I was taken back to the Hlobane and stopped there one more day and then was taken by four mounted men to Ulundi. I walked carrying their food. They had previously taken all my clothes except my hat. I tied a handkerchief round my middle, but a [Zulu] took it away. We were four days going, arriving on the evening of the fourth day. A messenger went forward to announce our arrival. I was left in the open, tied, till the next day. Then, about mid-day, I was taken before Cetywayo. Cetywayo is a very fat man, not tall, and walks with difficulty. Apparently about 40 years of age.

'A Dutch-speaking half-caste, black but with long hair, interpreted. There was also there a Portuguese making guns and lead for Cetywayo, and an English-speaking [Zulu] who also was able to read. I saw several newspapers. The [Zulu] was reading a paper.

'Cetywayo asked what the English wanted in coming to his country. He asked where Oham was, said he would kill him and Shepstone and everyone. He had plenty of men to do it. He asked the name of the commander of this column. Cetywayo showed me two cannons – they were both spiked – and asked me to put them in good order.

'The Portuguese stated that this was the only commando the Zulus feared.

'There were a large number of Martini Henrys lying about. I did not see any ammunition. I did not hear of any more Europeans being there, but I spoke frequently with the English-speaking Zulus and they appeared to know everything that was going on. There were about 160 men, which seemed as a personal guard to Cetywayo. I did not see any large numbers there.

'The king's kraal is surrounded by a double row of rough palisades, in a circular shape, there are no other fortifications. I was frequently beaten by the [Zulus], and only had mealies to eat.

'I was about ten days at Ulundi when messengers came in and reported Umbeline was killed as well as his brother, in the attack on the Kambula camp. I am certain this information is correct. Cetywayo on hearing this said he would send me to Umbeline's [men] to kill. On the 13th, early in the morning, I started under escort of two men, one armed with a muzzle-loading gun, both with assegais. About 12 mid-day we lay down, and the [Zulus] being rather sleepy, I snatched an assegai and killed the one with the gun. The other ran off.

'I travelled by night, and the next day I had to lie still a whole morning while there was a large impi passing. They were driving cattle towards Ulundi.

'I travelled each night and saw no one afterwards. Yesterday morning I was trying to see if I could recognise any of the hills, when I fell in with some of our people. The clothes I have I picked up on the way.

'I don't think the Zulus knew I was not an Englishman.'

*After a while, a number of contradictions became apparent in Grandier's story. It was true that King Cetshwayo had remonstrated with his commanders after Isandlwana, berating them for not having brought him an officer as a prisoner, whose hostage and intelligence value would have been considerable. Nevertheless, it was unlike the Zulus to spare anyone in the heat of battle, and it was soon being said that Grandier had in fact been found hiding amongst the rocks when the battle was over. And why should Cetshwayo have sent him back to Mbilini to be killed, when killings were hardly unknown occurrences at Ulundi? And if Grandier had escaped on the first morning of his return march, how had he found his way from the heart of Zululand without being detected? After the war, a number of Zulus were asked about the incident, and the traveller Bertram Mitford summed up their reactions:*

> *They said that a white man had been taken prisoner and brought to Ulundi; that Cetywayo had questioned him, and then sent him back under an escort, with orders that he should be let go near Hlobane, so that he could find his way to the English camp, but they knew nothing about the killing of the guard. Their statement agreed with that of other Zulus whom I interrogated in other parts of the country.*

*Grandier's story made him a hero, briefly, in the British press, but in fact Cetshwayo had probably realised that he was no use as a hostage and simply turned him loose. Nonetheless, Grandier had the distinction of being the only white man to have been taken as a prisoner of war by the Zulus throughout the war.*

CHAPTER FIVE

# THE SECOND INVASION

I N the immediate aftermath of Isandlwana, British garrisons
along the border huddled behind hastily erected defences
in daily expectation of Zulu attack. In fact, despite small
parties of warriors crossing to loot abandoned homesteads
– both black and white – no Zulu incursion took place, and
the tension gradually eased. With the arrival of reinforcements from home, the British were poised to renew the
offensive.

One of those who held the fort, quite literally, on the border
was Major Harcourt M. Bengough, 77th Regiment, commanding the 2nd Battalion 1st Natal Native Contingent. Bengough's
battalion had originally moved up to the Mzinyathi at Durnford's orders, but fell back on Helpmekaar when news of the
disaster reached them. On 24th January, Lord Chelmsford
ordered them to retire still further, to a spot near the magis-
tracy of Msinga, which commanded the road from the town of
Greytown to Helpmekaar. Here Bengough's battalion occupied and improved a stone redoubt which had been built on
a knoll beside the road, and which came to be known, in due
course, as Fort Bengough. Bengough's account of his experiences with the NNC, published in *Memories Of A Soldier's Life*
(1913), are of particular interest since, unlike Hamilton-
Browne, Bengough was a natural linguist, and took a keen
interest in both the culture and military potential of his men.
He understood something of their natural qualities, and how
they might best have been exploited.

*

It was now that I had the first real opportunity of studying the characteristics and the manners and customs of the interesting race of which my soldiers were composed.

And first as to the number of desertions. I found that most of the men after visiting their kraals returned and rejoined the ranks as if nothing had happened, so that it became impossible to punish them. The deserters were, however, generally hooted on their return.

With the recollection of the disaster at Isandhlwana fresh in their memories, it did not seem likely that they would be very reliable to stem the Zulu inroad over the border, and so to give them confidence in themselves and to find employment for them, I planned the outline of a small fort or redoubt for about a thousand men. The men took up the idea readily, and with the aid of two crowbars and a few spades and pickaxes the work was soon done. Our redoubt was composed of a plumb wall some six feet high, and between three or four feet thick, and with two flanking bastions in the centre of the fort. Alarm posts were assigned to each company. On the completion of the fort I took our chief Zulu to see it. He asked me, 'What is this for?' I said, 'This is a fort; if the Zulus from over the river attack us here, we go into the fort and shoot them down.' The old chief shook his head, looking very knowing, and said, 'No, you don't think that we are going to be caught here, like rats in a trap! Why, how are we going to run away?'

I may add that they afterwards began to appreciate, at any rate, the value of loopholes.

It was not long after the completion of our fort that an alarm was given of an attack by the Zulus. A picquet was sent out, and some rather indiscriminate firing was begun; and as I was going round the defences, an over-zealous member of the garrison fired his rifle from between my legs and wounded one of the picquet.

On going round the posts in the fort it was impressive to hear the men sharpening their assegais. I noticed this to my interpreter, Kinsman, who replied, 'Yes, sir, they mean to fight!'

We all slept in the fort ready dressed to turn out, boots and all. This we did for several months, and I never, I think, slept more soundly. In the daytime I had plenty to do, being my own commissariat officer, quartermaster, and paymaster. I will not add 'and cook', for the culinary art is one in which I have always signally failed to achieve any success.

Our bread for the officers' mess was baked with sour dough in an underground oven, often in an ant-hill, a barrel being sunk longitudinally half-way in the ground, the top covered with mud, and the wooden staves being set on fire.

I need not say that we were all teetotallers, or add that the health of the troops was excellent. I found a decided increase in my weight.

I was much impressed with the calm courage with which the district magistrate maintained his position on the frontier, as did also the members of the Scotch and German missions. The latter mission station was sacked by the Zulus, but the Argyle Presbyterian School mission was untouched. The minister thereof paid us several welcome visits, when we sang together 'Hold the Fort', with a vigour, inspired perhaps not a little by the accident of our material position at the moment.

The stage at which we have arrived in my story may be appropriate for the consideration of the much-debated question of the fighting qualities of the Natal Zulu. It must be granted, I think, that the fighting qualities of a body of men is not necessarily dependent on the aggregate courage of the individuals composing that body, but is rather subject to some exterior controlling power, as discipline, or some strong moral lever, such as patriotism, confidence in their cause, or their numbers, or their weapons, or their discipline, or their commander, or their position, or all or any of these combined.

In almost all these latter requisites the Natal Zulus were lacking. Discipline they knew not even by name; and to patriotism, they were fighting under an alien race against their own kinsmen, whom they knew to be vastly superior in numbers, and of the military training of their new leaders they understood nothing; moreover, by placing a foreign weapon in their hands their trust in the national weapon, the assegai, was discounted. The only point making for superiority was their hatred of the Zulus of Zululand, by whom, indeed, they had been expelled from their country. But this was hardly sufficient to make them fit to fight side by side of trained soldiers.

Thus the proper sphere for the Zulu battalions was undoubtedly that of outpost duty – spies and scouts – thus pitting native against native. It was in this way that they were eventually utilised on the advance to Ulundi. An English soldier fresh from a barrack square is useless opposed to a wily native. They are easily stalked and stabbed. My men used to take post on hills two or three miles from the encampment. There was a difficulty in recognising them in the case of an attack, and a plan of lanterns to be lighted by the picquets on retiring was tried, though not altogether successfully.

During our stay in the fort the reorganisation and re-armament of the Natal Native Contingent was carried out.

The new arms were 300 Martini-Henri rifles and 200 Sniders. The use of the arms and the breech action were quickly learnt by our men, and rifle practice was regularly carried out, badges being given to marksmen, and figures of merit were awarded to the companies, and were keenly contested.

The back-sight was never quite understood, and was, I believe, considered by the men to possess some magic power.

The drill was simplified, fives being used in the place of fours, and each company had a distinguishing flag.

The social customs of the Zulus are quaint. In a marriage contract the bridegroom pays the dower to the bride's father, who thus practically sells his daughter. In Natal the free choice of a girl bride is secured by the presence of a Government witness. In Zululand, regiments are only permitted to marry by order of the king, so that husbands are generally over forty years old, and love matches are not common. The strict virtue of Zulu girls is remarkable. The national religion is somewhat vague. The Great Creator (Nkulukulu), a spirit existing by itself, forms a beautiful maiden out of mud and water and takes her to wife. They believe in the transmigration of souls, their ancestors being transformed into snakes, to whom they pray. Their idea of right and wrong is the fear of offending these.

The witch doctors are an important element in the national belief. A candidate for the divining power retires into the bush, where he lives for months on roots, frogs, snails, and the like, until he becomes gifted with the divining power, or divine inflatus, and is able to detect a criminal by the process known as 'smelling out'.

Example: It is apparently something like the principle of 'Magic Music'. Some cows die suddenly in a village.

| | |
|---|---|
| Umzibu dwells in this village. | 'We hear, we hear.' |
| He has many wives, sons, and daughters. | Do. |
| „ many mealies in store. | Do. |
| „ many cattle in his kraal. | Do. |
| „ suffered a loss. | Do. |
| He has not lost a wife or child. | 'We hear, we hear.' |
| „ not lost any mealies. | Do. |
| Some of his cows have died. | Loud music. |
| Umzibu has enemies. | Do. |
| His cows have been bewitched. | Do. |
| His enemies are not of this kraal. | Do. |
| He has an enemy in Nolwengo kraal. | Do. |
| He is a relation (a shot in the dark). | Low music. |
| He is not a relation, but professes to be a friend. | Loud music. |
| His name is So-and-so. | |

The case is then reported to the king, who generally sends an 'impi' to kill the man and seize his goods and cattle.

A curious example of the above occurred among my men. A man was taken on suspicion of being a witch doctor one night, and Kinsman, my interpreter, intervened, knowing the summary manner in which such cases are generally settled. Suddenly a sort of wild cat appeared between the suspect's feet. There was a cry of 'There is his familiar.' The cat was killed, and I have the skin. The man somewhat mysteriously disappeared. It appeared afterwards that he had been suspected of stealing wood.

Though we certainly had not a very enlivening experience of life in our fort, yet I cannot remember that we found time hang very heavily on our hands. Our military exercises and rifle practice provided us with a certain amount of occupation, and there was always the possibility of a raid across the frontier by the Zulus, not unnaturally elated by their recent successes. There was some varied shooting also to be had by those who had a taste for sport, and did not mind working a bit for it.

I call to mind an incident that occurred to me when out shooting, which, though a small matter in itself, was not without significance to me in my then position.

The commander of an irregular force must trust to the personal opinion in which he is held by those under his command, rather than to the written or printed form of words appointing him to hold office, and this personal opinion is not seldom an intangible feeling, based upon apparently frail foundations. Hence the value, such as it is, of the following incident.

I was strolling about the country, mounted, one day in company with one of my officers, both of us carrying rifles, when one of the many sorts of African antelope got up in front of my horse and commenced quietly cantering away. More in the spirit of sport than otherwise, I checked my horse, threw up my rifle, and fired a chance shot. Much to my own surprise as well as to that of my companion, and no doubt to that of the antelope, the latter fell, shot through the back. 'Good shot, Major,' said my companion. 'A jolly fluke,' said I; but my reputation as a sportsman and rifle-shot was established, and I was careful to maintain it by not doing much rifle-shooting in public after that day.

*Meanwhile, Chelmsford's reinforcements were steadily arriving at Durban. Among them was Major Bindon Blood, RE, whose views on Zulu history we met in the first chapter. Blood's reaction on hearing the news of Isandlwana was typical of many officers in the UK: he immediately volunteered his services. The transports were crammed with staff officers en route to take up their new posts, and Blood found himself sharing the voyage with Major-General F. Marshall, who was to command a new cavalry brigade, and Colonel D. C. Drury-Lowe, commanding the 17th Lancers. He begins his story when he reports to the War Office:*

I went to the War Office by the next train to see our DAG about it. When I appeared he told me I was already in orders for Zululand with my company of the Royal Engineers, and that I was to move to Aldershot with it at once to mobilise, which I did in due course.

We were brought up to war strength very quickly and satisfactorily by the transfer to us of men from other companies of the corps, who, as it was 'all in the family', gave us of their best, so that we started – officers and men – a truly united and efficient lot, every man determined to do his best. I have before me a longish official letter addressed after the end of the campaign to the officer then in command of the company, and setting forth the authorities' strong approval of the company and of its work during the operations. So that our confident hopes at starting were – if I may put it so – justified as usual.

But the mobilisation of the rest of the force that went to Zululand in 1879, the infantry especially, was not so satisfactory. The battalions all required large drafts to bring them up to war strength, and in this case the drafts were provided by transfers from other corps, which were already short of trained men and could not part with them. Thus it came about that our battalions landed in Zululand full of incompletely trained men, a great proportion of whom had never fired a round of ball cartridge, while many had never fired a round of blank, before they embarked. I put it thus because great trouble was taken on the voyage in the instruction of the recruits on board the transports, so that in the harbour at St Vincent for instance, where our ship anchored for about twenty-four hours, the bullets were frequently heard singing somewhat unduly near our ears! And the same thing happened also at Simon's Bay, where, owing to bungling about coal, we wasted nearly a week.

Our ship, and I believe most if not all of those carrying men and horses, were despatched remarkably quickly from England, but with such short supplies of coal that many days were wasted in coaling them on the voyage, at St Vincent and Simon's Bay. In the case of our ship, according to our skipper, if twelve hours extra had been spent in coaling at Portsmouth before our start, we should have saved one day at St Vincent and nearly six at Simon's Bay, which we spent over coaling on the outward voyage; or nearly six days 'net' in time, besides considerable extra cost of coal. And moreover, the extra twelve hours at Portsmouth could have provided coal for our ship's return voyage, thus saving another considerable sum of money on account of time and cost of coal. I believe that much the same thing happened to many or most of the transports in this expedition.

At St Vincent we and our horses were inspected by the general commanding the cavalry of the expedition, a man universally liked and believed in, but without experience of active service. I had a slight acquaintance with him and he invited me to go with him to see some of the other transports lying in the harbour that were carrying mounted troops. The first ship we came to had on board the headquarters and several troops of the famous 'Death or Glory Boys', many of whom I knew. Just before this regiment had embarked, an unfortunate accident happened to their newly-appointed commanding officer – a fine soldier – which prevented his embarking, and so the previous colonel was brought back *pro tem*. He was a first-class man, being soon afterwards promoted to major-general, and he was also a bit of a character. Now in those days on embarking with troops we used to be served out – I think gratis – with a suit of 'sea kit,' coat and trousers, of stout naval serge, and a knitted cap, the same for all ranks. So when our cavalry general and I with his staff, boarded the nearest transport, we saw a smallish man in sea kit hurrying up to us, who saluted the General. The General shook hands with him and said, 'Why—, I quite thought you were one of the men!' 'So I am, Sir – so I am!' replied the Colonel. When the General said, 'Just the right answer, my dear—, to my stupid remark!' – very neat on both sides, as we thought!

At last we arrived at Durban and disembarked, with our 60 or 70 horses alive, but quite unfit for anything but rest and careful exercising during the next fortnight or more. We managed to get some mules and country horses locally, and started for our division, which was encamped at the mouth of the Tugela, about 60 miles to the north of Durban.

I was left at Durban to arrange for materials for a bridge over the Tugela near our divisional camp. This took several days, during which the King's Dragoon Guards and 17th Lancers arrived, dressed for the campaign in their tunics and booted overalls and gold lace all complete, except that Sam

Browne sword-belts had been imposed upon the officers, making them feel, as an old friend in the 17th said to me, 'Like a lot of damned tenors in an opera!'

At this time the Prince Imperial arrived, and I was presented to him. He had a charming manner, was very well informed and most promising as a soldier. He was also greatly interested in India, and I had several pleasant conversations with him about that country.

Durban in 1879 was a pretty little place consisting of a square and two or three streets near the sea, with some picturesque houses and country roads on the Berea, a ridge running along a mile or so from the sea and parallel to it. It was said to be hot in the summer, something like Bombay, but in the end of February and beginning of March we did not find it unpleasant. I was of course in camp with my company until it left, and then I stayed in a hotel where I was all right and enjoyed meeting many interesting and pleasant people.

As soon as I had finished the special work for which I had stayed behind at Durban, I started off at daylight one morning on horse-back, with my soldier groom on another horse leading a third which carried our kit; intending to get to our division on the second day, doing about 45 miles the first day and 15 or so on the second. It was a pleasant ride on an unmetalled track, through cultivated country and scattered trees. We crossed several shallow rivers with clear rapid streams and we rode through some picturesque villages with cottages covered by flowering creepers and gardens full of flowers. I specially remember one near Durban that was called by the famous name of Verulam.

We found an inn with breakfast at a suitable hour, and sat down to good plain food at a long table presided over by our hostess, who had a favouring eye for a soldier and put me beside her! On my other side was a pretty girl who was one of a party of four, made up by another girl and two men, travelling in an American 'spider' with a team of four nice horses that had passed us on the road. So I had a pleasant breakfast and the young lady was so kind as to say she hoped to see me again later on at dinner.

Accordingly we saddled up and went on by a bridlepath –

a short cut – so that we did not see the spider party again until we halted in a good-sized village for dinner, at which I again found myself next to the same young lady, to whom of course I proceeded to make myself as agreeable as possible. All went well until it was time to part, and I began some nonsense in the way of good-bye, when I noticed that the man on the other side of the young lady seemed uneasy, and presently said something that I did not quite catch. I asked if he had addressed me, and he observed that he had, and that if he had me outside he would do something or other, I forget exactly what. So I said I should be very glad to oblige him in any way, and we adjourned outside. There it became clear that he wanted a round or two with fists, to which I was quite agreeable, and calling up my hefty sapper groom, I gave him my coat to hold, and was ready for my friend, who was a bit bigger than I was, but clumsy-looking. It turned out that he was a duffer with his fists, and that as long as I did not allow him to close, he was in my hands; so I did not hurt him, and the matter ended amicably in a few minutes. I was informed afterwards that my adversary had been doing time in jail for selling guns to the Zulus, that he was on his way home therefrom when I met him, and that the young lady I had been talking to was engaged to him.

Next day I arrived at the headquarters of the 1st Division, Zulu Field Force, of which I had been appointed Commanding Royal Engineer.

*With two heavy defeats inflicted on the Zulus at either end of the country within a few days of one another, at Khambula and Gingindlovu, Chelmsford felt able to take the initiative once more. It was very doubtful that the Zulu army retained the capacity to mount an offensive campaign, so Chelmsford could begin a new invasion at as much leisure as the logistical situation would permit. Rather than advance from several different points along the border, he was now planning just two major thrusts. The first, consisting chiefly of troops from the old right flank and Eshowe relief columns, was to advance up the coastal strip, suppressing any local resistance, and perhaps opening a supply route via the sea. The second, consisting largely of men drawn from the reinforcements, would start from the frontier hamlet of Dundee, and cross the border north of Rorke's Drift, skirting the melancholy field of Isandlwana, and effecting a junction with Evelyn Wood's column, which would move down from the north. Although administratively separate, these two columns would march in concert, and fight as one army. Together they would be strong enough to deliver a devastating blow to the Zulu heartland.*

*The coastal column was designated the 1st Division, the new column the 2nd Division, and Wood's old column was restyled the Flying Column. As usual, the question of supply proved nightmarishly difficult, and throughout April the respective commanders struggled desperately to accumulate sufficient transport equipment. Army agents travelled the country buying up civilian wagons, oxen, horses and mules at inflated prices, only to have them break down or die in droves from overwork of the diseases which thrived in the insanitary conditions of the over-crowded camps. For the 1st Division, indeed, the transport crisis soon proved to be the real enemy, and remained so until the end of the campaign. Under the command of Major-General H. H. Crealock, the 1st Division began to move forward towards the end of April, but its advance was painfully slow. Crealock planned to establish a series of strongly fortified posts at strategic points along his route, where he could stock-pile his supplies, leap-frogging forward between them. In the event the scheme literally bogged his advance down. Building the forts was time-consuming, and they and the cumbersome convoys tied down many of his troops in escort and garrison duties. It rained incessantly, and the stream of traffic soon destroyed the roads and churned up the river drifts beyond repair. Dead oxen littered the tracks, and men began to fall ill with disease. Crealock had orders to destroy a number of important amakhanda in the region, but there was little Zulu resistance to alleviate the boredom. Those Zulus who still had the will to resist had gone to Ulundi to join the king, whilst the remainder quietly surrendered as the juggernaut of the 1st Division rolled over them.*

*Life with the 1st Division was hardly fun, a monotonous round of hard work with little hope of glory, but the irrepress-*

*ible Bindon Blood still found humour in human nature, as well as time to reflect on the death of the Prince Imperial:*

Our General's health was not good, and he suffered from various disabilities which showed up during the time he commanded us, one of the worst being a painful ailment which frequently prevented his mounting a horse for days together! He was a very accomplished amateur artist, being particularly clever at depicting horses, dogs, deer and similar subjects.

I remember that one day I was with him when he was on a horse, seeing a lot of men, white and black, bathing, and that he perpetrated a fairly good joke. You must know, good reader, that the Zulus had a great opinion of the virtues of salt water when taken internally, but as this could not be comfortably managed by the mouth, it was arranged otherwise, by the interposition of a long bullock's horn through which the water was poured. The General on seeing many operations of this sort being performed on the Zulu bathers, on all fours in ridiculous poses, exclaimed – 'Behold! The Zulu horn is exalted!' He did an excellent sketch of the scene afterwards.

I remember that on this and other similar occasions I was much struck with the superiority of our men to the Zulus, and all other natives, in muscular and physical development generally. Owing to the eugenic and other special arrangements in Zululand, the Zulus were taller, better-looking and better made generally than the ordinary [blacks]; but even they did not compare well with our men in muscular development. All the black men were smooth-bodied, like women; whereas our men made a very fine show! This was curious, as in our illustrated papers and books we had been accustomed to see African natives, and especially Zulus, depicted as of Herculean proportions!

The last time I know of white soldiers being flogged (I carefully avoided *seeing* it) was during the time we spent at the mouth of the Tugela in 1879. One Sunday in the middle of the day we of the staff were all busy in our tents, when suddenly there was a tremendous hullabaloo and a rush of men through the camp, some tumbling over tent ropes and others pulling up the pegs and throwing tents down. On looking out I saw a large party of men, madly drunk, and making the disturbance, while an increasing number of others were trying to stop it, and to seize the disturbers. With our help and that of our soldier servants this was soon done; and we learnt that the delinquents were a party of the old 'Faugh-a-ballaghs', wild Connaught 'boys', who being on commissariat 'fatigue', were rashly entrusted with the conveying of kegs of rum from one place to another. In doing this they managed to annex and hide a keg, and so got blind drunk on the contents. They all were tried by drum-head court-martial and got a couple of dozen apiece well laid on, which I have no doubt did a lot of good to them and to others like them who had to see it.

We had a most interesting man attached to our staff as a guide and adviser, and, as we should have said in India, a 'Political Officer'. His name was John Dunn and he was the son of a retired Indian Navy officer, who had finished his life in South Africa, where he had come on retirement with his wife and family. John Dunn found his way to Zululand in Panda's time, soon established a character for honesty and trustworthiness, and lived among the Zulus for many years, farming and doing a sort of agency business for them, chiefly in connection with the sale of their cattle. One constantly heard the natives say, 'Jone Doon he good man – Jone Doon he honest man.' He was a friend to Ketchwayo and I am sure did his best to prevent the war; and when it broke out he joined us with his flocks and herds and followers, many of them ladies and children of various ages. He built a regular kraal a mile or so from our camp and we often went to have meals of sorts with him, when he used to give us excellent food, more or less à la Zulu.

In those days the Zulu young ladies before marriage wore nothing in the way of clothes – only belts of woven grass or leather round their waists, after marriage they indulged in petticoats! So one day I was at Dunn's kraal talking to one of his married ladies who knew some English, and remarked to her that a girl of about fifteen – her daughter as it turned out – was nice-looking. So she said, 'Yes – very good figure – you can crack a flea on her—,' not mentioning anything hard, like the thumbnail, as might have been expected! I was informed

213

afterwards that the expression used by the lady was quite usual among the Zulus, and I must say I thought it to the point.

Another day I was riding towards Dunn's kraal with a large escort behind me, when we met a party of Zulu women and girls carrying milk to a depot we had arranged for it, and among them was the young lady I have mentioned above. I had turned my escort off the road, and halted a moment to talk to the women, who were full of remarks, complimentary and otherwise, of which we understood some! Presently I noticed that the young lady had on a very smart waist-belt, and I offered to swop my sword-belt – an old gold-laced one with a silver-mounted clasp – for her belt. To my surprise she jumped at the deal, so I took off my belt (my sword was on my saddle) and gave it to her, when she slipped behind a bush, made the change, and came back with her belt in her hand ready for me. As she had nothing on her besides the belt and some bracelets with a piece of muslin like a sash round her neck, one did not see the necessity for the retirement behind the bush – however, custom ordered it, so there was no more to be said. The girl was wonderfully pleased with my belt; especially the 'slings', swinging against her legs, seemed to delight her. I still have her belt.

Of course the shocking affair of the death of the Prince Imperial was a dreadful blow to us all and to our pride in the service. I felt it specially, as I had been presented to the Prince at Durban and met him frequently there, liking very much what I saw of him.

The story of the disaster is simple. On the 1st June 1879, Lieutenant Carey of the 98th, attached to the QMG Department of the 2nd Division of Lord Chelmsford's army, was sent out to inspect the site for a new camp, with an escort of six mounted white men of Bettington's Horse and a [African] guide. The Prince Imperial obtained leave to accompany the party and went with them. At luncheon time the party halted near a village close to a small stream and off-saddled, meaning to halt for an hour. There was an open space close to the village, but high grass and crops were near and there was a deep ravine with jungle running down to the stream and forming an easy approach; and by this ravine a party of Zulus did approach, lay hid in the grass and waited for a good target. Meanwhile the reconnoitring party acted as if they were in Hyde Park, and took their ease without any precaution whatever. Presently the [African] guide while carrying water, put up one of the hostile ambuscade in the grass near the stream, who bolted and disappeared. But even this did not disturb the equanimity of our reconnoitring party. They saddled up at leisure, formed up and had 'prepared to mount,' when, as they doubtless gave the target waited for, the ambuscaders fired and hit nobody. But Carey and five of his men got on their horses and galloped off helter-skelter for some miles, losing one, who was shot directly after the start, deserting him as well as another whose horse broke away, and also the [African] guide and the Prince, whose horse was awkward to mount. The man whose horse had bolted was promptly killed, the [guide] also was surrounded and killed, while the Prince's horse knocked him down and broke away, the Prince being killed with assegais. The usual story was and is that 50 or 60 Zulus attacked the party, forty of them firing a volley at 20 yards; but I was told by John Dunn and others what was much more likely to be the truth, namely that the attackers were only nine at most in number, and that they were not all armed with fire-arms. It is inconceivable that 'a volley fired from forty rifles at a distance of twenty yards,'[1] at eight men and eight horses close together, even if fired by Zulus, should have missed them all.

Carey and his party apparently did not fire a shot, their carbines being unloaded when they were attacked, and the two officers' revolvers being doubtless carried, as is usual with us in our army, in a manner that rendered them useless at short notice. At all events Carey and the Prince appear not to have used their revolvers, with which, if they had kept their heads and could shoot, they could have easily held off the Zulus and defeated them ultimately, even if there had been a good deal more than nine of them.

Of course I have frequently seen men lose their nerve on active service, as well as when hunting dangerous game; and an amusing instance occurred under my observation soon after

---

[1] *History of the Zulu War*, by A. Wilmot, F.R.G.S., 1880, p. 150.

Carey's case. After the 1st Division moved, towards the end of June 1879, I rode out in the afternoon one day with an escort of a couple of hundred mounted men to look at a river five or six miles ahead which we intended to bridge next day. At a short distance from camp I came across an officer doing a sketch of the road, and he asked to be allowed to go on with me to see the road further on. So he came and we rode on together till we came to the river, which was narrow and deep with a bluff on the other side. There was a ford which was deep at the time, and the best place for the bridge was said to be at the bluff; so I halted and disposed my escort to cover me, and my friend and I rode on to the river with a few files scouting a little in front of me and on both flanks. We halted on the bank of the river opposite the bluff and my friend and I were making notes, when suddenly a volley was fired on the top of the bluff and there was some shouting there. We did not see anyone at first, but my friend said, 'Hullo! this is a bad business,' turned his horse and galloped off to the escort. I much admired the way his horse, a nice English hunter about 15.2 high, went over the bad ground, and I thought what a good pig-sticker he might make, if one had him at Roorkee or Meerut. However I signalled my scouts to join me and fell back at a discreet pace, utilising the cover, and we all reached the escort safe and sound. In fact I doubt if the Zulus on the bluff saw us until we were too far off for their limited markmanship.

My friend always used to look unhappy afterwards when we met, although I never said a word about the occurrence to him, or anyone else, for at least fifty years.

*Strictly speaking, the Prince had no right to be in Zululand at all. Prince Eugène Louis Jean Joseph Napoleon Bonaparte was the son of Napoleon III, who had fled to Britain when the Third Empire collapsed at the hands of the Prussians in 1870. Queen Victoria had taken the exiles under her wing, and, on the death of his father, Louis became the heir to the Bonapartist claim to France. As a child, Louis had been raised in the glorious tradition of his famous forebear, and revelled in all things military. He was allowed to undergo military training as an officer cadet at the Royal Military Academy at Woolwich, but there was never any hope that he might hold a command in the British Army. When, in due course, he passed out, he settled into the empty life of a leader in exile. Then the news of Isandlwana broke in the British press. Louis was thrilled, seeing an opportunity to gain the military experience and adventure he craved. Clearly, it would be politically impossible for him to ever fight in Europe, but surely there could be no objections if he took part in an obscure war in Africa? He had to use all of his charm and influence to persuade the British establishment to let him go, but at last he was given permission to join Chelmsford's force in the capacity of an observer, with no official rank. He set sail from Southampton on 28th February: two months later he was at the front.*

*Chelmsford, who had more than enough on his plate, was not pleased to have an added responsibility, and struggled to find something useful for the Prince to do. Finally, he hit upon the idea of attaching him to the staff of the Acting Quartermaster General of the Headquarters, Colonel Richard Harrison. Harrison was responsible for securing the 2nd Division's inevitable transport, as well as planning the route of advance, and there would be ample opportunity to employ Louis on duties which would be interesting, useful, and above all, safe.*

*Harrison's memoir,* Recollections of a Life in the British Army *(1908), describes the gruelling task of keeping the 2nd Division in the field as it began its advance, and the tragic fate that befell the young Prince:*

Starting on May 2, we had a look at the preparations then in progress for the 2nd Division camp at Landman's Drift, passed some men of the 80th Regiment from Wood's camp cutting firewood on the Doornberg, and a little farther on the 94th Regiment and the 5th Company RE (in which was Chard of Rorke's Drift fame). We arrived in the evening at Baltee Spruit, where we found the headquarters of the 80th in an old Dutch laager. The next day we crossed the Blood river and reached Wood's camp at Kambula, which he had defended not long before against a determined attack by a large Zulu 'impi'. After a ride to Zunguin Neck, and a look at Inslobani Mountain, where Wood's mounted troops were so severely handled the day before the Kambula attack, we saw an alarm practised at the camp; and on the 6th we went to Utrecht, where head-quarters were to be established until the troops were ready for the advance.

Now, the little party that left Dundee in light order on May 2 had not been idle. Not only had it travelled fast and far, but it had taken part in long animated discussions with all whose opinions were worth having about the conditions of the country, and the best manner of carrying out the approaching war.

There were already in Natal quite sufficient troops to subju-gate the Zulus, but there were more than the usual difficulties in regard to transport. The rivers were not navigable; the only railway ran from Durban to Pietermaritzburg; and all move-ment depended upon sufficient wheel and pack carriage being obtainable to keep the troops supplied with food and ammu-nition and such other stores as were necessary for the campaign.

Many people think that in a temperate climate you have only to send enough horses and mules with an army to enable it to go anywhere. There was never a greater mistake. Given a seat of war in which no food can be furnished for horses by the country, and it is a simple matter to calculate the distance from the base of supplies that a horse or mule can carry or draw a useful load. It must be borne in mind that under these conditions each animal must bring along his own food as well as whatever else he has to carry; and, even if there are good roads, he will not take a useful load beyond four or five marches – say sixty miles.

In Natal and Zululand it cannot be said that there was no food to be obtained for horses. Some mealies are usually grown on white men's farms as well as by [African] kraals; and at certain times of the year there is plenty of grass. But English horses had to be taught to eat the grass of the country; and mealies, unless carefully administered, often disagree with them. Besides which there was the terrible horse-sickness, not to mention various tormenting flies; so they could not be considered good transport animals.

Although the fact may be overlooked by those who have only

known South Africa since it has been crossed and recrossed by railways, the real transport animal in that country is the bullock. You must treat him properly if you want to get good work out of him. You must not try and make him go too fast; you must give him time to eat the grass that he finds by the roadside, and drink the water of the streams, and also to take periodical rests, and he will be to you on the veldt of South Africa what the camel is in the north – the ship of the desert.

The problem before Lord Chelmsford and his staff, while the columns were concentrating and organising for the advance into Zululand, was how to bring to the various rendez-vous the necessary supplies, and where to get the bullock wagons required to move those supplies across the dongas of Zululand as far as the capital of that country – the king's kraals at Ulundi.

Transport being the ruling factor, only such troops could be taken as could be fed; and the farther the troops marched from the bases of supply, the more difficult it became to feed them. This meant organisation. Which troops were to form the columns of the moving army, and which were to serve in the line of communications? How were the columns themselves to be formed, and what was to be the organisation of the guiding and controlling staff? These questions had, no doubt, been carefully considered by the general commanding ever since he knew what troops were coming out from England to take part in the war. Now was the time to put the finishing touches to the machine, and to set it in motion.

On the morning of May 8 Lord Chelmsford came into my tent and told me that he had determined to appoint me acting quartermaster-general of the Army, pending approval from England. Of course I was much honoured by the confidence thus shown in me, and I said I would do my best; but I was well aware of the difficulties that had to be faced. At that time there was no quartermaster-general's department in the country. The work was supposed to be done by the adjutant-general's staff and a new organisation which had charge of the base and the lines of communication, of which General Clifford was the head.

The troops were scattered along a line of communication

over 300 miles, which had to be kept up chiefly by runners or special orderlies. No road reports or military sketches of the country existed. There was very little information regarding the enemy, and I had no office whatever, only Lance-Corporal Martin, whom I had brought with me from Pietermaritzburg, and my own private sketching case and stationery.

I knew that three matters were urgent, viz. First, the completion of the organisation of the forces; second, the collection of supplies and transport; third, reconnoitring the enemy's country.

That same afternoon an officer, Lieutenant Carey, 98th Regiment, was appointed to assist me in military sketching; and the Prince Imperial was lent to me to collect and compile information in regard to the distribution of troops and depots. Having set these two officers to work I drafted and sent off a number of telegrams regarding the collection of supplies.

It was known that the country between the Black and White Umvaloosi Rivers was very difficult, if not impracticable. At the same time it was known that there were tracks practicable for wagons between Rorke's Drift and the capital. What was required was to ascertain if sufficiently good roads could be made between the rendezvous of the 2nd Division and Wood's column, to enable these forces to join hands and then advance as one army on Ulundi.

The troops available for escort duty were the Cavalry Brigade at Dundee, the mounted troops of Wood's column under Lieutenant-Colonel Buller, and Bettington's Natal Horse, at that time at Conference Hill. The Cavalry Brigade were still somewhat unfit for work after their long voyage from England, and they had not yet learned the ways of campaigning in South Africa, while Wood's mounted troops were in good condition, thoroughly acquainted with Zulu customs, and moreover were under the command of an officer who had an eye for country second to none in the Army, and who was an exceptionally good leader of mounted men. So I arranged that for the first reconnaissance I should accompany a mounted party led by Buller. We were to rendezvous at Conference Hill, and a small detachment of Bettington's Horse were also to go with us.

On May 13 the General Officer commanding, with his military secretary, left the headquarter camp at Utrecht for a trip to Newcastle, and I went off to take part in the reconnaissances in Zululand. I was accompanied by two officers of the headquarter staff, viz. the Hon. J. Drummond, chief of the Intelligence Department, and the Prince Imperial, extra aide-de-camp to Lord Chelmsford. Each of us took one servant and three horses; all our requirements were carried in saddle-bags.

An easy day's march took us to Conference Hill, where we drew rations for men and horses. The next morning Colonel Buller arrived with some two hundred frontier Light Horse and Basutos, and we went all together to Koppie Allein, where we bivouacked in a deserted farm. The horses were knee-haltered and turned into a mealie field for the night. Fires were lit and food prepared, each one for himself, and then we lay down and slept, in great coats and blankets, on the mud floor of the farmhouse.

At daylight on the 15th we were off in a southerly direction, Buller leading. At about 10.35 we halted to rest the animals, and boil water to make tea or coffee. All meals on these occasions are much the same – a little tinned meat, some ration bread or biscuit, occasionally as a treat a little potted meat or, perhaps, jam, and then the fragrant and soothing cup of tea or coffee, after which a talk round the smouldering fires, and, if there is time enough, a pipe or cigar.

About the middle of this day we saw a few Zulu scouts among the hills, some on foot and one or two mounted. We pursued them for some distance and then gave it up, because they did not go in the direction that we wanted to spy out. Once we entered a kraal from which the inhabitants had departed, leaving only a few diseased cattle; and then we continued on our way until it was quite dark, when we made a ring of our horses, heads inwards, saddles and bridles on, riders lying down by them on the grass. It was not safe in such a situation to feed by night, because the horses might stray away too far in the darkness; and we could not light fires, because so doing might attract attention. As a rule, the time for rest and food during a reconnaissance is in the daytime, and in a position that can be protected by outposts.

On the 16th we arrived at a new camp that had been established for Wood's column, near Wolf Hill.

Now the three days' march that we had just accomplished, under the guidance and direction of Buller and his mounted men, had no doubt been useful to all of us, and it had established certain facts in connection with the Zulus; but it had not discovered a route for the 2nd Division, and so I determined to make a further reconnaissance. This matter I discussed with Colonel Wood when we got in, and we had a long talk regarding plans for the campaign, and then I wrote to Lord Chelmsford and others until far into the night. The next morning Wood went off early to Utrecht to see the commander-in-chief, and I went to Conference Hill, to make arrangements for the further reconnaissance. Drummond went back to headquarters, but the Prince Imperial, having obtained leave from the commander-in-chief, returned to go with me. My immediate party for this expedition consisted of the Prince and his servant, Captain Carey, DAQMG, Captain Bettington with five of his men leading spare ponies, and twenty Basutos under an officer. We had arranged to meet Colonel Buller and some four hundred mounted men at a point eastward of the Ingutu Mountains, but on arrival there we saw nothing of them. The day wore on while we were searching, and we had to spend the night in that vicinity, taking all precautions in case our position and circumstances should become known to any of the Zulus who lived in the neighbourhood.

The next morning, after a further fruitless search for Buller's men, we had to make up our minds what to do: should we return to Conference Hill or get back on to the Ingutu Range, and, proceeding eastward along the ridge, endeavour to find a road leading into the valley of the Nondweni River, and so to Ibabanango Mountain? Captain Bettington told me that he had frequently been in that part of the country with quite a few men, and that safety lay in proper precautions rather than in the size of the escort. So I agreed to go on. The Prince and Captain Carey were both sketching, and Captain Bettington took immediate command, under me, of the mounted men.

Our order of march was as follows: Bettington leading; in front and on the flanks, guided by their leader's hand, Bettington's troopers; close behind, taking notes of the ground as we went along, the Prince Imperial; then myself; and behind me Carey and the Basutos. Our direction was south-east, and our object to find a way up to the top of the Ingutu Ridge.

When ascending a very steep path, up which our horses could hardly scramble, some Zulus lined the rocks at the top and opened fire. The Prince dismounted and drew his sword; Bettington pressed on in front, his men firing as they went; and I waved my helmet to urge on the Basutos. Two of the latter galloped up at once, and joined us in the attack, but the rest hung back a little and did not come up until we had won our way to the top. The Zulus began their usual tactics of trying to surround us, but the side of the hill, except on the path, was too steep even for them. Moreover, I think they were surprised by our rapid attack, and did not know what our strength was. Anyhow, they gave way in the centre as we mounted the path, and then the Basutos came up and completed their discomfiture.

At the top we found a large kraal, and in it some saddles and other stores taken at Isandlwana. After a short halt there we continued our march. I had started slightly ahead of the escort, when I saw three men in red coats advancing towards me. They were coming along in a leisurely manner, evidently returning to the kraal in ignorance of the skirmish that had taken place there, and thinking that it was still occupied by their own people. Their only arms, as far as I could see, were assegais.

Not realising at first who they were, whether Natal [natives] in British service or followers of Ketchwayo, I approached nearer to them, at the same time changing direction slightly to the right in order to avoid being caught on the path they were using, which ran along the edge of the steep northern slopes of the Ingutu Ridge. At that moment I heard a shout behind me, and saw Bettington, the commander of my escort, coming along the path at a gallop, with his revolver in his hand. Clearly he did not want any nearer approach to show him who my three friends were, and, riding past me, he shot one of them, while the other two jumped into the bush on the mountain side and disappeared. When the war was over I was asked to verify this little incident; and, in connection with other service, it obtained for Captain Bettington the honour of a decoration. Later on we came upon some horses grazing and captured some of them.

We then went on again along the ridge, descending into the valley of the Nondweni, and reconnoitring up to the slopes of Alarm Hill, near which ran the wagon track from Rorke's Drift to Ulundi. It seemed to me that we had found the road we wanted for the 2nd Division; the 'going' on the top of the Ingutu Hills was good and easily protected, and the only difficulty along the route was the descent to the valley at the eastern end.

Having done what we started to accomplish, we retired. Towards evening we found some wood in a kraal, and were able to cook. Then, leaving our fires alight, we went on again. Some Zulus followed us, and when they came to one of our fires they danced round it, making the most hideous noise. So we did not think it safe to stay long anywhere, but worked our way by stars and compass throughout the night, and early the next morning reached Conference Hill. Even then our troubles were not quite over. We knew that it was the custom of British troops in South Africa, at that time, to turn out before daybreak, and man the defences around the laager that they had occupied during the night, as a precaution against possible attacks at dawn of day.

We were aware also that many of the troops were young and inexperienced, and did not always await their officers' orders to fire. So we approached the laager at Conference Hill with caution. It was well we did so. The men were lining the trench that had been dug around the encampment, and we could hear their colonel talking to them: 'Now, boys, be ready– when I give the word to fire, fire low – I see them coming – look out, boys – remember to fire low'; and so on, until, by signals, without showing our bodies, we convinced the gallant defenders of the post that we were not Zulus, but only hungry and tired comrades anxious to obtain food and rest.

The same afternoon the Prince and I rode back to headquarters at Utrecht, leaving our companions at Conference Hill.

Since we left a week ago we must have ridden over 200 miles. During the last thirty-six hours we were twenty-five in the saddle, but the Prince enjoyed it all immensely, and, besides making a very good report, which I forwarded to Lord Chelmsford, he wrote a long account to the Empress of the French in England of all he had seen and done.

At our bivouacs, and elsewhere, we frequently discussed military and other matters, and I had to reply to his many questions about what was the organisation of this and that in the English Army by telling him that the word with us was hardly understood – the usual custom being for our generals to make such arrangements, in the field, as they thought most likely to meet the circumstances of the time. Then he took great interest in hearing from Captain Bettington how he had spent his early life in New Zealand, driving cattle, assisting as a dispenser, keeping a livery stable, and for a time even acting as 'boots' at an hotel, until he found himself in Natal at the time of the Zulu War, and obtained the command of the irregular mounted corps that bore his name.

Arrived at Utrecht, I reported to the General commanding the result of our reconnaissances, soon after which Buller came in, and said that he had gone to what he thought was the rendezvous where I was to meet him, and, not finding us there, had reconnoitred on his own account. His recommendations in regard to the route for the 2nd Division differed from mine, and as he had had considerable experience in the country, and I had had none, the General naturally inclined to his.

At this time the Cavalry Brigade, under General Marshall, made a reconnaissance on a large scale into Zululand; but they did not go much beyond the battlefield of Isandlwana, and their reports threw no light on the best line of advance for the columns. So it was settled that the 2nd Division was to enter the country by way of Koppie Allein, and to follow generally the route taken by Wood's column, each force being complete in all arms and forming its own laager for the night bivouac. Headquarters were to accompany the 2nd Division. The general line of advance being settled, it became necessary to make detailed reconnaissances, and road sketches, for the convenience of the troops. To carry out this I had at my disposal Captain Carey, who worked from Conference Hill, and the Prince Imperial, who was to remain at headquarters, but was to be held available to carry out such quartermaster-general's work as from time to time I might entrust to him. By direction of Lord Chelmsford I gave the Prince written instructions that he was never to leave the immediate precincts of the camp without a proper escort. His ordinary work was to sketch the camps occupied by headquarters, and the roads they traversed when on the march.

The latter part of May was spent in carrying out the details connected with the organisation of the forces for the combined march, in collecting supplies, and in training the troops of all arms for the anticipated fighting. Wood's column was moving steadily southward, and on May 28 the 2nd Division and Army headquarters moved to Koppie Allein.

On June 1 the 2nd Division made its first march into Zulu-land, and the same afternoon one of the most unhappy events in this or any war took place – the death of the gallant young Prince, who had come out to share with his comrades of the English Army the risks and dangers of war.

The evening before, he came to me and asked that he might extend his sketch beyond the camp to be occupied the next day, and make a reconnaissance of the road to be traversed the day following. I saw no objection to this, provided he took with him the usual escort. Many of us had been over the ground, and we knew there was no 'impi' in the neighbour-hood. Moreover, I thought that the cavalry which accompanied the division, would be extended over the country far in advance of the camp, so I gave permission. Shortly afterwards Captain Carey came to my tent, and asked that he might go with the Prince's party, as he wished to verify his sketch of the country, and I said 'yes', and added that he could look after the Prince, and see that he did not get into any trouble.

On the morning of the 1st I was told that Carey and the Prince were ready to go, but that the escort had not turned up. So I walked over to see the General of Cavalry, and he sent his brigade-major to make the necessary arrangements. I then took in hand my own work for the day. I rode ahead with the staff officer of the division, and showed him the site for their camp on the ridge between the Incenci and the Itelezi Hills. I then went to see to the watering arrangements. While so engaged I came across Carey and the Prince, and found that they had with them the European part of their escort, a detachment of Bettington's Horse, but none of the Basutos, whom I had specially ordered to be detailed, because they have a much keener sense of sight and hearing than Europeans, and consequently make better scouts. They told me that they were to get their Basutos from the regiment that was out scouting in front of the camp, and I enjoined them not to go forward without them. Returning to camp, I accompanied Lord Chelmsford round the laager, and then went to my tent and drafted the orders for the next day's march.

About six o'clock in the evening Captain Carey came to see me, and reported that the reconnoitring party he was with had off-saddled the other side of the Ityotyozi River, and had been surrounded by Zulus, and that the Prince, two of the white men, and the interpreter were missing, as well as five horses. I said: 'You don't mean to say you left the Prince?'

And he replied: 'It was no use stopping; he was shot by the first volley.' And I said: 'You ought to have tried, at all events, to bring away his body.'

Much overcome by what I said to him, he told me, as far as he could remember, the story of what had happened, accepting full responsibility for what had taken place. Immediately afterwards I went to see Lord Chelmsford, and asked him to allow me to go out at once and look for the Prince. After what Carey had said I hardly expected to find him alive, but anyhow I thought I might bring home his body. The Chief, however, would not let me go; all he said was, 'I don't want to lose you too.'

Later on it was settled that the cavalry were to go out at daybreak and search the spot where the fight had taken place; and reports were called for from Carey, Bettington's men, and myself.

The story as it evolved itself was briefly as follows:

When Captain Carey and the Prince left me on the Itelezi Hill, they did not, as I had instructed them, look for the Basuto escort, but went on without them. The party consisted of these two officers, six troopers of Bettington's Horse, and a native interpreter (told off by the chief of the Intelligence Department). The Prince did not, as usual, take his servant with him on this occasion, and Captain Bettington did not accompany his men. If either of these had gone, matters might have been different.

[1]About half-past twelve they reached a flat-topped hill, on the summit of which they dismounted while the Prince made a rough sketch of the surrounding country. After spending an hour on this hill they moved along the ridge between the Tombokala and Ityotyozi Rivers, and about 2.30 p.m. descended from the high ground towards a kraal some 200 yards from the latter stream. This kraal was of an ordinary type, and consisted of a circular stone enclosure outside of which there were five huts. The huts were unoccupied, but some dogs were prowling about, and fresh remains of food could be seen, and it was evident that the inhabitants had only recently gone away. The ground near the kraal was covered with coarse grass and Indian corn, growing to a height of five or six feet, and surrounding the huts on all sides except the north and north-east. Here the ground was open for about 200 yards, but at that distance from the kraal there was a donga or dry watercourse, some six or eight feet deep, by which, in the rainy season, the storm waters found their way into the Ityotyozi. On arriving at the kraal, at about 3 p.m., the Prince ordered the escort to off-saddle and knee-halter the horses for grazing. This was done, and the men made coffee and rested until nearly four, when the native guide reported that he had seen a Zulu come over the hill. The horses were at once caught and saddled, and the men prepared to mount. The Prince gave the word to 'mount', and as the word was uttered a volley was fired at the party by a number of Zulus who had crept unobserved through the long grass to within fifteen yards of the huts. Though no one was hit by this volley, the surprise was complete, and the troopers, not yet settled in their saddles,

[1] This paragraph and the four following ones are taken from the published official accounts of the war.

could hardly control their horses, which, terrified by the shots and yells of the Zulus, bore them across the open ground towards the donga. The Prince himself was in the act of mounting when the volley was fired, but his charger becoming restive he appears to have failed to get into the saddle, and to have run alongside the animal, which followed the horses of the escort. The Prince, who was extremely active, now endeavoured to vault on to his horse while in rapid motion, but his efforts seem to have been foiled by the tearing of the wallet which he had seized, and on this giving way he fell to the ground, and his horse broke away from him.

As the escort were galloping away from the kraal the Zulus kept up a fire by which one trooper was hit in the back and fell. The native guide and another trooper, who had not mounted with the rest, were left behind at the kraal, and neither was again seen alive. The remainder of the party, consisting of Captain Carey and four troopers, crossing the donga at different points, galloped on for several hundred yards. Captain Carey, after crossing the donga, was joined by the rest, and learnt that the Prince was not with them, and that he had been last seen between the kraal and the donga, dismounted and pursued by the Zulus.

Many of the enemy being now on the ground, and the Prince's horse being seen galloping riderless at some little distance, Captain Carey came to the conclusion that the Prince must have fallen and that it would be useless for the few survivors to return. The party accordingly proceeded in haste to bear the news to the camp of the 2nd Division.

The next morning, early, General Marshall, with a cavalry escort, went to the kraal where the reconnoitring party had been surprised. The dead bodies of the two troopers were first found – one in the donga and the other between it and the kraal; and soon afterwards the body of the Prince was found in the donga, where he had made his way on foot. Being overtaken there, he had evidently turned on his pursuers, but after emptying his pistol his sword had been of little use against the assegais of the enemy, and he had fallen where he stood.

The body, which bore sixteen wounds, all in front, was

placed on a bier formed of lances and a blanket, and was carried to an ambulance, on which it was conveyed to the Itelezi Hill Camp. There it was received with all honour, and a service read at a parade of the whole division. Then it was despatched by way of Landman's Drift and Dundee to Pieter-maritzburg and Durban, and from thence conveyed in HMS *Orontes* to England, and laid to rest in the mortuary chapel at Chislehurst, from which place it was eventually transferred to Farnborough.

A few words on the events that followed the death of the young Prince, and my connection therewith, and then I will return to the march of the columns on Ulundi.

The reports furnished by those who were associated with the Prince Imperial, or who accompanied him on his last fatal ride, led to a court of inquiry, and the court of inquiry led to a court-martial on Captain Carey. While this was in progress war correspondents and others wrote many letters to the papers, and the people in England took much interest in the matter. It was so sad a thing that a gallant young prince, whose mother lived in England, who had been educated in an English military school, and who had gone out to South Africa to take part in the war that was being carried out there by the land of his adoption, should not only have been killed in a reconnais-sance, but have been left behind among the enemy, when some of his comrades galloped off and escaped! Questions innumerable were discussed: Why was he employed on a reconnaissance at all? Why was not the escort larger? Why was it not composed of regular cavalry? What was Captain Carey's business in the matter? &c., &c., and, without waiting for the report of the court of inquiry, or the court-martial, many drew their own conclusions and added to the correspondence.

Among soldiers in South Africa the whole blame for the disaster rested on Captain Carey. In England, at first, it was the same; but when Carey's friends joined in the correspondence, some of the press took up the line that he was being made a scapegoat of, and, in order to foster this idea, it was necessary to suggest that there were others who were not blameless. I was attacked because there had been a mistake in regard to the escort, and because the duties of the Prince when he went out were not defined with greater clearness. Naturally I saw nothing of these press criticisms until long afterwards, and, even then, I did not think it my duty to answer them; and so blame rested on me until I returned to England.

I have already said that the court of inquiry led to a court-martial to try Captain Carey. The charge preferred against him by the adjutant-general in South Africa was to effect that he had shown cowardice in the face of the enemy when in command of an escort.

Naturally Carey did all he could to refute the charge, directing his attention particularly to that part of it which combined the alleged act of cowardice with the fact that he was in command of the party. He was assisted in his defence by an able officer detailed for the purpose, and no one connected with the court-martial thought it necessary to take exception to the statements made in his defence, even though, in trying to save himself, he threw blame on others.

When the court-martial had completed their work, the proceedings were sent to the Horse Guards for the decision of the commander-in-chief. On August 16 an official letter was written to the General commanding in South Africa, stating that the charge against Captain Carey was not sustained by the evidence, and that he was to be released from arrest, and sent to do duty with his regiment.

This letter was sent to me when I was commanding the troops in the Transvaal, and as it contained some observations on my conduct, evidently based on statements made by Captain Carey and others at the court-martial, I replied in full, giving my own version of the occurrence.

The answer to my protest was to the effect that the matter should now be allowed to rest. So I tried to forget the circumstance, and turned with all the zeal in my power to the work that I had to do in the Transvaal. When that work was over, I was offered a renewal of my appointment by the High Commissioner. At the same time he said that, as he anticipated that I should only have ordinary routine peace work to carry out, and no opportunity for active service, he would advise me not to take it, but to go home. I acted on his advice and returned to England. Not long afterwards I was given one of the best appointments open to a young officer in England – that of assistant quartermaster-general at Aldershot.

*Chelmsford held the first of many funeral services for the Prince the day his remains were brought into camp. His body was drawn on a gun-carriage past rows of troops, with Chelmsford walking solemnly behind. Louis was not to be buried in the field, however, and his body was sent back down the line with due ceremony. In Pietermaritzburg, it was led through the streets by a military band with black-draped instruments. At Durban, mourning crowds turned out to watch the coffin placed on board a transport for England. At home, the Prince's mother, the Empress Eugénie, had collapsed with grief, and the Queen herself was deeply shocked. News of the Prince's death touched the public far more than had the disaster at Isandlwana, and sympathetic crowds greeted the coffin at the docks. Louis was buried with full military honours alongside his father, in the chapel at Chislehurst, Kent. Years later, his devoted mother had both tombs moved to Farnborough Abbey in Hampshire, which she considered a more appropriate resting place.*

*For a while, the press seethed with indignation, and recriminations flew thick and fast. Harrison was at last vindicated, but a cloud still hung over Carey, and he sank back into obscurity within his regiment. He died in India in 1883.*

*Tragic as it was, Louis' death was little more than a sideshow compared to the invasion of Zululand, and Chelmsford could hardly allow it to interfere with his advance. The 2nd Division and Flying Column had converged on 2nd June, and marched alongside one another to the Nondweni river, where Chelmsford intended to establish a major supply depot. Near here, on 5th June, the British had their first significant encounter with the Zulus since the second invasion had begun. Scouting ahead of the Flying Column as usual, Buller had run into a Zulu concentration apparently preparing to block the advance in the Upoko valley. Buller rode out to clear the way, and a fire-fight ensued amidst the long grass and bush. The 17th Lancers came up from the 2nd Division, and deployed to support Buller, but as they did so a sniper's bullet struck their young adjutant, Lieutenant Frith, clean through the heart. He died instantly. The cavalry disengaged, and returned to camp with Frith's body draped across the saddle. The death of Frith, coming so soon after that of the Prince, seemed to weigh heavily on the nerves of the inexperienced men of the 2nd Division, and the following night there was a bad scare, as Molyneux relates:*

This night, the 6th, was a lively one in our laager. Some groups of natives were posted with the outlying pickets, and one of these began firing at about eight o'clock; whereupon the pickets retired into the unfinished forts, the tents outside the trench and laager were struck, and the men fell in to resist an attack. Now the camp-kettles had been left on their tripods at the usual cooking-places on the outer side of the tents, and presumably this deceived the men of one regiment, for they gave them a warm independent fire, and even the artillery assisted with two rounds of case. Horses and oxen galloped round the interior like mad things: all who were not firing shouted to all those who were, to cease; and the din was tremendous. When quiet was restored it was found that the enemy consisted of a stray ox or so; that two sergeants and three men of the outposts had been hit; and that all the camp-kettles, tents, and kit left outside one face were perforated. Fort Newdigate got the slang name of Fort Funk, and one regiment did most of its cooking in mess-tins afterwards. This was rather a disreputable affair, as showing what exaggerated ideas the new troops from home had of their foes, and how easily panic increases at night. There was a bright moon with fleeting clouds; so there was really no excuse for a stray bullock, or even the shadow of a cloud, being mistaken for an impi.

*Despite the fact that the alarm proved false, and the widespread knowledge that the Zulus preferred to avoid night attacks, false alarms happened all too frequently on the final advance to Ulundi. In fact, unbeknownst to the British, King Cetshwayo had lost faith in a military solution, and was making a desperate attempt to ward off the final confrontation by seeking a diplomatic settlement. As the columns pushed forward, the king sent a stream of messengers asking what terms Chelmsford would accept to end the fighting. But the king had missed his chance; the tide of war was now flowing firmly in Chelmsford's favour, and he was not to be cheated of his final revenge for Isandlwana. The Zulu envoys were sent away with terms which were impossible for the king to accept. Richard Harrison describes the inexorable British advance:*

Wood's column led, as it had done from the commencement; but orders for the operations were issued from headquarters, which accompanied Newdigate's force. Some instructions were issued for the posts on the line of communications, and also for Major-General Marshall, who, with the larger part of the Cavalry Brigade, was put in charge of the general defence of the country, and the line of communications of the advancing columns.

On the 18th I accompanied Buller on a reconnaissance to within a mile or two of the Umlatoosi River. We saw a few Zulu scouts on the hills, burning grass.

Comparatively speaking, short marches were made by both columns on the 18th, 19th, and 20th. The inexperience of the troops, officers and men, to which I have already alluded, was very evident, especially in the 2nd Division. I find a remark in my journal to the effect that 'I used to take far more pains about the march-out of the pontoon troop that I commanded at Aldershot than is shown here by the staff in arranging for the march of a division in an unknown country, with such an active enemy as the Zulu in our front. The whole Army requires instruction in the art of war.'

But Lord Chelmsford was indefatigable in his endeavours to put things straight, and established some system in the business.

On June 21 I made the usual arrangements for the marches, and selected a site for the new fort on the line of communications. In the afternoon I took a few Royal Engineers out to blow up rocks on the road. The next day I rode out reconnoitring with some of Buller's cavalry, and we had a good view of Ulundi. The quartermaster-general's work was nearly complete – that is to say, the troops had been brought safe and sound to within sight of the enemy, and it only remained to issue the orders for the battle, which, as a rule, is the business of the adjutant-general's branch. At this juncture Major East arrived at our camp, and took charge of the quartermaster-general's duties. At the special request of Lord Chelmsford I remained as his assistant; but it was not the same thing. Whenever I reconnoitred I could not go straight to the General Commanding, as I had done hitherto, and tell him what I had seen, and settle at once any required action. I had to report through my new chief. Moreover, not being the head of a department, I no longer attended at staff conferences, and consequently did not always know what was going on. Nearly the last thing I did, while I was still in charge, was to send a special messenger to General Crealock, who commanded the 1st Division in the south of Zululand, directing him what action to take in concert with the northern columns.

As assistant quartermaster-general I continued to carry out the daily reconnaissances in front of the columns, usually in company with Buller, who commanded the mounted troops of the leading column. East came part of the way with us on June 24, along what was known as the Jackal Ridge. The next two days there were some skirmishes with the Zulus, and one or two military kraals were burned.

On the 27th both columns reached the end of the Entonjaneni Range, from whence we looked down over the bush country to the valley of the White Umvolosi River, on the left bank of which lies Ulundi.

Here we made a fortified laager, and left all weak men as well as a large number of wagons and oxen, and about one hundred effective horsemen; and, with the balance of the force, lightly equipped, without tents, but with ten days' food, and a good reserve of ammunition, we marched down from the high ground to come to close quarters with the Zulu king. Some oxen and tusks had been sent out from Ulundi as a peace offering, to try and detain us; but Lord Chelmsford would not stop unless all the conditions laid down when we crossed the frontier were fulfilled to the letter.

While we were forming the laager, alarming but quite

unnecessary reports were circulated about an 'impi' being near at hand. Those of us who had been constantly with the mounted troops in touch with the Zulus, and had learned something of their manners and customs, knew better. The alarms were started by officers provided with telescopes, who mistook the meaning of the drills and 'doctoring' going on in Ulundi.

On June 20 the two columns, each with one hundred wagons, left the Entonjaneni camp at 9 a.m. More reports were received of possible 'impi' attacks, and the oxen were hurried along as quickly as possible, and laager formed by 1 p.m. More messengers came from the Zulu king, bringing the Prince Imperial's sword, but our chief would no longer delay the advance. At this time it was quite warm in the plain, compared to what we had experienced on the hillsides during our advance.

On July 1 we started again at 7 a.m., Wood's column, as usual, in front. I went ahead to choose camping-ground, or ground to fight on, if fighting became necessary. I arrived at a koppie near the drift across the Umvolosi at 10.40, and from there watched the Zulu Army manoeuvring in and around Ulundi.   ·

Every now and then it looked as if they were coming against us, especially about 11.40; but those who knew their habits felt pretty sure that these demonstrations did not mean an attack, so I proceeded to choose the camping-ground for the two columns close together, about three-quarters of a mile from the drift, and directed the staff officers on them. But before the flying column had completed its laager, and while the 2nd Division wagons were on the road, an order came to me from Lord Chelmsford to complete the laagers in half an hour, 'as the Zulus were advancing rapidly towards us, and were then only three miles off.' I knew that both the laagers could not be formed at the place I had chosen under two or three hours, and so I ordered the 2nd Division wagons to park on a hill which I remembered about a mile back. This was done, and the troops formed round them, and set to work with a will to dig the usual defence trenches, so that by the time given both columns were ready for the attack. The Zulus, however, halted near us and did not come on. The laagers were then finished with more or less regularity.

That evening we received messages from Sir Garnet Wolseley that he had arrived in Natal, and was going to join General Crealock's column, and from Crealock that he was 'burning kraals'.

*The imminent arrival of General Sir Garnet Wolseley was, indeed, a goad that spurred Chelmsford on. Chelmsford was notified in the middle of June that he was about to be replaced, and that Wolseley had been given his job. In Britain, the Home Government had become tired of the war and its expense. Isandlwana had destroyed the political credibility of the confederation scheme, which was seen to be resting on the shaky foundations of false assumptions. Chelmsford seemed unable to bring the war to a swift conclusion, or to work amicably with the civilian administration in Natal. Worse, the cost was escalating beyond all bounds. Their solution was to appoint one man as a special commissioner, with both civil and military powers to resolve the whole South African crisis.*

*Sir Garnet was the darling of the radical, progressive movement within the Army, the hero of the Asante ('Ashanti') War, dubbed by the press 'Britain's Only General'. He was not popular with the military establishment, but then Chelmsford had been approved by the establishment. Wolseley was an obvious choice for the appointment, and he accepted with alacrity. He arrived in Durban in late June, and began bombarding Chelmsford with messages urging him to stop his advance. Wolseley was determined to be at the front in time for the final confrontation; Chelmsford, after coming so far and enduring so much, was equally determined not to be cheated of his kill.*

*The problem facing Wolseley was which column to join in order to reach the front quickest. The 2nd Division and Flying Column were deep in the heart of Zululand, and it was impossible to control them from Durban, especially as Chelmsford had no wish to be controlled, and it would take several days of hard riding to reach them. The 1st Division had by now, however, established a beach head at a lonely stretch of coastline optimistically named Port Durnford, where supplies were*

237

*being carried ashore from transports by surf-boats. Wolseley gambled that once he was in Zululand, Chelmsford would no longer be able to ignore him, so he decided to sail up the coast and land at Port Durnford. His plan was to order Chelmsford to halt from there, and galvanise 'Crealock's Crawlers' into moving rapidly on Ulundi. Nature, alas, thwarted him, as Bindon Blood relates:*

At the end of May 1879, Sir Garnet Wolseley was appointed to the supreme civil and military control of the eastern part of South Africa, and he consequently arrived at Durban on the 27th June. Some time before this a landing-place had been selected at Port Durnford, about 30 miles or so north of the Tugela, and the sappers had arranged for Sir Garnet's landing there, according to a local plan which was most simple and ingenious.

First there was a boat with a keel-less bottom, just like a spoon, decked, with a shallow well aft; rigged with one mast, shrouds and a fore-stay, all with slip-knotted lanyards, and a shifting lug-sail. She was also fitted with a large sheave on the stem and another on the stern-post, to take a five or six inch rope cable on board, under which the boat could travel ahead or astern; and an arrangement in the well for a stopper on the cable with which to control her movement.

Secondly there was a manila rope cable fixed to a bollard, above high water mark on land, and at the other end to an anchor straight out in the sea outside the surf, with buoys at suitable places between.

When passengers or stores, or both together, had to be landed, and the surf was not too heavy, they were stowed below in the boat and battened down; the boat making sail to the cable which was picked up outside the surf. Then everything was made snug, the crew took to the rigging, except one man for the stopper, and the boat was committed to the surf, which, thanks to the skillful manipulation of the stopper, took the boat to land and bumped her into shoal water. There the cargo was landed with the greatest ease by the smart boatmen and natives, who were used to the arrangements and were in attendance. The boat went out to sea in a similar manner, the stopper being handled so as to utilise the outdraft of the surf. All of us, sappers especially, were delighted with this beautifully simple dodge, and with the smartness of the boatmen who worked it.

But unfortunately Sir Garnet was not able to land at Port Durnford, and had to go round by Durban and Pietermaritzburg to the front after all.

He came to Port Durnford and was battened down with his staff and baggage in the landing-boat and spent two or three hours trying to land. But although the surf had been all right up to about six o'clock that morning, it got bad afterwards, and there had been so much delay about the start that landing was too dangerous when the boat came to the surf, and so Sir Garnet had to go back to his warship. He and his staff undoubtedly had a shocking time for two hours or so while battened down in the landing-boat, in rather a rough sea, and they would not hear of trying again, but were off to Durban at once! Of course next morning there was a flat calm, and they could have landed in row-boats if they had stayed.

*Wolseley had missed his chance. On 30th June Chelmsford's columns descended from the Mthonjaneni heights towards the White Mfolozi river. This was the last barrier before Ulundi; across the river lay the Mahlabathini plain, the heart of the kingdom, where the great amakhanda nestled among the surrounding hills. Ulundi, the prize, was in sight at last. Chelmsford established a camp on the south bank of the river, and paused to make his final preparations. There was a final flurry of diplomatic activity. Cetshwayo had once more called up his army, and the British could see the dark masses of the regiments moving between the amakhanda in the distance, but the king no longer had any faith that his warriors could check the British advance. He was prepared to listen to any reasonable demands Chelmsford might make of him. But Chelmsford had no need to be reasonable; he held all the aces, and his position was uncompromising. Finally even the Zulus themselves realised there was no further point in talk; on 2nd July Cetshwayo sent a herd of his prized white cattle to Chelmsford as a gesture of good will, but warriors of his own Khandempemvu regiment intercepted it and turned it back. The die was cast.*

*As the amabutho gathered for one last gesture of defiance, the sonorous chants and sudden frenzied yells of their pre-battle purification rituals rolled across the hills, unsettling the British in their camp. The veterans of Flying Column understood their significance, and that there was no immediate fear of attack, but the sound preyed on the minds of the 2nd Division men who'd not yet proved themselves in action. The spectre of Isandlwana was on the prowl again, and that night there was another scare, vividly described by Harrison:*

About 12 o'clock at night there was a scare in both laagers. One of the sentries on outpost duty over the 2nd Division fired at an officer who had not answered his challenge, and this so alarmed the native troops that they rushed helter-skelter into the laager. I shall not easily forget the occurrence. I was lying down with my great coat on, under one of the wagons, my head sheltered in my saddle, as was the usual custom in South Africa, when I was awakened from my first sleep by the noise of the rush, and saw a naked Zulu dripping with blood, his assegai in his hand, standing over me. In my waking moments the truth flashed upon me, that my visitor was one of the Natal Zulus fighting on our side, who had been frightened by the outpost fire, and had dashed through the thorny abattis, which accounted for his appearance. But others did not come so quickly to the same conclusion, and there was a considerable stampede, that it took some time to settle. Among others, the officer who was bivouacking next to me disappeared with my sword, and I did not find it until the next day. Directly I got up I went to where I knew Lord Chelmsford was lying, and I found him just starting round the laager, and so I accompanied him. We were pleased to find the regulars all at their alarm-posts and everything ready for a real attack if one had taken place.

*Bengough, Smith-Dorrien and Molyneux were all in the camp that night, and shared the same experience. 'I was lying dressed with the rest of my officers on the border of the camp', wrote Bengough, 'and was awakened about midnight by a suc-*

*cession of fiendish yells, followed by a trampling of many feet.
I tried to rise, but was knocked down by a rush of men. I felt
sure the Zulus had broken into the camp, and tried to clutch
my revolver, which was by my side, but in vain. I remember
expecting vaguely the thrust of an assegai in the small of my
back, but nothing happened ... and then the truth dawned
on me! It was only another false alarm!' Molyneux, at least,
saw a certain humour in Harrison's predicament, though the
real war was about to begin again in earnest:*

That night was a noisy one in both laagers. In that of the
Second Division an officer of the Native Contingent was fired
at by a sentry when visiting his pickets. In a minute the whole
of our natives outside made a wild rush at the abattis and
laager; and it says much for the discipline of the soldiers opposite them that they were not shot down and bayoneted, as
occurred near Ginghilovo. The soldiers were driven back by
the rush to the waggons, and the natives came clean over both
into the interior. Headquarters were in bivouac just inside the
waggons, and we were lying about in various positions when
the black avalanche came down. For a minute we could not
tell what was up; but the noise tended to reassure us. The
rush of panic-stricken feet only requires to be heard once
to be remembered: no enemy attacks with such velocity as
the frightened attain in running away; and so the jumpers
were given blows from sticks and fists instead of cuts from
swords and shots from pistols. A burly native landed full on
the adjutant-general's prostrate form, who at once forgot all
about his published work on *The Treatment of Natives*. He
forgot to call them '*Abantu* (people),' '*Amadoda* (men)', or
'*Amabuti* (soldiers)': he did not recollect to tell them that
they were behaving like '*Amakafula* (common [blacks])'; but
he called them '[—]' (with the addition of an adjective) and
other things; and he beat them till we regained our good
temper, which had been temporarily lost with the disturbance of our beauty-sleep.

Next day a fort was built on a knoll between the two laagers,
and then the waggons of the Second Division were moved
down and formed into two lines, one end of each line resting

on a side of Wood's laager and the other ends converging on the fort. Throughout the day the Zulu marksmen, posted in the rocks on a high hill over the Umvolosi just below the drift, fired at our watering-parties and wounded several men and horses. Large bodies of them were seen moving about over the river during the day. Our men were employed felling the bush for one hundred yards round the laagers and making a huge abattis of the thorny stuff round the waggons. I got a welcome present from home that day by a friend of the Engineers who arrived at night, bringing me two silk pocket-handkerchiefs in a letter. All mine had been stolen, and a towel cut in four pieces had been their substitutes for some time; so they were useful presents indeed.

On the 3rd the Zulus were still firing on us. This was clearly a breach of the agreement. Accordingly, when noon came and the time allowed the king had expired, the cattle sent to us at Entonjaneni were driven across the Umvolosi as a sign that negotiations were at an end. An hour later Buller crossed the river with his mounted men, drove the Zulus from the hill, and pursued from over the open towards Nodwengu kraal. From the waggons at the highest point of the laager we could see with our glasses most of what was going on. When Buller reached the Imbilane stream a large force of Zulus appeared suddenly in front of him, while at the same time other large forces rose out of the valleys on his right and left. It looked as if he must be cut off, or would at least have to fight his way through, as the Zulu wings were closing behind him. It was an exciting moment, and right glad we were to see him retiring. Two nine-pounders were got into position and some infantry sent to the drift to cover his retreat. Some of his men left on the hill checked the pursuit, and he got back with a loss of only three killed and four wounded.

It was a most successful affair. He had noted an excellent position for the next day's fight: he had shown us where the Zulus were in force, and that they were posted in horseshoe form ready for us to enter the trap; and he had returned, when nearly surrounded by many thousand men, with a very small loss indeed.

*The irregular cavalry had had a lucky escape: the Zulu trap had been planned to perfection, and only Buller's unerring instinct had prevented it being sprung to better effect. As it was, three men were killed and a number were snatched to safety under the very noses of the Zulus. It was the sort of adventure that would delight the public back home, and there were several journalists in the camp to ensure that it would not pass unnoticed. The eyes of the press had been elsewhere in the world when the Zulu War broke out, and to the chagrin of his rivals, only one correspondent, Charles Norris-Newman of* The Standard, *had been present to cover the dramatic events of 22nd January. When news of Isandlwana had reached London, however, the top papers had hurried their best men to the scene. In the age before instant photography, the 'special correspondent' was king, and he was not only a journalist, but an artist who made rough sketches on the spot, which were worked up into complex engravings for publication at home. The famous Melton Prior, a veteran of the steamy forest bloodletting of Asante, represented the* Illustrated London News, *whilst* The Graphic *had sent Charles Fripp, who would later paint one of the most enduring images of the war,* The Last Stand Of The 24th At Isandlwana. *Most of the 'specials' had arrived too late to cover the early fighting, but the death of the Prince Imperial had given them ample copy. Now they were thirsting for revenge no less than the soldiers. Archibald Forbes, the correspondent of the* Daily News, *was perhaps the master of them all. Widely regarded as the best war correspondent of his day, Forbes was not an artist, but he provided a dramatic written picture of Buller's skirmish, and of the gallantry of Captain Lord William Beresford, which was to win him the Victoria Cross:*

The arrangements were simple; and there was no delay down by the Umvaloosi bank, where the accelerated fire from the Zulus in the kopjie over against them whistled over the heads of the horsemen; over whom too screamed the shells from the guns in front of the laager that were being thrown in among the crags where the Zulus lurked. The spray of the Umvaloosi dashed from the horse-hoofs of the irregulars, as they forded the river on the right of the kopjie, and then bending to the left round it, took it in reverse. The Zulus who had been holding it had not cared much for the shell fire, ensconced among the rocks as they were, but were quick to notice the risk they ran of being cut off by the movement of the horsemen, and made a bolt of it. Beresford's fellows galloped hard to intercept them, Bill well in front, sending his chestnut along as if he were 'finishing' in front of the stand at Sandown. The Zulu induna, bringing up the rear of his fleeing detachment, turned on the lone man who had so outridden his followers. A big man, even for a Zulu, the ring round his head proved him a veteran. The muscles rippled on his glistening black shoulders as he compacted himself behind his huge flecked shield of cowhide, marking his distance for the thrust of the gleaming assegai held at arm's length over the great swart head of him. Bill steadied his horse a trifle, just as he was wont to do before the take off for a big fence; within striking distance he made him swerve a bit to the left – he had been heading straight for the Zulu, as if he meant to ride him down. The spear flashed out like the head of a cobra as it strikes; the sabre carried at 'point one' clashed with it, and seemed to curl round it; the spear-head was struck aside; the horseman delivered 'point two' with all the vigour of his arm, his strong seat, and the impetus of his galloping horse; and lo! in the twinkling of an eye, the sabre's point was through the shield, and half its length buried in the Zulu's broad chest. The brave induna was a dead man before he dropped; the sword drawing out of his heart as he fell backward. His assegai stands now in the corner of Bill's mother's drawing-room.

Beresford's Zulu was the only man slain with the 'white arm' in hand-to-hand combat during the day, but of the fugitives whom the dead induna had commanded, several fell under the fire of the fellows who followed that chief's slayer. The surviving Zulus ran into the nearest military kraal, Delyango. Out of it the irregulars rattled them, as well as the few Zulus who had been garrisoning it. A detachment had been left behind – a fortunate precaution taken by Buller – to cover the retreat by holding the kopjie in the rear; and then the force – Beresford and his scouts still leading, the main body spread out on rather a broad front – galloped on through the long grass across the open, bending rather leftward in the direction of the Nodwengo, the next military kraal in the direction of Ulundi. In front of the horsemen there kept retiring at a pace regulated by theirs, about two hundred Zulus, all who were then visible anywhere on the face of the plain. These shunned Nodwengu, leaving it on their right, and heading straight for Ulundi. The irregulars drew rein long enough for a patrol to ride into Nodwengu and report it empty. Then the horses having got their wind, the rapid advance recommenced. It really seemed a straight run in for Buller and Beresford as they set their horses' heads for Ulundi and galloped on. The idea had occurred to many in the force that Cetewayo must have abandoned his capital and withdrawn his army into the hill country close behind Ulundi.

Those irregular horsemen had no very keen sense of discipline, and in a gallop, a forward gallop especially, were rather prone to get out of hand. Buller's hardest task was to restrain this impulse, and it was well that day that he was exerting himself all he knew to curb the ardour of his fellows. Beresford's advance-detachment, scouts as they were, were of course straggled out rather casually over the whole front. Everything seemed prosperous. No enemy showed anywhere save the two hundred fugitive Zulus, falling back ahead of our fellows at the long easy run which takes the Zulu over the ground with surprising speed and which he can keep up hour after hour without a symptom of distress.

Their flight was a calculated snare; those fugitives were simply a wily decoy. Suddenly from out a deep, sharply-cut water-course crossing the plain, and invisible at two hundred yards' distance, sprang up a long line of Zulus, some two thousand strong, confronting at once and flanking the horsemen. Simultaneously the whole plain around them flashed up into vivid life. Hordes of Zulus had been lying hidden in the long grass. Buller's alert eye had caught the impending danger, and his voice had rung out the command 'Retire' ere yet the bullets of the sudden Zulu volley whistled through and over his command. Three men went down smitten by the fire. Two were killed on the spot and never stirred; we found their bodies next day shockingly mangled. The third man's horse slipped up in the abrupt turn, and his rider for the moment lay stunned. But Beresford, riding away behind his retreating party, looked back at this latter man, and saw him move up into a sitting posture.

He who would succour in such a crisis must not only be a brave man, but also a prompt man, quick to decide and as quick to act. The issue of life or death hangs at such a time on the gain or waste of a moment. The Zulus, darting out from the watercourse, were perilously close to the poor fellow; but Beresford, used on the racecourse to measuring distance with the eye, thought he might just do it, if he were smart and lucky. Galloping back to the wounded man, he dismounted, and ordered him to get on his pony. The wounded man, dazed as he was, even in his extremity was not less full of self-abnegation than was the man who was risking his own life in the effort to save his. He bade Beresford remount and go; why, he said in his simple manly logic – why should two die when death was inevitable but to one?

Then it was that the quaint resourceful humour of his race supplied Beresford with the weapon that prevailed over the wounded man's unselfishness. The recording angel perhaps did not record the oath that buttressed his threatening mien when he swore with clenched fist that he would punch the wounded man's head if he did not allow his life to be saved. This droll argument prevailed. Bill partly lifted, partly hustled the man into his saddle, then scrambled up somehow in front of him, and set the good little beast going after the other horsemen. He only just did it; another moment's delay and both must have been assegaied. As it was, the swift-footed Zulus chased them up the slope, and the least mistake made by the pony must have been fatal. Indeed, as Beresford was the first gratefully to admit, there was a critical moment when their escape would have been impossible, but for the cool courage of Sergeant O'Toole, who rode back to the rescue, shot down Zulu after Zulu with his revolver as they tried to close in on the rather helpless pair, and then aided Beresford in keeping the wounded man in the saddle until the safety of the laager was attained.

There was danger right up till then; for the hordes of Zulus obstinately hung on the flanks and rear of Buller's command, and the irregulars had over and over again to shoot men down at close quarters with the revolver; more than once the fighting was hand-to-hand and they had to club their rifles. If the Zulus had kept to their own weapon, the assegai, the loss among Buller's men would have been very severe; but they had extensively armed themselves with rifles that had fallen into their hands at Isandlwana, with the proper handling of which they were unfamiliar. They pursued right up to their own bank of the Umvaloosi, and blazed away at our fellows long after the river was between them and us. Of course, cumbered with a wounded and fainting man occupying his saddle while he perched on the pommel, Beresford was unable to do anything toward self-protection, and over and over again on the return ride, he and the man behind him were in desperate strait, and but for O'Toole and other comrades must have gone down. When they alighted in the laager you could not have told whether it was rescuer or rescued who was the wounded man, so smeared was Beresford with borrowed blood.

It was one of Ireland's good days; if at home she is the 'distressful country', wherever bold deeds are to be done and military honour to be gained, no nation carries the head higher out of the dust. If originally Norman, the Waterford family have been Irish now for six centuries, and Bill Beresford is an Irishman in heart and blood. Sergeant Fitzmaurice, the wounded man who displayed a self-abnegation so fine, was an Irishman also; and Sergeant O'Toole – well, I think one runs no risk in the assumption that an individual who bears that name, in spite of all temptation, remains an Irishman. So, in this brilliant little episode the Green Isle had it all to herself.

*It was clear to everyone that the last great confrontation of the war would take place the next day. That night, the Zulus across the river provided an appropriate choral accompaniment as the British soldiers tried to snatch a few hours' fitful sleep. The grey dawn came at last, however, and reveille sounded on 4th July 1879. Taking only their ammunition carts with them, and leaving a garrison to guard the camp,*

247

*Chelmsford's men marched out across the Mfolozi. Molyneux was with them:*

The night of the 3rd was rendered hideous by the war-songs which proclaimed the enemy's intention of fighting next day; by '*Umlungu wahlab' inkosi* (the white man struck at the king) among others. We could gather from the volume of sound that there was a goodly host assembled, and between the roars of the men came the shrill cries of the women, which told the old hands that they had got hold of the three bodies of the troopers killed that day and were mutilating them. Perhaps it was well that they made a night of it, for they were very late rising next morning. They said afterwards that, seeing our laager standing, they thought we should not move that day; but I doubt whether they could see if for the fog, though they might have listened for the rumbling of the waggons, and not hearing that thought we were not moving.

We were up next morning at five, to find everything shrouded in a thick white mist. Five companies of the 1st battalion 24th, one company of Royal Engineers, with detachments from other corps, some six hundred men in all, were left to defend the laager under Colonel Bellairs, deputy-adjutant-general. At six the rest of the force advanced to the Umvolosi in the following strength:

| | |
|---|---:|
| Cavalry (17th Lancers and Irregulars) | 1,344 |
| Infantry (1st batt. 13th: 2nd batt. 21st: 58th, 80th, 90th, and 94th) | 2,840 |
| Native Contingent | 958 |
| | 5,142 |

With twelve guns and two Gatlings

Buller's mounted men were to lead: the infantry, with the guns, were to follow in a rectangle, natives, ammunition and tool carts, and bearer-company in the centre; and the 17th Lancers were to bring up the rear. We were all across the river by seven, and at half-past eight had reached the knoll selected by Buller on the previous day for our position. The Chief now took personal command of the united force, wheeled the rectangle half-right, so as to face Ulundi kraal, halted it, faced the men outwards, and ordered the ranks to be dressed, and the ammunition-carts to be placed handy and opened. Wood proposed to entrench, but the Chief refused. 'No,' he said, 'they will be satisfied if we beat them fairly in the open. We have been called ant-bears long enough.'

The Zulus did not keep us waiting long. The ranks were scarcely dressed before our mounted men on the right commenced firing at the back of Nodwengu kraal, and almost immediately it was taken up all along the line of scouts. Buller and Drury Lowe brought in the Irregulars and 17th Lancers at a gallop, so as to clear the infantry front. 'Volleys by companies' was the order when the square was closed again. The Chief refused to dismount, so all staff-officers, including Newdigate's and Wood's, remained on horseback throughout the action; and a very fine view we had of the whole battle.

The Zulus had remained in the horseshoe formation of the previous day, and now joining the two horns, they came with a tremendous rush at our rear face. This was held by two companies of the 2nd battalion, 21st, and two of the 94th, the greatest rush coming at the right rear-angle held by the 21st. There was a patch of bush and long grass thirty yards off it behind which the enemy were assembling; so the Chief brought the 5th company Royal Engineers up behind the 21st to help them in case of need; but company volleys and case from two nine-pounders scattered the Zulus at this point and stopped a closer rush. The guns this day were in action in line with the infantry; the two Gatlings in the centre of the front face, and the others, two together, either at the angles or at the intervals between the regiments. The flank and front faces were the next engaged, and it seemed to me, from horseback, that the Zulus killed many of their own men. At one time I was watching the enemy opposite the left face. They were in a hollow, and our men, being unable to see them, were not at that moment firing; yet two or three threw up their arms and fell, which could only have been from shots fired by their friends opposite, who were attacking our right face and whose bullets had passed over our heads and hit them.

Shortly after nine o'clock a dense black mass of Zulus emerged from Ulundi kraal and moved down the slope, east of the Imbilane stream and towards us; it was the reserve, or the 'Loins' of the Zulu army, consisting of the royal regiments of the Undi corps at least five thousand strong. Two nine-pounders had been moved from the left rear to the left front angle, and they had taken the range to a solitary euphorbia tree on this slope about two thousand yards off. Down the slope came the Zulus in a wide rectangle, fifty deep, beating their white shields and shouting their war-cry. The two Gatlings in the centre of our front face, after playing havoc in the black ranks, had now jambed and were out of action; but the nine-pounders were equal to the occasion. Loading with shrapnel they fired, both shells bursting in the centre of the front of this mass which was once opened out into two wings; two more shells followed, one into the heart of each wing; they hesitated, then closed again; two more shells sent them all to the right about, and we saw no more of Cetewayo's reserve that day. It had at no time been within a mile of us.

After three quarters of an hour the foremost Zulus began to waver. Seeing this the Chief told Colonel Drury Lowe to take his Lancers out and disperse them. Just as he had mounted, a spent bullet hit him on the spine and benumbed him, so Major Boulderson took command. Leaving by the left face, where a company of infantry was wheeled back to form a gateway, he took his men out towards Nodwengu kraal, and then, wheeling into line to the right, charged the still unbroken part of the Zulu right horn. Poor Wyatt Edgell was shot dead almost before the Lancers had cleared the square. One Zulu regiment stood firm and even gave the cavalry a volley; the fire was wild, however, and the ensuing shock when horse met foot could even be heard by us. The Zulus broke and fled, followed fast by the Lancers; but some rallied on the rocky hills to the north-west where the cavalry could not follow, and they were dispersed by shrapnel shells. The lance-pennons were a sight that night; there was not one that had not done its work. Buller's mounted men, who had left the square after the Lancers, dispersed several other parties of the enemy; and within an hour there was not a Zulu to be seen.

So ended the fight at Ulundi. We all at once crowded round to congratulate the Chief: the soldiers cheered their generals, and every one rejoiced. Of the Chief's staff Milne only was wounded, but General Newdigate had both his aides-de-camp hit. Our total loss was one officer and ten men killed, nineteen officers and sixty-nine men wounded, twenty-eight horses killed and forty-five wounded. The Zulus, whose total strength that day was certainly over twenty thousand, were estimated to have lost fifteen hundred. Cetewayo did not witness the fight, having left Ulundi the day before; the commanders were Mnyamane Tshingwayo and Dabulamanzi.

We halted till half-past eleven to bury our dead and attend to the wounded, and then moved forward to the Imbilane stream, where the men dined.

There was a tremendous cloud of smoke all over the country, for Ulundi and all the smaller kraals near the Mhlabatini Plain were fired that day. I got leave to ride on, reached Ulundi before it was quite destroyed, and got some of the white shields out of a shield-house. The kraal was an enormous place in the form of an oval, one diameter being about seven hundred yards and the other five hundred. There were seven rows of beehive huts round it, facing inwards; but the heat was so intense from the burning mass that little looting could be done before it was all destroyed.

The troops now returned by the way they had marched, slowly, for all the wounded were carried in litters. Our Basutos (who were Christians) held a most elaborate musical service over the grave of one of their men who had been killed; their hymns could be heard quite a mile away. They have the most splendid voices, and every morning and night on the campaign they used to sing a hymn in their own musical tongue. We were back again in our laager by half-past three, and then commenced the drudgery of writing. But it was nothing now; we all felt so light-hearted at having completed the business without interference.

*The great battle of Ulundi had lasted scarcely an hour from beginning to end. Evelyn Wood felt that the Zulu Regiments came on in a hurried, disorderly manner, which contrasted strangely with the methodical, steady order in which they advanced at Kambula on 29th March, for now not only bat-*

*talions, but regiments, became mixed up before they came under fire.' He commented: 'having seen the Zulus come on grandly for over four hours in March, [I] could not believe they would make so half-hearted an attack.' Perhaps the Zulus had hung back a little; no doubt the memory of their losses at Isandlwana and Khambula daunted them. Yet they had given Lord Chelmsford more of a run for his money than Wood cared to admit: afterwards, the leading bodies were found just nine paces from the square.*

*Yet the Zulus knew now that they were beaten. They had hoped that by catching the British in the open, without entrenchments or laagers, they would triumph, but they had been unable to withstand the terrible storm of fire unleashed by Chelmsford's massed ranks. And the pursuit had been particularly severe: after the 17th Lancers broke up the retreating Zulu formations, the irregulars and NNC followed behind, shooting or stabbing the wounded. Perhaps as many as 2,000 Zulus died altogether, and the army was scattered.*

*King Cetshwayo had not stayed to witness the fight, but, after issuing his last instructions to his warriors, he retired north to the homestead of his chief minister, Mnyamana Buthelezi. Behind him, the British looted the great royal homesteads on the plain, and put them to the torch. There were no great riches to be taken from Cetshwayo's palace, so officers had to content themselves with shields, spears and curiosities. Lt-Colonel Grenfell, Chelmsford's Deputy-Assistant Adjutant and Quartermaster-General, provided a macabre touch to the hunt for souvenirs in his account published in* Memoirs of Lord Grenfell *(1925). He fought at Ulundi, and two years later, after the disastrous Transvaal War, he returned to the battlefield:*

On the signing of the Convention and the break up of the camp at Newcastle, I was ordered to Durban to conduct the embarkations, but before doing so, I made long ride with Buller and Donald Browne into Zululand to see our old fighting ground at Ulundi. When we arrived, we found the old track across the Umfolozi River where the grass had grown up very high on the place where our square had stood. I stood at the place, which was still marked by cartridges, at the corner of the square where the Zulus had made their last attack. I told Buller that I had seen a Zulu induna shot in the head by Owen's machine-guns, of which there were two at this corner. He was leading his men on and got as close as eighteen yards from the square, for I had measured it after the action. I again paced the eighteen yards and came to my old friend, a splendid skeleton, his bones perfectly white, his flesh eaten off by the white ants. I felt I could not part with him, so I put his skull into my forage bag, and brought it home with me. It now adorns a case in my collection of curiosities.

*Chelmsford did not stay at Ulundi. After tending his wounded and burying the dead, he retired back across the White Mfolozi to his camp. That night, Archibald Forbes approached him and asked if he could send his account of the battle with a military courier. Chelmsford refused; his own report was not yet ready, and he would not be sending a courier that night. 'Then, sir', snapped Forbes, whose temper was legendary, 'I will start myself at once!' And so he did, though he later admitted, 'I was sorry for myself the moment I had spoken.' The nearest telegraph station was the best part of a hundred miles away, at Landman's Drift, across rough country alive with parties of warriors returning home after the fight. Someone bet Forbes five pounds he'd never make it, and when Forbes accepted the bet, insisted he left his stake behind. But Forbes did make it, reaching Landman's Drift at sunrise, and carrying not only his own report, but Prior's sketches and some military despatches. His colleagues enthusiastically hailed his adventure as a 'Ride of Death', and Forbes found himself depicted on the front pages alongside his own reports.*

*For Chelmsford, Ulundi had at last exorcised the ghost of Isandlwana, and Sir Garnet was welcome to what remained of the war. The British forces began to withdraw. Over the next few days the 2nd Division began to climb up the Mthojaneni heights once more, back the way it had come, whilst the Flying Column moved south-east, towards the 1st Division and Wolseley. Chelmsford himself was happy to resign his command. There was nothing left for Wolseley to do but pacify the country and supervise the peace settlement. Several important chiefs*

*needed to be bullied into submission, whilst King Cetshwayo
was still at large. Bindon Blood describes the last weeks of the
war, and the evacuation of troops:*

A day or two after this scare I was ordered to join Sir Garnet's
Staff at Ulundi, halting one night on the way with another
column, which curiously enough had a scare on the night we
were with it, quite insignificant however compared with that
I had described. When we arrived at Ulundi arrangements
were being made to capture Ketchwayo who was still at large
some 40 or 50 miles to the north. Several mounted parties
were sent out, and among the rest was one under Herbert
Stewart, then a major I think, consisting of fifteen officers with
[black] guides. I was sent with this, and we had about ten days
of riding long distances and roughing it. At last we picked up
Ketchwayo's tracks – or rather his pony's – and got within a
few miles of him. I followed him down to a river where he
had come to a quicksand and turned off half a mile or so to a
ford which he had crossed the same day. As soon as I was
certain about this, I halted and sent for the rest of the party,
which had got scattered. Meanwhile, before my message about
the ford had reached him, Herbert Stewart had arrived at the
river bank and not knowing of the quicksand, etc., had ridden
in and promptly gone over his head, his horse being got out
with some difficulty. This caused so much delay that we bivouacked for the night near the ford, and when we took up Ketchwayo's tracks next morning they led us straight to him in the
camp of the party under Major Marter of the King's Dragoon
Guards, to whom he had surrendered that morning. So we
returned to Ulundi rather sad at our bad luck!

I had a very pleasant and interesting time at Ulundi before and
after I went surveying, as Sir Garnet Wolseley sent for me to
ride with him and talk about India almost every evening. He
was very well read and well educated both as a soldier and
otherwise, and he had had much war experience, and since I
also was not unqualified in the former respects, I could and
did appreciate, enjoy and profit by his conversation. He was a
man of very high ideals of duty and of loyalty, and I came to

regard him with respect, admiration and strong personal liking. I have always felt that England did not have her usual luck with Lord Wolseley, in that he did not synchronise with the Boer War and the Great War.

I only remember one amusing incident on the march to Pinetown. We halted at the Tugela mouth for a couple of days, and I was taking a stroll with one of my subalterns one evening when we stopped and sat down to see a kit inspection, a little way off, of a squadron of Bettington's Horse. Colonel Bettington rode up and proceeded with the inspection, in the course of which he knocked down two of his troopers quite neatly. I was told that they were all in great awe of him. I met him that evening at dinner with the Commandant of the Post, that best of good fellows whom his friends called Reggie Thynne. Bettington was medium-sized, very strong, a fine horseman, good-looking and a good fellow, in fact a first-class fighting man, as he had learnt to be handy with his weapons from long experience in South American Republics. I had a very pleasant talk with him and wished I had met him sooner. I was very sorry to see an announcement of his death from fever in South America, two or three years later.

At Pinetown we found the King's Dragoon Guards and 17th Lancers both literally very much out at elbows and armpits – as they had been soldiering in their tunics – I think the last corps in our army that did so on active service. But if they were out at elbows they were not out of spirits, and we all amused ourselves in various ways. I remember that we had quite good fun paper-chasing, as we could ride over the country in September without doing damage, and the neighbouring farmers were most kind and good-natured to us.

I had instructions to embark at once for home, en route to Kabul, where fighting was going on, and where a place was waiting for me. So I hurried back to Pinetown and embarked at Durban on the next mail steamer for home.

The ship was lying in the open sea, the harbour of Durban being too shallow then for large vessels, as ships of 3,000 tons or so were considered in those days, and I went on board in a tender, after bidding adieu to many friends and last of all to my faithful Zulu orderly Adona, or Adonis as of course we called him. The last I remember of him was seeing him sitting weeping on the shore, in an old suit of khaki uniform I had given him. He sat there for an hour or more, and after that he disappeared. He was a good fellow and feared nothing except ghosts!

The ship rolled deeply as there was a long swell, and to my astonishment I was sea-sick for a couple of hours after I got on board. However I was all right after a little sleep, and soon discovered that two of the male passengers were soldiers and old friends. Of course we arranged to sit together, and having chosen a table in a retired corner, we were (at first unpleasantly) surprised at dinner-time to find a lady, who turned out to be an American actress, and her duenna established at our table. I am quite certain that no-one of us showed the least trace of surprise or disappointment – especially as the lady was good looking. But she at once apologised for invading our table, saying, 'You see I couldn't sit with those cats'! and was otherwise pleasant and amusing, so we thought ourselves very lucky long before dinner was over, and still more so later on.

*And so the glittering panoply and pomp of the Great White Queen's victorious Army moved on, now rather shabby and down at heel, and relieved, no doubt, at the prospect of new duties to perform in different climes, and new glory to be won. Major William Butler, who had served on the lines of communication in the closing stages, and was a Wolseley partisan, included a darkly humorous post-script to the whole adventure in his* Sir William Butler; An Autobiography *(1911):*

Some of the battalions and batteries had been a long time up country, and very large arrears of pay were due to them, as well as to the very numerous irregular corps which had been recruited for service after the disaster at Isandula. It would be difficult to imagine anything more irregular than the majority of the rank and file of these latter bodies: the Turkish title, Bashibazouk, seems alone suited in its sound adequately to describe them. Their regimental titles were also suggestive in many instances of the general trend and direction of their

256

discipline and methods – Sham-buckers' Horse, Raafs' Rangers, the Buffalo Border Guards, etc., etc.

To pay off, disarm, and embark those worthies was a work requiring some little tact and method on the part of the officers who had to deal with them under their respective heads. These various units of raffish swashbucklers now came to the port of embarkation to be paid their reckonings and to pay them again into innumerable public-houses of Durban. I devised many plans by which the evil might be lessened. Sometimes I put a pay officer and his paysheet, with a good guard of regulars, on board a transport in the outer anchorage, and informed the men that they would only be paid on board ship. Another plan was to encamp the corps six or eight miles out of Durban, in the vicinity of a railway station, by means of which they could be fed and supplied from the port. The scenes which were daily taking place were often of a very ludicrous description. A battalion of infantry, to whom some five or six thousand pounds had to be paid, would reach the wharf for embarkation, having been made the recipients on the march through Durban of a public luncheon and innumerable quantities of large water melons – the latter a most innocuous fruit on any ordinary occasion, but somewhat embarrassing when presented to a man after a hearty meal and many libations *en route*. I had prepared, however, for the dangers of the embarkation from the wharf in the large flat boats, and a dozen steady men with boathooks stood ready to gaff the men who fell into the water – a precaution which bore fruit in more senses than one, for many of the men deemed it a point of honour to hold on by their water melons even when they were in the sea. The acme of confusion was, however, reached on the occasion when some eighteen hundred 'details,' prisoners, 'insanes,' sick, and absentees from previous embarkations had to be put upon a troopship in the outer anchorage.

At the last moment a train had arrived from Maritzburg with six 'insanes' for shipment to England. The transport was still in the roadstead, so a boat was sent out to her. The corporal in charge had just time to run up the gangway with his charge; the anchor was already up. On reaching the quarterdeck, crowded with eighteen hundred men, the six 'insanes' saw their chance, and while the corporal was handing his papers to the staff officer on board they adroitly dispersed themselves among the miscellaneous crowd of men thronging the decks. Identification was entirely impossible in that mixed crowd: the corporal had to get back to his escort in the boat as quickly as possible, and the big troopship moved off to shake her motley collection of men into that subsidence which only grows more complete as the sea grows more restless.

But the hour came when the staff officer asked the sergeant of the guard, 'Where are the six insanes?' No man on board could say where; and soon the rumour passed from deck to deck that there were six madmen at large among the troops. Every man began to take a strange interest in his neighbour. 'And who is thy neighbour?' asks the catechism. 'Mankind of every description' is the answer, so far as I can recollect it over the lapse of years. But surely that reverend and estimable namesake of mine, when he penned that question and answer, can never have contemplated a contingency such as this crowded troopship, with twenty different corps represented in its human freight, and at least two unknown madmen at large upon every deck! And yet never could there have been a time when men regarded their neighbour with more lively interest. A council of the leading authorities on shipboard was rapidly assembled, and a course of action decided upon. Practically it came to this, that the whole mass of military was placed under observation; a select corps of observers was organised, and the work began. Any man who was sitting apart in the anticipatory stages, or after effects, of sea-sickness found himself walked round and suspiciously regarded; at frequent intervals a man would be tapped on the shoulder and told to come before the doctor. When the vessel reached Cape Town there were twenty-six men under observation, and it was afterwards found that not one of the six 'insanes' was among them. A curious thing now happened: after a while, some sergeant or corporal, more observant than his comrades, remarked that there were certain men in the crowd who were ready on all occasions to lend a hand in running in the suspected ones, first to the doctor and afterwards to the 'observation' hold. The eagerness and alacrity of these few men attracted first praise and then suspicion. There was an expression of self-satisfaction on their features which was peculiar to them alone among those whose duty it was to discover the missing madmen. Then their off moments were watched, with the result that when the ship reached St Helena the 'observation' hold was cleared of its former inmates and the six insanes were duly installed therein.

At last the weary work of sweeping up the wreckage of a war which was unusually fertile in shipwrecks drew to an end. A crowd of contractors flocked to the base to batten upon the expected spoil when the time for selling surplus stores came. Enormous accumulations of food, forage, and all the other paraphernalia of war had to be got rid of. At first high prices were obtained; then the usual rings were formed. We had some thousands of tons of food-stuffs to sell, and the dealers saw their chance: they would only give first one shilling, and then sixpence, for a heavy sack of Indian corn. I had two large transports sailing with troops, the cargo decks of which were empty. 'All right, gentlemen; we will put these two thousand odd tons of excellent food-stuffs on board these empty vessels and send them to London.' Then the counter-attack began. The dealers worked hard to prevent this move; the departments were also hostile to my proposal. It had not been done before; it would complicate departmental accounts; it was a new departure, etc., etc. 'But is it not common-sense?' I said. 'These innumerable sacks of food, for which we can get sixpence here, will sell in London for ten or twenty times that figure. We are already paying enormous prices for the freightage of these ships; it will cost us nothing to send all this food to England.' This and a lot more I urged. At last sanction was given, and I saw the enormous stacks of supplies vanish into the empty ships, the cargoes to fetch in London even more than I had anticipated.

*Perhaps it is not altogether inappropriate to end a tale of the Zulu war on a note of cynical profiteering. Though the men whose voices are heard in this book had their fair share of courage and honour, like thousands more on both sides, Frere's policy had been one of expediency. When the pro-*

*fessional soldiers had departed, and the irregulars had been disbanded to pick up the threads of their civilian lives, the Zulus alone remained, and few concerned themselves with their fate.*

*In London, Disraeli's administration had fallen, and the new Gladstone government had firmly turned its back on Frere's policies. Opposed to colonial expansion, it refused point-blank to annex Zululand. Wolseley was left to cobble together a hasty peace-settlement, and to extract Britain from the entanglement as cleanly as possible. Cetshwayo was sent into exile, and his kingdom was divided up between thirteen chiefs appointed by the British, one of whom was John Dunn. Wolseley had designed his policy to exaggerate political stresses inherent in the old kingdom, hoping thereby to prevent Zululand emerging as a united power in the future. It was partly successful: it awakened bitter rivalries between those who supported the old royal house, and who agitated for the king's return, and those, like Dunn, who had waxed fat in its absence. With no strong British administration to control the tension, Zululand slid into anarchy and a civil war which would cost as many lives as the war with the British ever did. And in the end, within a decade, British red-coats would once more have to march into the green hills of Zululand, to pick up the pieces of past imperial ineptitude.*

# Biographical Notes

*Listed alphabetically*

**Bengough, Sir Harcourt M**. Bengough was born in 1837, and, as an ensign in the 77th Regiment, served in the Crimea. A long period of peacetime soldiering followed, chiefly in India, before Bengough was sent to South Africa as a special service officer, and given a command in the Natal Native Contingent. During the second invasion he was attached to the 2nd Division, and was present at the battle of Ulundi. He finished the war as a lieutenant-colonel. In 1880 he returned to India, and subsequently took part in the Burma campaign of 1885–6. The rest of his career was spent largely in garrisons around the Empire, including Madras and Jamaica. In 1894 he was made a major-general, and commanded the 1st Infantry Brigade at Aldershot. He died in 1922.

**Blood, Sir Bindon:** Of Anglo-Irish ancestry, Blood was born in 1842, and entered the Royal Engineers in 1860. Much of his early service was spent in India, though he saw no service until the Jowaki Expedition of 1877. He returned home on leave thereafter, and no sooner had he left than the 2nd Afghan War broke out; regulations prevented his returning to India immediately, so, when the news of Isandlwana reached England, he volunteered for service in South Africa instead. He served throughout the later stages of the campaign as senior Engineer with the 1st Division. From Zululand he returned to India and the Afghan War, and in 1882 joined the Egyptian Expedition, and was present at Tel-el-Kebir. Between 1895 and 1897 he took part in a number of important actions on the North-West Frontier, including the Chitral Relief Expedition, and rose to the rank of major-general. In 1901, during the Anglo-Boer War, he was appointed commander of the Eastern Transvaal, organising columns in pursuit of the fast-moving Boer commandos. In late 1901 he returned to India as commander of troops in the Punjab, a post he retained until his retirement in 1907. He lived until 1940.

**Butler, Sir William:** Born in Ireland in 1838, Butler was commissioned into the Army in 1858, and, despite a number of overseas postings, did not see active service until the Fenian Raids in Canada in 1870. This was the beginning of a long association with Sir Garnet Wolseley. Indeed, Butler is counted a member of the 'Wolseley Ring', the group of young and progressive officers the General gathered about him, and Butler served under him again in Asante in 1874. He was also on his staff during Sir Garnet's brief tenure as lieutenant-governor of Natal in 1875. During the Zulu War Butler's responsibilities were confined to the lines of communications and base, but he played a more prominent role in the Egyptian campaign of 1882, and was present at Tel-el-Kebir. In 1884 he served on the unsuccessful Gordon Relief Expedition, and commanded a brigade at Ginniss a year later, which checked the Mahdist advance. His later career consisted of a series of peacetime appointments, culminating in the post of Acting High Commissioner to the Cape in the difficult days before the Boer War. He returned to Britain to take up a home command shortly before the outbreak of hostilities. He died in 1910. In 1877 Butler married Elizabeth Thompson, who, as Lady Butler, achieved fame as the leading painter of battle scenes in the Victorian period.

**Chard, John Rouse Merriott:** Chard was born near Plymouth in 1847, and joined the Royal Engineers in 1868. He was posted for a while to Bermuda, and then to South Africa with No. 5 Company for the Zulu War. Attached to the Centre Column, he was responsible for supervising the ponts at Rorke's Drift, and was the senior officer present when that post was attacked on 22nd January. He fell ill shortly after, but recovered sufficiently to rejoin his company on the march to Ulundi. He was promoted captain for his part in the defence, and awarded the VC which was presented by Sir Garnet Wolseley at St Paul's in Zululand on 16th July 1879. Despite being received by the Queen and feted as a hero by the Victorian public, Chard did not see active service again, and retired in poor health 1897, with the rank of colonel. He died in November 1897.

**Forbes, Archibald:** Forbes was born in Scotland in 1838, and served in the Royal Dragoons between 1859 and 1864, when he bought himself out. He cut his journalistic teeth in the Franco-Prussian War of 1870, and later covered various uprisings in the Balkans, and the Russo-Turkish campaign. A tall, powerful man with a notoriously quick temper, he soon established a public reputation, not only for the quality of his writing, but for his ability to get his despatches home even under the most trying conditions. He was sent to Zulu-land by the *Daily News* when word of Isandlwana reached England, and covered the closing stages of the fighting. After the war, he waged a bitter campaign against Whitehall, claiming that he was entitled to the South Africa campaign medal, on the grounds that he had carried Chelmsford's military despatch along with his own after Ulundi. He was unsuccessful. Perhaps as a result of this, he retired from the 'active service' of the war correspondent, and wrote books about his experiences and lectured. He died in delirium in the arms of his editor in March 1900, crying out 'Those guns, man, don't you see those guns? I tell you, the brave fellows will be mowed down like grass...'

**Grenfell, Sir Francis Wallace:** Born in Wales in 1841, Grenfell joined the 60th Rifles in 1859, and in 1873 was appointed ADC to the General Officer Commanding in South Africa. He took part in the Griqua-land West expedition, the Cape Frontier, Zulu and Transvaal Wars. In 1882 he served in the Egyptian campaign, and was present at Tel-el-Kebir. From 1884 he was primarily involved with the Egyptian Army and the campaigns against the Sudanese Mahdists. He commanded a division at the battle of Ginniss in 1886 and again at Toski in 1889. He was Sirdar of the Egyptian Army from 1885–1892. After a spell in Britain with the Army Headquarters, he returned to Egypt in 1897, supporting Kitchener's advance on Khartoum. In 1899 he was appointed Governor of Malta, and from 1904 to 1908 he was commander-in-chief of Ireland. He died in 1925.

**Hamilton-Browne, George:** Born in 1847 to Anglo-Irish ancestry, Hamilton-Browne first saw action as a member of the volunteer corps fighting the Maoris in New Zealand in the 1860s; he recalled his adventures in his first book, *With the Lost Legion in New Zealand* (1911). In South Africa, he served with an irregular unit, raised by Colonel Pulleine of the 1/24th, 'Pulleine's Rangers', in the closing stages of the Ninth Cape Frontier War. In Zululand, where he held the rank of commandant in the Natal Native Contingent, he served with the ill-fated Centre Column, and later the Eshowe relief expedition, where he was present at Gingindlovu. He was briefly involved in the subsequent BaSotho War, and accompanied Sir Charles Warren's Bechuanaland Expedition in 1885. For a while he held a command in the Diamond Fields Horse, and in 1888 returned to Zululand with the forces sent to put down Prince Dinuzulu kaCetshwayo's rebellion. In later years he moved north of the Limpopo in the wake of Cecil Rhodes' attempt to colonise Rhodesia (Zimbabwe).

**Molyneux, William C. F.** Molyneux was gazetted as an ensign in the 22nd Regiment in 1864. He attended the Staff College between 1872 and 1874, and on passing out was appointed ADC to General Thesiger, later Lord Chelmsford. At the end of January 1878 Thesiger was sent to South Africa as GOC, with Molyneux on his staff. Molyneux therefore saw active service in the closing stages of the Frontier War. He missed the beginning of the Zulu War, having been sent home because of ill health, but returned in April 1879, in time to accompany the Eshowe relief expedition. He continued to serve as Chelmsford's ADC throughout the war. He returned to England at the end of the war, but again saw active service in Egypt, in 1882, where he was present at Tel-el-Kebir. He took part in the Bechuanaland Field Force in 1885, but retired in 1887 with the rank of major-general. He died in 1898.

**'Harry O'Clery of the Buffs':** O'Clery remains the most enigmatic of the contributors to this volume. Although all the internal evidence in his account suggests that it is authentic, there is no O'Clery to be found on the 3rd Regiment's medal roll, quoted in D. R. Forsyth's *Medal Roll for South Africa General Service 1877–8–9*. Forsyth comments that the original roll for the Buffs is particularly illegible, but it seems likely that, like many of his colleagues in the ranks, O'Clery had simply enlisted under a different name. By his own account, he went on to serve two years in the Straits Settlements, 'and three years in Hong Kong; after which he returned to England, and I quitted the Army'.

**Parr, Sir Henry Hallam:** Born in Somerset in 1847, Parr was gazetted into the 13th Light Infantry in 1865. In 1877, with the rank of captain, he was appointed military secretary to Sir Bartle Frere, and sailed to the Cape. He saw something of the Cape Frontier War, and was temporarily released onto the staff of the Centre Column at the start of the Zulu War; after Isandlwana, he resumed his duties with Frere. After leave in England, he was sent back to South Africa to join Sir George Colley's staff during the Transvaal crisis, but arrived after Colley's death at Majuba. In 1882 he took part in the Egyptian campaign, where he was severely wounded; curiously, he was found on the field by Molyneux. Nevertheless, he served in the Red Sea campaign in 1884, being present at the battle of Tamai, and in the unsuccessful Gordon Relief Expedition. Although his work in Egypt was held in high regard, his health broke down completely in 1888, and he spent the remainder of his career in a series of peace time postings, rising to the rank of major-general. He died in 1914.

**Shervington, Charles Robert St Leger:** Born in 1852 to a military family of Anglo-Irish stock, Shervington had an adventurous youth, which included training in both the Army and Navy, and a spell seeking his fortune in the Indies. When the Cape Frontier War broke out, Charles Shervington sailed out from England with his younger brother Tom to volunteer. Both men served throughout the campaign, Charles with 'Pulleine's Rangers'. With the outbreak of the Zulu War, both men joined the NNC with the Coastal Column, and Charles was present throughout the siege of Eshowe, where his daring on patrol brought him to the attention of Pearson on several occasions. After the relief of Eshowe, Charles served with the 1st Division. Another brother, Will, joined Charles and Tom during the closing stages of the war, so no less than three Shervingtons fought in the campaign. Tom, unfortunately, died of disease in February 1880, at the age of 21. Charles went on to serve with the Cape Mounted Rifles in the BaSotho 'gun war', and later went to try his luck in Madagascar, where he rose to the rank of colonel, commanding Malagasy troops in their struggle against the French. His efforts were ultimately unsuccessful, however, and he returned home in poor health, and died in April 1898.

**Smith-Dorrien, Sir Horace:** Born in 1858, Smith-Dorrien joined the 95th Regiment in 1877, and, at Chelmsford's request and despite the disapproval of his commanding officer, sailed to South Africa to join the impending war against the Zulus. As a transport officer with the

Centre Column, he survived Isandlwana, but fell ill shortly after, although he recovered in time to join the second invasion, and was in the camp on the White Mfolozi during the battle of Ulundi. His subsequent career reads like a list of Victorian colonial campaigns: in 1882 he commanded a unit of mounted infantry in the Egyptian campaign, and, with the Anglo-Egyptian army, he fought against the Sudanese Mahdists around Suakin, at Ginniss and finally Omdurman. He saw more action on the North-West Frontier, and served throughout the Boer War, being present at the battle of Paardeburg, and prominent in the pursuit of Botha and De Wet. Having by now risen to the rank of general, he was appointed Adjutant-General of India in 1901, where he served until 1907, when he was given a command in Aldershot. With the outbreak of WWI he was sent to France in command of II Corps of the BEF. During the retreat from Mons, he fought a holding action at Le Cateau against the orders of his superior, Sir John French, which, although successful, ultimately led to his resignation. He did, however, go on to command the East African forces in 1915, and after the war he became Governor of Gibraltar. On 11th August 1930 he was badly injured in a car accident outside Bath, and he died the next day.

**Tucker, Sir Charles**: Born in 1838, Tucker joined the 80th Regiment in 1855. As a captain he served in the Bhutan Expedition of 1865, and again saw action in Perak in 1876. Tucker served with his regiment throughout the Sekhukhune campaign and Zulu War, commanding the garrison at Luneburg, and the regiment on the march to Ulundi, at which he was present. In the 1890s he was in command of the Secunderbad District in the Madras Presidency, and subsequently served throughout the Boer War, where he was promoted lieutenant-general. His later appointments were principally in the UK. He died in 1935.

**Wood, Sir Henry Evelyn**: Born in 1838, Wood's unusual career took him from midshipman in the Royal Navy to field marshal in the British Army. He joined the Navy in 1852, and saw active service in the Crimea, where he was wounded in the attack on the Redan, and invalided home. He then transferred to the Army, in the hope of seeing more active service. He did so and in 1859 won the VC in the closing stages of the Indian Mutiny, rescuing a captured landowner from a rebel band. In 1874, now a lieutenant-colonel, he took part in Sir Garnet Wolseley's Asante ('Ashanti') campaign in West Africa. He fought in the Ninth Cape Frontier War and Zulu War, and in 1880 led the Empress Eugénie's party on a pilgrimage to the spot where her son, the Prince Imperial, was killed. In 1881 he conducted the peace negotiations at the end of the disastrous Tranvaal War. A year later he took part in the 1882 Egyptian campaign, and was appointed the first British sirdar of the Egyptian army. During the Gordon Relief Expedition, he commanded the lines of communication. Returning to England, he held a series of vastly influential staff posts, including, from 1897, Adjutant-General of the Forces. Evelyn Wood, as he was universally known, was a highly capable, energetic and popular commander, despite a tendency to vanity, and a propensity to suffer bizarre accidents: he was once trampled by a giraffe. He died in 1919.

# FURTHER READING

The Anglo-Zulu War has probably attracted more attention from writers and historians than any other Victorian military campaign, with the possible exception of the Anglo-Boer War. This list is not intended as a comprehensive bibliography, but the following books are particularly recommended: between them, they represent both the best contemporary accounts, and the most up-to-date and balanced research, and cover many aspects of the war. Furthermore, they should be readily available; only those contemporary works which have been recently reprinted are listed here.

Bennett, Lt-Colonel Ian: *Eyewitness in Zululand: The Campaign Reminiscences of Colonel W. A. Dunne*, London, 1989.

Child, Daphne (ed): *The Zulu War Diary of Colonel Henry Harford*, Pietermaritzburg, 1978.

Coupland, Sir Reginald: *Isandlwana: Zulu Battle Piece*, 1948, reprinted London 1991.

Emery, Frank; *The Red Soldier*, London, 1977.

Holme, Norman (comp): *The Silver Wreath*, London, 1979.

Knight, Ian: *Brave Men's Blood*, London, 1990.

Knight, Ian: *The Zulus*, London, 1989.

Knight, Ian: *British Forces in Zululand 1879*, London, 1991.

Knight, Ian, and Castle, Ian: *The Zulu War: Twilight of a Warrior Nation:* London, 1992.

Laband, John: *Fight Us In The Open: The Anglo-Zulu War Through Zulu Eyes*, Pietermaritzburg, 1985.

Laband, John (ed): *Moodie's Zulu War*, Pietermaritzburg and Cape Town, 1988.

Laband, John and Wright, John: *King Cetshwayo kaMpande*, Pietermaritzburg, 1980.

Laband, John, *The Battle of Ulundi*, Pietermaritzburg, 1988.

Laband, John, and Matthews, Jeff, *Isandlwana*, Pietermaritzburg, 1992.

Laband, John, and Thompson, Paul; *Field Guide To The War In Zulu-land And The Defence Of Natal*, Pietermaritzburg, revised edition, 1987.

Laband, John, and Thompson, Paul: *Kingdom And Colony At War*, Pietermaritzburg and Cape Town, 1990.

Mitford, Bertram: *Through The Zulu Country*, 1883; reprinted London, 1992.

Morris, Donald R. *The Washing of the Spears*, London, 1966.

Mossop, George: *Running the Gauntlet*, 1937, reprinted Pietermaritzburg 1990.

*Narrative of the Field Operations Connected With The Zulu War of 1879*, War Office, 1881, reprinted London, 1989.

Norris-Newman, Charles: *In Zululand With The British Throughout The War of 1879*, 1880, reprinted London, 1988.

Vijn, Cornelius: *Cetshwayo's Dutchman*, 1880, reprinted London 1989.

# INDEX

270